Table for Two

by Joanne Stepaniak

Book Publishing Company
Summertown, Tennessee

Cover art and interior illustrations by Sheryl Karas
Back cover photo by Michael Stepaniak
© 1996 Joanne Stepaniak

01 00 99 98   5 4 3 2

Published in the United States by   Book Publishing Company
                                   PO Box 99
                                   Summertown, TN 38483

ISBN 1-57067-019-6

Stepaniak, Joanne, 1954-
        Table for two / by Joanne Stepaniak
              p.   cm.
        Includes index.
        ISBN 1-57067-019-6 (pbk.)
        1. Vegetarian cookery. 2. Cookery for two. I. Title.
   TX837.S76   1996
     641.5′61--dc20   95-26091
                                   CIP

Our Lay-Flat Binding
The binding of this book will make it easier for the book
to lay open as you use it and will increase its life span.
By opening the book to any page and running your finger down the spine, the pages will lay flat without
breaking the spine.

Calculations for the nutritional analyses in this book are based
on the average number of servings listed with the recipes and
the average amount of an ingredient, if a range is called for.
Calculations are rounded up to the nearest gram. If two options
for an ingredient are listed, the first one is used. Not included
are optional ingredients, serving suggestions, or fat used for frying, unless the amount of fat is specified in the recipe.

Contents

Hunger only for a taste of justice;
Hunger only for a world of truth.

Tracy Chapman

Several people were instrumental in helping me complete this book. My deepest gratitude is extended to my sweet husband Michael who patiently tolerated the same dishes day after day after day until I "got them right." He's been an ace kitchen prepper, taste-taster, proofreader, advisor, clean-up specialist, and maintenance engineer, and has always performed each and every task with a smile.

Karen Bernard has been abidingly inspirational and supportive. She generously contributed numerous ideas and suggestions, and endured my countless phone calls and questions—for all of which I am extremely appreciative.

Matt Ball, Paula Barry, Karen Bernard (and Rachel), Scott Frizlen, David Gaydos, Anne Green (and Ellen), Glenn Grodin, Billy Pepmeyer, Susan Richter (and Eli), and Mary and Ray Schinhofen shared their special recipes and/or tips for how they manage to fit healthful, compassionate cooking into their busy schedules. Their sage advice and useful recommendations were kindly donated so that others might benefit from their experiences. I am grateful to each of them for their generosity, insight, and wisdom.

Special thanks to Laraine Flemming who contributed her family's recipe for Grandmother's Peppers & Tomato.

My warmest gratitude is also extended to Louise Hagler and Dorothy Bates for their pioneering work adapting tofu, tempeh, and seitan to American vegetarian cuisine, and to all the early vegetarian cookbook authors who gallantly paved the first inroads to a saner and more compassionate way of eating.

Dedicated to the memory of
Glenn Grodin,
with endless admiration, affection, and love.

INTRODUCTION

It seems, at times, that the art of cooking is spiraling toward extinction. Many of us have schedules that are too demanding and energy that is in too short supply to take the time needed to prepare regular meals or teach our children the importance of this valuable craft. This is unfortunate because meal preparation and mealtimes have traditionally been opportunities for families and household members to socialize, share information, and reaffirm their ties. Parents and grandparents at one time took great pride in passing down recipes to their offspring and took great pleasure in sharing their skills and secret techniques with a new generation.

I remember my grandmother carefully guarding her special recipes—the ones all her grandchildren adored. She wanted to wait to give us the actual recipes until we were older. That way she would have the joy of preparing them for us and be able to indulge our squeals of delight for as long as possible. I was fortunate to have been able to spend time with my grandmother the day before she died. My mother and I knew she was aware of her limited time left on earth, because it was only then that she shared with us her prized recipes. That was her bequest to us.

It isn't that those of us who don't cook aren't eating. Indeed we are. But we are eating a lot of high-fat, low-fiber, high-calorie foods that are hardly nutritious by anyone's standards. More and more of us are eating out at restaurants or picking up take-out meals daily. "Home cooked" is fast becoming a misnomer for most of the foods we eat. Perhaps "home heated" or "home reconstituted" would be more accurate terms.

If the art of cooking is allowed to wither, our children and their children will forever miss the simple pleasures of licking the mixing bowl, inhaling aromas of real food cooking, requesting a special birthday meal, or tugging on a grownup's apron in order to have "just a taste." And we will all be denied the sensual thrill of preparing wholesome foods, seasoning them to perfection, and basking in appreciation as our creations are devoured with gusto.

In deference to realistic pressures, I created this book of simple recipes so the art of cooking could be preserved. The recipes are quick (most can be on the table in under thirty minutes!) and nutritious. And did I mention easy? Even if you are a novice cook, you should have no problem with these recipes. The directions are simple enough for older children and teenagers to follow (although adult supervision is always recommended). The ingredient lists are short, and the procedures are uncomplicated. There is a brief glossary of a few ingredients which may be unfamiliar, a section on setting up your kitchen and pantry so you will be ready to start cooking at a moment's notice, and even a listing of "kid-pleasing" recipes.

Most cookbooks have recipes that will serve four, six, eight, or even ten people. According to statistics, however, few of us are in living situations where quantities of this size would be needed. Transitional living arrangements and established two-person households have rapidly become the norm. Whether you live alone, with a child, or with another adult, this cookbook can provide a host of ideas that won't fill your refrigerator or freezer with a month's worth of leftovers. Regardless if you are a seasoned cook or are one whose pots are still in the carton, you'll find these recipes easy to understand, easy to prepare, and far from boring.

When I first told my husband I was going to write a cookbook for smaller households he was aghast. You see, my husband likes to eat—a lot. He was concerned that a reduced number of servings would mean a reduction in portion size as well. Since my "experiments" always end up being our meals, the thought of leaving the table hungry was a major concern. I assured him that he would be satisfied—not to worry. And so I went about the task of creating recipes that would appease the appetites of two hungry adults. Granted, some of the portions might be a little large for a young child or a very light eater, but that is a minor tradeoff. The small amount of food left over could easily be eaten later or served as a snack or lunch the following day.

In order to make these recipes not only easy but extremely quick, I have incorporated a few convenience foods throughout. (Remember—always recycle commercial packaging whenever possible!) Canned beans, frozen vegetables, quick-cooking rices, packaged non-dairy milks, etc., help to speed up meal preparation. However, they are always harmonized with fresh fruits, vegetables, and other whole foods so that nutrition and good taste are never compromised.

I encourage you to select the highest quality foods you can afford—whether fresh or packaged. This includes seeking out certified, organically grown fruits, vegetables, grains, non-dairy milks, and frozen and canned products whenever you can. It makes sense to buy organically grown foods for several reasons:

•Organically grown food is more healthful;

•Organically grown food tastes better;

•Organic farming helps to maintain the health of our soil, air, and water supplies which have become polluted by chemical-dependent agriculture;

•Organic farms help to preserve wildlife because they do not pollute or interfere with animal habitats;

•Organic farming provides a safer work environment for those who grow our food;

•Organic farming encourages the use of composting which, if implemented on a large scale, would significantly reduce the garbage which now ends up in our landfills.

Cooking is an art. Whether your masterpieces are abstracts (creative combinations of whatever you have on hand), reproductions (careful duplications of tried and true standards), or paint-by-numbers (simple combinations of frozen and prepackaged foods), they are your specialties. Whatever you put into your food is what you will get out of it. Put your heart into your cooking—even if you only cook a few times a week.

If it hasn't happened yet, I hope one day you'll know the joy of being asked for one of your treasured recipes. As my grandmother would say, "Food is life. Cooking is love."

TIPS FOR SMALL PORTION COOKING & DINING

Whether you have downsized a formerly large household, are a single-parent, have an alternative living arrangement, share your space with roommates, cook daily or occasionally for one or two children, have always lived by yourself or with just one other person, or are venturing out on your own for the very first time, establishing a system for planning meals and cooking can be a challenge. Large households are accustomed to cooking large quantities, and with so many mouths to feed and varying tastes to appease, they also tend to have a wide variety of foods and snacks on hand. Running a smaller household is not unlike running a larger one. The pantry and herb and spice cabinets still need to be stocked, and meal preparation still needs to be coordinated.

The most significant differences between large and small household cooking are 1) small households require lesser quantities to fill the pantry, and 2) smaller pots and pans are more appropriate. One distinction that is not so obvious, however, is that people who live in one-person and two-person situations have more difficulty getting motivated to cook. This is especially true for people who live alone and for people who are roommates but who are not close friends, lovers, or marriage partners. Most recipes make quantities substantially larger than most small households can consume, and since cooks in small households often receive less support for their culinary expertise, it almost seems easier just to heat up a frozen, prepackaged dinner, open a can of soup, warm up a frozen veggie burger or hot dog, make a quick sandwich, eat at a restaurant, or bring home take-out instead of cooking. Because of outside pressures and time constraints, these shortcuts sometimes make perfect sense. Nevertheless, as a steady diet they can drain both one's health and wallet.

There are many ways to make small-quantity home cooking enjoyable and interesting without consuming all your time. The following are a few cooking and dining suggestions for two-person and single-person households which I hope you will find helpful:

•**Think small.** Pack away any large cooking vessels you may own and keep the smaller ones in a convenient, easy-to-reach place.

•**Keep a light touch with your seasonings.** Small quantity cooking demands gentle care when flavoring foods. If you are most familiar with cooking for larger groups, it may at first be difficult to switch from a teaspoonful of a seasoning to just a pinch. However, a heavy hand with seasonings can oftentimes destroy an otherwise perfectly delicious dish. Remember, it's easier to add more seasoning later than it is to mask too much.

•**If possible, plan your meals ahead of time.** This way you can give yourself ample opportunity to stop at the store and pick up any fresh items you may need. Planning several days' worth of meals in advance will allow you to do all your shopping at once, and you can avoid the need to stop at the store on a daily basis.

•**Look for smaller-sized produce when shopping.** For example, instead of selecting a large eggplant, pick a small eggplant or try to find Asian eggplants which are naturally petite.

•**Buy small-portion canned and packaged goods.** For instance, search for 8-ounce cans of tomato sauce or beans. If you have difficulty finding them, ask your grocer to stock more small-size packaged goods. If there is a demand for them, your grocer will be happy to stock them for you. (Yes, it does consume more energy and resources to package goods in small containers. However, it's far less wasteful to purchase exactly what you need than to throw away excess.)

•**Seek out unpackaged produce** such as potatoes, tomatoes, mushrooms, onions, and fresh fruit so that you can purchase only the amount you will use.

•**Freeze leftovers.** If you live alone, this can be a boon on nights you don't feel like cooking. Keep several storage containers on hand with snug fitting lids so you can store leftovers properly. Foods that will be frozen need to be packed in airtight containers or storage bags in order to prevent freezer burn. All the muffins, soups, and casseroles made from the recipes in this book can safely be frozen for up to one month. Remember—thaw frozen foods in the refrigerator, not at room temperature, to avoid contamination from bacteria.

•**Reheat only what you need.** If you are storing leftovers in the refrigerator, take out from the storage container only the amount you will be using for that particular meal instead of reheating the entire batch. This way your food will not become overcooked from reheating it several times.

•**Freeze sliced bread,** especially if your bread tends to get stale or moldy before you are able to work your way through the loaf. If bread is sliced before it is frozen, you can easily remove the exact number of slices you need. You can make sandwiches using the frozen slices in the morning, and the bread will be defrosted and fresh tasting in time for lunch. You can also toast the bread immediately without defrosting it, or for "fresh" bread, wrap it in a clean kitchen towel (to absorb any excess moisture), and allow it to come to room temperature.

•**Make the full recipe as listed in this book, even if you live alone.** The extra portion can be placed in the refrigerator and heated up a day or two later.

•**Serve soup for dinner one or two times a week.** Leftover soup is great for lunch the following day. If you pack your lunch (or are packing lunch for a partner or child), heat the soup in the morning, and pour it into a wide-mouth thermos designed for hot foods. A good way to ensure that the soup stays hot until lunchtime is to pour boiling water into the thermos while the soup is heating on the stove. When the soup is ready, pour the water out and spoon the hot soup into the preheated thermos.

•If you live alone and have a friend or acquaintance who also lives alone, **consider sharing meals a few times a week.** You can eat your meals together or trade off delivering meals to each other.

•**Pack something special in your lunch**—a low-fat cookie, muffin, or other tasty treat that you can look forward to. A pleasant "surprise" can make you feel loved and well taken care of.

•**Make your meals as visually appealing as possible.** A sprig of parsley, a grinding of nutmeg, a carrot curl, or a sprinkling of paprika can make a bland-colored dish look much more vibrant and appetizing. Garnishes with color and/or texture contrasts add excitement and interest.

•**Set the table attractively, even if you are dining alone.** Use a beautiful place mat, utensils that have a nice feel and are in good condition,

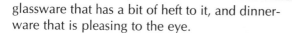

glassware that has a bit of heft to it, and dinner-ware that is pleasing to the eye.

•**Use cloth napkins.** They can be turned over or inside out and refolded to get several uses from them before they need to be laundered. Cloth napkins are also much more environmentally sound—no need to toss away paper products made from trees. As an added bonus, cloth napkins feel more "elegant" and special, even for everyday use.

•**Eat your meals slowly.** Chew thoroughly and try to savor the flavors of your food. If you have a dining partner, use this time to engage in pleasant conversation. If you are alone and desire some companionship during mealtime, play soft, beautiful music or turn on a mellow radio station. Avoid watching television while eating, though, because it will distract you from what you are putting into your mouth. Dining solo, however, can provide a good chance to catch up on your reading.

THE COOK'S TIPS

•Frozen fruit juice concentrates are excellent sweeteners. Unless they are solidly frozen, it is not necessary to defrost them before using. Store the frozen concentrate in the freezer. Once opened, transfer the concentrate to a jar or a plastic storage container with a tight fitting lid, and return it to the freezer. Another option is to cover the top of the original container tightly with plastic wrap secured with a rubber band.

•If a recipe calls for fresh juice and you only have juice concentrate on hand, you can make the exact amount you need by mixing the juice concentrate with water using a ratio of 1:3. For example, if you need 1 cup of juice, use 1/4 cup of juice concentrate mixed with 3/4 cup of water.

•If a recipe calls for tomato sauce and you only have tomato paste on hand, you can make the exact amount you need by mixing the paste with water using a ratio of 1:2. For example, if you need 1 cup of tomato sauce, use 1/3 cup of tomato paste mixed with 2/3 cup of water.

•A 14.5-ounce can of whole tomatoes equals approximately 1 2/3 cups with juice, or approximately 1 cup of tomatoes and 2/3 cup of juice. If a recipe calls for a 14.5-ounce can of whole tomatoes and you only have larger cans on hand, measure out the appropriate amount.

•A 6-ounce can of tomato paste equals approximately 2/3 cup. If a recipe calls for a 6-ounce can and you only have an 8-ounce can, measure out 2/3 cup.

•A 10.5-ounce package of silken tofu contains approximately 1 1/2 cups. If a recipe calls for a 10.5-ounce package of silken tofu and you want to cut the recipe in half (or if the recipe calls for half a 10.5-ounce package), you will need to measure out 3/4 cup of tofu.

•If you do not have oat flour, you can make it yourself from rolled oats. Just put 3/4 cup of rolled oats in a dry blender, and whirl them around for a minute or two. This will yield about 1/2 cup of oat flour.

•Two small bananas, mashed, will equal approximately 1/2 cup.

•When making pancakes and crêpes, cook one or two half-dollar-size ones before cooking those you will be serving. The first batch usually does not cook quite as thoroughly or beautifully as later batches, because the pan has not yet had a chance to become fully seasoned from the heat and oil. You can eat this first small batch yourself or offer it to your meal mate. Although it will not be very pretty, it will still taste delicious.

•When serving individual casseroles directly from the oven, place them on serving plates that are topped with a clean, folded terry washcloth, a thick kitchen towel, or a cloth napkin. This will protect your table from the heat of the casserole dish and keep your serving plates safe as well. Be sure to warn your dining partner not to touch the casserole directly. If you are serving young children, the food may be scooped out of the casserole dish into a bowl or onto a plate and allowed to cool slightly before serving.

•Approach cooking as an opportunity to have fun. Attitude is the secret ingredient to turn a mediocre meal into something magical.

•Read through a recipe completely at least once before jumping in. Then check to be sure you have all the ingredients you need on hand, and take them out ahead of time along with the utensils you'll be using.

•Don't set yourself up for failure—start with simple recipes. Remember—good cooks aren't born, they're cultivated. Anyone can learn to be a good cook!

•Try a recipe as it is written at least once before experimenting with it on your own.

•Always wear an apron! Too often trying to take "the easy way out" ends disastrously with stained and ruined clothing.

•Never sprinkle dried herbs or spices directly from the container into your simmering dish. The steam will dampen and destroy them, measurements could be inaccurate, and too much could spill into your dish. Transfer the seasonings first to your hand or to a measuring spoon away from the heat of the stove.

•To effectively chop parsley, scrunch the bunch together very tightly at the top. Then slice what you need, including the tender stems, while holding the bundle together as compactly as possible. Slide your fingers back very slightly to expose just a small portion of the parsley while you chop.

•To peel a clove of garlic, crush the clove slightly with the flat side of a chef's knife. This will crack the peel and allow you to remove it more easily.

•As the saying goes, "A watched pot never boils." So, if you need to boil water, cover the pot with a lid to speed the process along. This is especially useful when you are bringing a large pot of water to a boil for pasta.

•To save energy when baking, turn off the oven near the end of the baking time, and let the residual heat do the remainder of the work.

•Do not open the oven door during baking until the specified baking time has elapsed. Opening the oven door will cause the oven temperature to drop significantly, thereby affecting the outcome and quality of the baked product.

•If your baked goods are not turning out as expected, it may not be the recipe that is at fault —it could be your oven. Check your oven's temperature with an accurate oven thermometer after your oven has been heated for about 15 minutes. If the thermometer registers higher or lower than the temperature you have set for the oven, you will need to adjust your settings accordingly. For instance, if you set your oven at 350°F but the oven thermometer registers it as actually being 300°F, you will need to set the oven dial for 400°F for any recipe calling for a 350°F oven.

•Always match the burner with the size of the pot you are using for more efficient heating and energy conservation.

•Whenever a recipe instructs you to remove a saucepan or skillet from the heat, turn the burner off completely, and put the cooking vessel on a cool part of the stove or on a trivet placed on the countertop. The burner should always be turned off, even if you will be returning the saucepan or skillet to it in a short time.

•Always make sure lids fit tightly on your pots. A loose fitting lid is inefficient and may extend the cooking time or cause uneven results.

•In order to keep cleanup to a minimum, measure dry ingredients first, wipe off the measuring utensil with a clean, dry cloth, and then measure out the wet ingredients. Always use the fewest number of cooking utensils needed, and reuse pots whenever feasible to help make cleanup a breeze.

•Keep at least two cutting boards on hand —one for onions and savory foods, and one for fruits and sweet breads. This will eliminate the unwanted transfer of flavors (so your apples won't taste like onions and your sweet rolls won't be garlicky).

•Always allow your pans to cool thoroughly before washing them or putting water into them. Otherwise, hot metal pans could bend out of shape and glass containers could crack.

•Canned beans are efficient and inexpensive and are a fine alternative to cooking up a batch of beans at home, especially if you only need a small quantity. They are nutritionally comparable to dried beans cooked at home and certainly as tasty. Draining off the liquid and rinsing the beans well will wash off much of the sodium used in processing and may also help to improve their digestibility. More varieties of dried beans are available than canned beans; nevertheless, almost every supermarket has a wide range of canned beans to choose from. (Just be sure to recycle the cans!) If you opt to use home-cooked beans when canned beans are called for in a recipe, keep in mind that each 15-ounce or 16-ounce can of beans generally contains between 1 1/2 to 1 2/3 cups of beans after draining.

•Whenever a recipe calls for bringing a mixture to a boil and cooking it for a specified amount of time, be sure to begin the timing after the mixture has come to a full rolling boil.

•Make fresh bread crumbs by grating slices of bread on a hand grater or whirling torn pieces of bread in a food processor fitted with a metal blade.

•To ease the task of cleaning your blender, place a few drops of dish detergent in the bottom of the blender jar and add 1/2 cup of water. Blend for one or two minutes on low before thoroughly washing the jar.

•Juice several lemons at a time, and keep the juice in a tightly sealed, non-metal container in the refrigerator. Fresh lemon juice will keep for about two weeks, and it's very convenient to have on hand, especially if a recipe calls for just a small quantity. The bright flavor and tartness of fresh lemon juice is incomparable to the dull, stale taste of bottled or even frozen lemon juice.

•Always follow the food preparation instructions in the ingredient list prior to measuring an item. For example, when an ingredient is listed as "1 cup onions, chopped" be sure to chop the onions first, then measure them. An easy way to prepare the exact amount you need is to chop in small quantities, place the ingredient in a measuring cup, and add more to it as needed. This way you can "measure as you go."

•Always use a glass measuring cup to measure liquid ingredients. Place the cup on a stable, flat surface, pour the liquid into the cup, and crouch down so your eye is level with the marker on the cup. If the liquid is not at the correct marker, add more liquid or remove some of it until the quantity is exactly what the recipe requires. Remember—crouch down so your eye is level with the markers; do NOT lift the glass up so it is level with your eye. When you lift a glass of liquid it can imbalance the contents. Because you can't be sure if you are holding the glass level, it will be impossible to get an accurate reading.

•Never measure liquid or dry ingredients directly over the bowl or pot that contains your other ingredients. If what you are measuring spills into the bowl, your measurements will not be accurate, and your recipe could easily be ruined.

•When you measure sticky ingredients, such as molasses and other syrups, coat the measuring cup or measuring spoon lightly with oil. This will help the sticky food slide off easily. It will also help to keep your measurements accurate and speed cleanup.

•For dry measurements (i.e. flour, cornmeal, grains, etc.), always use high-quality metal (preferably stainless steel) or plastic measuring cups. Dry measuring cups come in nested sets that can include 2-cup, 1-cup, 1/2-cup, 1/3-cup, 1/4-cup, and 1/8-cup (2 tablespoons) sizes. Spoon the dry ingredient into the appropriate measuring cup, and use the straight edge of a table knife to level off the contents. This same method can be used to level off measuring

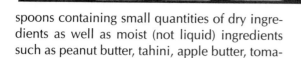

spoons containing small quantities of dry ingredients as well as moist (not liquid) ingredients such as peanut butter, tahini, apple butter, tomato paste, etc.

• It is not necessary to sift whole grain flours. In fact, doing so will separate out the bran. In some recipes you may desire this in order to make the flour "lighter," but in most cases sifting will merely defeat the purpose of using whole grain flour in the first place. Instead of sifting, simply stir the flour in the bag or canister to aerate it before measuring—I find that a dry wire whisk works best. Then lightly spoon the flour into a dry measuring cup (metal or plastic), and level off the top with the straight edge of a table knife.

• To test if a skillet or saucepan is properly heated or if the oil you are heating in it is ready, moisten your fingertips with water, and flick a few droplets into the pan. If the droplets sputter and steam, the pan is ready. If the droplets skitter rapidly across the bottom of the pan, then the pan is extremely hot, and the heat may be turned up too high.

• Wash your pots and pans as soon as possible after using them, once they have cooled. Sometimes, however, a long, overnight soaking in soapy water can do miracles for loosening burnt, baked-on or hard-to-remove food. Just fill the pots or pans with very hot water and a few drops of dish detergent. In the morning, wipe them out with a soft cloth to remove any loosened food, and finish the cleaning with soap, hot water, and a nylon scrubber.

A Word About Seasonal Cooking

Although all of the recipes in this book are appropriate any time of the year, certain recipes are more suitable for particular seasons. Lighter fare that contains predominantly fresh fruits and vegetables is most welcome during warmer months or in hot climates, whereas heavier foods, canned items, and recipes which require longer cooking times are preferred in colder weather. What recipes are best for you will depend on your personal preferences, the climate where you live, and the foods that are prevalent in your region at various times throughout the year.

BASIC COOKING TERMS

If you are new to cooking, the following definitions of cooking terms which are used throughout this book should prove helpful.

Al Dente (al-DEN-tay): This is an Italian phrase meaning "to the tooth." It is used to describe pasta or other food that is cooked only until it offers a slight resistance when bitten into, but which is not overdone or soft.

Baste: To flavor, glaze, or moisten food by brushing or spooning on a liquid during cooking.

Beat: To combine thoroughly or make smooth by vigorously stirring with a spoon, wire whisk, rotary or electric beater, or electric mixer.

Blanch: To briefly cook fruits, vegetables, or nuts in boiling water in order to loosen their skins so the skins can then be removed easily. Blanching is also done to wilt leafy greens or to soften vegetables prior to incorporating them in a recipe.

Blend: To gently mix ingredients with a spoon, electric blender, electric mixer, or food processor until evenly smooth in texture and uniform in color.

Braise: To cook food slowly in a small amount of liquid in a tightly covered pan.

Broil: To cook food under direct, dry heat.

Broth: A thin, clear liquid in which vegetables or beans have been cooked.

Casserole: A round, oval, or rectangular covered dish made of glass, ceramic, or metal which may be used for cooking in the oven. Casseroles frequently have slightly curved sides and may also be used as a serving dish. The word casserole also refers to the food which is cooked in a casserole.

Chop: To cut food into small, irregular shaped pieces, about the size of peas.

Cream: To beat a combination of ingredients until the mixture is smooth and homogenous, showing no separation nor indication of any particles.

Cube: To cut food into uniform pieces that are about 1/2 inch on all sides.

Cut In: To mix a fat with dry ingredients (such as a flour mixture) until the combination is in the form of small particles. This technique can be accomplished by using a wired tool called a *pastry blender*, two knives, a fork, or fingers.

Dice: To cut food into 1/8-inch to 1/4-inch cubes.

Dust: To lightly sprinkle food with a dry ingredient such as cornmeal or paprika in order to improve its flavor or appearance.

Fold: To delicately mix ingredients that cannot withstand stirring or beating. To fold, use a rubber spatula or wooden spoon, and gently cut down through the mixture, move across the bottom, and come back up pulling along some of the mixture from the bottom.

Garnish: To add visual appeal to a dish by decorating it with food, herbs, or other edible seasoning.

Grate: To reduce a firm piece of food to small particles or thin shreds by rubbing it against the coarse, serrated surface of a kitchen utensil called a *grater*, or by running it through a food processor fitted with a special shredding disc.

Grill: To cook food by direct heat (such as on a griddle) or indirect heat (such as on a barbecue grill) using very little or no fat in order to produce a browned surface. The word grill also refers to a piece of cooking equipment (i.e. barbecue grill) consisting of a rack placed over a heat source.

Julienne: To cut food into thin strips about 2 to 3 inches in length.

Knead: To mix and work a dough with a pressing-folding-turning action performed by pressing down into the dough with the heels of the hands, then pushing the dough away from the body. The dough is then folded in half and given a quarter turn. The process is continued for 5 to 15 minutes, or until the dough is smooth and elastic.

Mash: To press or beat food using a fork or potato masher to make a smooth mixture.

Mince: To cut food into very tiny, irregular pieces.

Moisten: To add enough water or other liquid to a dry ingredient to dampen it but not make it runny.

Pare: To remove the thin skin or outer covering of a food using a small knife or vegetable peeler.

Peel: To remove the thick skin or outer covering of a food using a small knife or vegetable peeler. The term *peel* also refers to the outer covering of a fruit or vegetable.

Pinch: A term of measurement referring to a small amount of a dry ingredient that can be held between the tips of the thumb and forefinger, approximately 1/16 of a teaspoon.

Purée: To mash or blend food into a smooth, heavy paste. The term *purée* also refers to the mixture that results when a food is mashed or blended into a smooth paste.

Ramekin (RAM-ih-kihn): A small container (usually about 3 to 4 inches in diameter) which is used for baking, has straight sides, and resembles a small soufflé dish. It is used as an individual, uncovered casserole.

Rind: The thick skin of fruits such as melon or citrus fruits.

Roast: To cook by dry, indirect heat in an oven.

Rolling boil: A liquid that is boiling so vigorously that the bubbles cannot be stirred down.

Sauté: To cook or brown food in a small amount of hot oil, stirring often to prevent scorching.

Scald: To heat a liquid to just below the boiling point when tiny bubbles begin to appear around the edge of the liquid.

Sear: To brown a food quickly using high heat to seal in its natural juices.

Shred: To cut food into long, narrow strips using a knife, grater, or food processor.

Simmer: To gently cook food in a liquid that is kept just below the boiling point so tiny bubbles form slowly and burst at or just before they reach the surface.

Sliver: To cut food into long, thin pieces.

Slice: To cut food into flat, thin pieces.

Spread: To apply a thick, soft mixture over the surface of another food, usually with a knife or spatula.

Steam: To cook food in a special steamer basket or saucepan insert over simmering water, covered with a lid.

Stir-fry: To quickly cook small pieces of food in a wok or skillet placed over high heat using a small amount of hot cooking oil. The food is stirred or tossed constantly to keep it from sticking or burning.

Stock: A thin, clear liquid containing herbs in which vegetables or beans have been cooked.

Tender-crisp: Foods that are cooked until barely tender and are still somewhat crunchy.

Zest: The colored portion of the peel of citrus fruits which does not include the bitter white portion beneath it. Zest may be removed with a special citrus zester or a vegetable peeler and is sometimes referred to as *grated peel* in recipes.

GLOSSARY OF SPECIAL INGREDIENTS

The recipes in this book may introduce you to ingredients that are unfamiliar. Most of the following are available in natural food stores, large supermarkets, or ethnic grocery stores.

Balsamic vinegar: A dark brown vinegar with an exquisite, delicate, sweet flavor.

Brown rice vinegar: A delicately flavored, amber colored vinegar made from either fermented brown rice or unrefined rice wine.

Bulgur: Pre-cooked, dried, and cracked whole wheat berries. It is available in coarse, medium, or fine grinds and needs only to be soaked in boiling water or simmered briefly to prepare. Store bulgur in a tightly sealed container at room temperature for brief periods or in the refrigerator for longer storage.

Capers: The cured flower buds of a bush indigenous to the Mediterranean and parts of Asia. The small buds are picked, dried in the sun, and then pickled in a vinegar brine. If desired, capers may be rinsed before using to remove excess salt and brine. Their peppery flavor lends a piquant tartness wherever they are used. Capers will keep indefinitely when stored in the refrigerator.

Carob powder: Made from the dried and ground pods of the locust tree (a Mediterranean evergreen), roasted carob powder has a rich, chocolate-like flavor and is often substituted in recipes measure-for-measure for cocoa powder. The recipes in this book call for only unsweetened, roasted carob powder. Store it in a tightly sealed container at room temperature away from heat and moisture.

Cilantro: Sometimes called *Chinese parsley*, cilantro leaves are the small, fragile leaves of the coriander plant. Cilantro has a pungent, distinctive flavor. It is an essential ingredient in many authentic Latin American, Asian, and Indian dishes. Store fresh cilantro in the refrigerator, and use it within three days.

Garlic granules: Made from dried, ground, fresh garlic and, unlike garlic powder, have no starches added. If you cannot find garlic granules, garlic powder may be substituted measure-for-measure. Store garlic granules at room temperature in a tightly sealed container away from heat and moisture.

Instant gluten flour: Also called *vital wheat gluten*, the protein part of the wheat kernel obtained from wheat flour that has had the starch and bran removed. Instant gluten flour is used to make *seitan*, also known as *wheat meat*, which has been a popular food in Asian countries for hundreds of years.

Traditionally, seitan has been time-consuming and labor-intensive to prepare, but with instant gluten flour, which needs only to be mixed with seasoning and a liquid, you can prepare seitan quickly and easily at home. (See recipe on pp. 156-57.) Instant gluten flour will keep indefinitely stored in an airtight container at room temperature. You can obtain instant gluten flour (vital wheat gluten) from natural food stores or bakeries. If you can not find instant gluten flour locally, it may be ordered directly from The Mail Order Catalog, P.O. Box 180,

Summertown, TN 38483. Call first for current price information at 1-800-695-2241.

Liquid smoke: This handy flavoring is used to replicate the smoky taste of ham, bacon, or other smoked meats. Try to find brands that contain only water and natural hickory smoke (some brands may contain sugar and caramel coloring). Just a few drops are usually sufficient to effectively flavor most dishes.

Miso: A salty, flavorful, fermented soybean paste which often contains rice, barley, or another grain or bean. Used primarily as a seasoning, miso ranges from dark and strongly flavored to light, smooth, and delicately flavored. The recipes in this book call only for light miso. Store miso in a tightly covered container in the refrigerator where it will keep for several months.

Non-aluminum baking powder: Most commercial brands of double-acting baking powder contain sodium aluminum sulfate, which may be harmful to your health. Two common non-aluminum brands are Rumford and Featherweight.

Non-dairy milk: A generic term which refers to any creamy, milk-like beverage such as soymilk, nut milk, or rice milk that is produced from non-animal sources.

Although my recipes call for low-fat, non-dairy milk only, you can substitute full-fat, non-dairy milk without affecting the outcome of the recipes. Most non-dairy milks will keep for up to a week when stored in a tightly sealed container in the refrigerator.

Nutritional yeast: A natural, whole plant grown on a molasses base. As opposed to torula or brewer's yeast, nutritional yeast is prized for its delicious, cheesy taste as well as its high content of B-complex vitamins. Some varieties have vitamin B-12 added; check the package label. Nutritional yeast is an *inactive* yeast (meaning it has no fermenting or leavening power), making it acceptable for use in yeast-free diets.

Nutritional yeast is available in flake or powdered form, although the recipes in this book call only for the flakes. If flaked nutritional yeast is not available in your area, use half as much of the powdered form. Some brands of packaged nutritional yeast have been combined with whey, a by-product of cheese processing. Pure nutritional yeast does not contain whey or any other dairy products, so read all product labels carefully. When kept in a cool, dry place, the physical characteristics and nutritive values of nutritional yeast will remain unchanged for at least one year.

If you are unable to locate nutritional yeast in your area, it may be ordered directly from the following source: The Mail Order Catalog, P. O. Box 180, Summertown, TN 38483. Call first for current price information at 1-800-695-2241.

Onion granules: Made from dried, ground fresh onion and similar in consistency to garlic granules (see page 16).

Pine nuts: (also called *pignolia nuts* or *piñon nuts*): The small, creamy white seeds from one of several pine tree varieties. They turn rancid quickly, so store them in the refrigerator in an airtight container for up to two months or in the freezer for up to six months. Pine nuts can be found in the spice, nut, or gourmet section of food stores.

Poultry seasoning: This seasoning blend consists of several ground herbs, generally thyme, sage, marjoram, nutmeg, rosemary, and black pepper. Store poultry seasoning at room temperature in a tightly sealed container away from heat and moisture.

Seitan (say-TAN): Also called *wheat meat,* seitan is made from cooked gluten, one of the concentrated proteins in wheat or spelt (see **Instant gluten flour**, p. 16, and recipe, p. 156).

Soy sauce: What many people think of as "soy sauce" is little more than hydrolyzed vegetable protein, sugar, and caramel coloring. However, excellent, naturally fermented Chinese and Japanese soy sauce (labeled as *shoyu* or *tamari*) is readily available in natural food stores and most supermarkets.

Check the labels closely and make sure the product contains only soy beans, salt, water, and possibly wheat. Good soy sauces with reduced sodium are also available. If you have a sensitivity to yeasted or fermented foods, look for *liquid aminos*, a rich, beefy-tasting soy product that has not been fermented.

Sweeteners: A variety of pure vegetarian sweeteners abound which provide a delicious alternative in taste and texture to white table sugar. Some choices for granulated sweeteners include unbleached granulated sugarcane juice (a lovely amber sweetener with a light molasses taste; some brands such as Sucanat are made from organically grown sugar cane), turbinado sugar (granulated sugar cane that has been steam cleaned, with coarse crystals that are blond-colored and have a delicate molasses flavor), or granulated maple sugar.

Options for liquid sweeteners include pure maple syrup, molasses, sorghum syrup, corn syrup, rice syrup, frozen fruit juice concentrates, and concentrated fruit juice syrups. Peruse the shelves of your local natural food store for these and other commercial sweeteners. Experiment with them to see which ones have the flavors you most prefer. You may wish to invest in a small quantity of several different sweeteners and try them in various recipes.

Tahini: A smooth, creamy, tan-colored paste made by finely grinding hulled, raw or roasted sesame seeds. It is an essential ingredient in many Middle Eastern recipes and adds a wonderful texture and nutty flavor to spreads, sauces, and dressings. Tahini may be very thick, like peanut butter, or thin and slightly runny depending on the brand. As with all unrefined nut and seed butters, store tahini in the refrigerator to keep it from becoming rancid and to keep the oil from separating out. (However, if the oil does separate out, simply stir it back in.)

Tempeh (TEM-pay): A protein-rich food made from split and hulled soybeans that are cooked and fermented. Grains such as millet and quinoa are often added. Tempeh is excellent steamed, baked, or sautéed, and when it is grated it can easily replace ground meat in traditional recipes. If the package does not state that the tempeh is fully cooked and ready to use, you will need to steam, sauté, or bake it for 20 minutes before eating it or make sure that the recipe in which you are using it involves cooking it for that length of time. Tempeh is available refrigerated or frozen in natural food stores.

Tofu: A delicate, mild, white cheese made from soymilk curds and pressed into block form. Although there are many flavored and marinated tofus on the market, there are essentially two basic types of unflavored tofu: *regular* and *silken*.

Regular tofu tends to be grainier and firmer than silken tofu and adds texture and chewiness to recipes. Depending on the manufacturer, regular tofu may come in only one firmness or may be available in a range of firmness from soft to firm to extra firm. You can easily recognize "regular" tofu, because it is always packed in water. It is available in bulk or vacuum sealed tubs or packages, usually containing a one-pound portion. The packages should be stamped with a freshness or expiration date.

Silken tofu is actually made right inside its aseptic package. Each package weighs 10.5 ounces and, as long as the package is not opened, aseptically packaged silken tofu will keep for many months without requiring refrigeration. Silken tofu also comes in a range including soft, firm, and extra firm. Silken tofu's overall consistency is very smooth and custardy, and it works best when it is blended with sauces and dips to add creaminess.

Both regular and silken tofu are available in fat-reduced (lite) versions, and those are the ones I recommend using in this book. However, full-fat tofu products may be substituted if necessary or desired, without affecting the outcome of the recipes. Once the package is opened, tofu should be stored submerged in water in a clean, covered container. Rinse the tofu and replace the old water with fresh water daily. Stored this way, tofu will keep for about five days in the refrigerator. Always rinse tofu and pat it dry before using.

BASIC EQUIPMENT

What you'll need in your "kitchen for two" to make the recipes in this book:

1 or 2 sets of measuring spoons
1 or 2 sets of mixing bowls with at least 3 bowls each of differing sizes
1 or 2 sets of measuring cups for dry ingredients (including 1/4-cup, 1/3-cup, 1/2-cup and 1-cup measures)
1 or 2 1-cup calibrated glass measuring cups
1 2-cup calibrated glass measuring cup
1 large slotted spoon
several wooden spoons in various sizes
1 large wire whisk
1 flat metal spatula
2 rubber spatulas
1 high-quality, well-sharpened, all-purpose utility knife with a 5-, 6-, 7-, or 8-inch blade (select a knife with a comfortable weight, a comfortable size blade, and a handle that suits the size of your hand)
2 solid wood cutting boards (one for onions and vegetables; one for fruits and breads)
1 vegetable peeler
1 vegetable brush (a stiff bristled brush designed for scrubbing potatoes and other vegetables)
1 sturdy garlic press
1 colander
1 large wire mesh strainer
1 1-quart saucepan with lid
1 2-quart saucepan with lid
1 4 1/2-quart Dutch oven or saucepan with lid
1 6-quart Dutch oven or saucepan with lid
1 9-inch or 10-inch skillet with lid (stainless steel or cast iron)
1 4-quart or 6-quart casserole with lid
1 stainless steel, collapsible steamer basket or 1 steamer insert designed to fit into a lidded saucepan

2 15-ounce or 16-ounce ramekins or individual casseroles
1 baking sheet
1 cooling rack
1 9-inch or 10-inch glass pie plate
1 6-cup stainless steel or nonstick muffin tin
1 blender
1 small food processor
1 box-style grater
1 can opener
2 aprons
2 potholders or oven mitts
6 stainless steel, glass, or plastic storage containers of various sizes with tight fitting lids
plenty of dish towels, hand towels, dish detergent, dish sponges, and nylon pot scrubbers

Optional Equipment: (your particular kitchen set-up and cooking style will determine whether these are optionals or necessities)
1 lemon reamer
1 citrus zester
1 salad spinner
1 kitchen timer
1 kitchen scale
1 flame tamer (also called a "heat diffuser")
1 toaster oven
1 potato masher
1 stovetop or outdoor grill
1 oven thermometer
1 9-inch or 10-inch nonstick skillet with lid
1 4-quart or 6-quart pressure cooker
1 sturdy peppermill
1 electric spice and seed mill (to grind whole spices)

A Note From Anne & Matt:

Buy a food processor, the best one you can afford. A good food processor has saved us time and also given us many more menu options.

SETTING UP YOUR PANTRY

Because tastes, lifestyles, and personalities differ greatly, there is no "right way" to approach meal planning. Some people like to shop at the last minute, while others prefer to have a week of meals scheduled in advance with every item pre-purchased. Either way, having a well-stocked pantry, spice and herb cabinet, refrigerator, and freezer will be a great asset when trying to plan meals, especially if your time is limited.

I recommend setting aside a few minutes one evening or weekend morning to take stock of what you already have on hand. Use the following charts to determine what's on your shelves and what you need to purchase. Make a list and take it with you to the store. Once you have a well-stocked kitchen, meal preparation will be much easier. When you are almost out of a particular item, write it on your weekly shopping roster—this way you will always have ample supplies available.

A well-stocked pantry is advantageous for several reasons:
• You will be less tempted to make impulse purchases;
• You will be able to more easily maintain a healthful, low-fat, well-balanced diet;
• You will be able to plan ahead or prepare last minute dishes depending on your schedule or personal style;
• Although setting up a pantry initially can be slightly costly, especially if you have very little on your shelves to begin with, once you have established your pantry, maintaining it is easy and relatively inexpensive.

The following is a master list to be used as a general guideline. Adapt it to suit your kitchen needs and personal preferences.

CUPBOARD STAPLES

Canned Goods
2 15-16-ounce cans pinto beans
2 15-16-ounce cans garbanzo beans
2 15-16-ounce cans great northern beans
2 15-16-ounce cans black beans
any additional canned beans of your choice
3 8-ounce cans sliced beets
3 8-ounce cans whole kernel corn
4 14.5-ounce cans whole tomatoes
4 8-ounce cans tomato sauce
4 6-ounce cans tomato paste
1 8-ounce can crushed unsweetened pineapple packed in juice
1 8-ounce can unsweetened pineapple chunks packed in juice

Grains, Pasta & Dry Goods
1 package quick-cooking rolled oats
2 boxes quick-cooking brown rice
1 pound long-grain brown rice
other rices of your choice (arborio, basmati, short-grain brown rice, wild rice, etc.)
1 pound couscous
1 pound bulgur (medium ground)
1 pound millet
1 pound quinoa
2 pounds instant gluten flour (vital wheat gluten)
2 to 4 pounds pasta (elbow macaroni, linguine, penne, rotini, spaghetti, ziti, etc.)
1 container non-caffeinated coffee substitute (i.e. Pero, Kaffree Roma, etc.)
1 or 2 boxes low-sugar, whole grain cereals
1 container non-aluminum baking powder (such as Rumford)
1 box baking soda
1 box cornstarch
1 container unsweetened roasted carob powder
2 boxes or bags instant potato flakes

Packaged & Bottled Goods

6 8-ounce or 2 1-quart packages aseptic, low-fat soymilk, rice milk, or almond milk

4 10.5-ounce aseptic packages low-fat, firm silken tofu

1 or 2 bottles fat-free or low-fat salad dressing

1 jar salsa

1 jar low-sodium sauerkraut

1 bottle fat-free barbecue sauce

1 jar applesauce

1 container nutritional yeast flakes

1 or more bottles vinegar (brown rice, red wine, apple cider, balsamic, etc.)

1 bottle naturally fermented soy sauce

1 bottle anchovy-free Worcestershire sauce

1 container prepared yellow mustard

1 jar Dijon mustard

1 container ketchup

1 bottle Tabasco sauce

1 or 2 packages dried fruit (raisins, currants, dates, apricots, prunes, etc.)

Oils

1 small bottle olive oil

1 small bottle canola oil

1 container nonstick cooking spray

Sweeteners & Jellies

1 or 2 containers granulated sweetener (i.e. unbleached granulated sugar cane juice such as Sucanat, turbinado sugar, granulated maple sugar, etc.)

1 or 2 containers liquid sweetener (i.e. brown rice syrup, pure maple syrup, sorghum, light molasses, corn syrup, etc.)

1 or 2 jars fruit-sweetened jam or jelly (apricot, raspberry, blackberry, etc.)

1 jar sugar-free apple butter and/or other fruit butters

Seasonings & Herbs

1 container ground black pepper (or whole peppercorns if you have a pepper grinder)

1 container each dried herbs (basil, bay leaves, dill weed, marjoram, oregano, sage, tarragon, thyme, etc.)

1 container each ground spices (allspice, chili powder, cinnamon, cloves, coriander, cumin, curry powder, fennel seed, ginger, nutmeg, poultry seasoning, turmeric, etc.)

1 container each whole spices (caraway seeds, cloves, cumin seeds, peppercorns, etc.)

2 bulbs fresh garlic

1 container garlic granules

1 container onion granules

1 container dried onion flakes

1 container salt (sea salt or rock salt)

1 container vegetable seasoned salt (such as Spike, Vegesal, or any other favorite brand)

1 container crushed hot red pepper flakes

Snack Foods

1 package baked tortilla chips

1 package baked potato chips

1 package pretzels

1-2 packages low-fat cookies

1-2 packages low-fat whole grain crackers

1 package rice crackers

1 package rice cakes

1-2 packages fruit leather

1 package plain popcorn

Fresh staples to be stored at room temperature or cooler (but not refrigerated):

1 bunch bananas

4 to 6 onions

4 to 6 potatoes

4 to 6 sweet potatoes/yams (in season)

2 to 4 tomatoes (in season)

grapefruit/oranges and other citrus fruit

Refrigerator Staples:
Produce
6 lemons
1 pound carrots
1 head celery
other assorted fresh vegetables
1 head romaine or leaf lettuce
fresh parsley
other fresh herbs as desired
assorted fresh fruits

Soy Products
1 pound fat-reduced, firm regular tofu
1 package light miso (preferably sweet white miso)
1 jar low-fat, egg-free mayonnaise

Flours & Grain Meals
4 to 5 pounds whole wheat pastry flour
2 pounds yellow cornmeal
2 pounds oat flour

Nut & Seed Butters
1 jar peanut butter
1 jar almond butter
1 jar tahini

Miscellaneous
1 pound seiten (may also be stored in the freezer)
1 package active dry baking yeast

Freezer Staples:
Juice Concentrates
2 containers unsweetened apple juice concentrate
1 container orange juice concentrate
other juice concentrates as desired

Breads
1 loaf sliced whole grain bread
1 package whole grain bagels

Fruit
1 small package sliced peaches
other frozen fruit as desired (blueberries, raspberries, strawberries)

Vegetables
2 10-ounce packages frozen chopped spinach
2 10-ounce packages frozen mixed vegetables
1 1-pound loose-pack bag green peas
1 1-pound loose-pack bag corn kernels
1 1-pound loose-pack bag green beans
1 1-pound loose-pack bag broccoli
other packaged vegetables of your choice

Nuts (Nuts should be stored in the freezer in an airtight container to maintain freshness for long periods of time. Frozen nuts can be used directly from the freezer in all recipes.)
1/2 pound shelled walnuts
1 small package slivered almonds
1 small package whole almonds
1/2 pound raw (not roasted) sunflower seeds

Soy Products & Burgers
1 package tofu frankfurters (hot dogs)
1 package vegetarian burger patties
2 8-ounce packages tempeh

Frozen Desserts
1 package frozen fruit juice bars
1 container low-fat non-dairy frozen dessert

HERB & SPICE SUBSTITUTIONS

If you want to experiment, or if you are in a pinch and do not have the herb or spice a recipe calls for, try some of the following alternatives. Start with a smaller amount than the recipe requires (about half), and then add more until the flavors taste right to you.

HERB SUBSTITUTIONS

Basil:
Oregano
Thyme

Chives:
Leeks
Onions
Scallions
Shallots

Cilantro:
Parsley
Any combination of basil, oregano, and rosemary

Marjoram:
Basil
Savory
Thyme

Mint:
Basil
Marjoram
Rosemary

Oregano:
Basil
Thyme

Parsley:
Chervil
Cilantro

Rosemary:
Tarragon
Thyme
Savory

Sage:
Marjoram
Poultry seasoning
Rosemary
Savory

Savory:
Marjoram
Sage
Thyme

Tarragon:
Chervil
Pinch of ground fennel seed

Thyme:
Basil
Marjoram
Oregano
Savory

SPICE SUBSTITUTIONS

Allspice:
Cinnamon
Pinch of ground cloves
Pinch of ground nutmeg

Aniseed:
Fennel seed
A few drops of anise extract

Cardamom:
Ground ginger

Cayenne Pepper:
Ground black pepper
Dash of Tabasco sauce
Ground white pepper

Cinnamon:
Pinch of ground allspice
Pinch of ground nutmeg

Cloves:
Pinch of allspice
Pinch of cinnamon
Pinch of nutmeg

Fennel:
Aniseed
A few drops of anise extract

Ground Cumin:
Chili powder

Ground Ginger:
Ground allspice
Ground cinnamon
Ground mace
Ground nutmeg

Ground Mace:
Ground allspice
Ground cinnamon
Ground ginger
Ground nutmeg

Ground Nutmeg:
Ground cinnamon
Ground ginger
Ground mace

Saffron:
Tiny pinch of turmeric (to add color)

White Pepper:
Dash of Tabasco sauce

A Note From Glenn:
I've had little instruction in cooking, which I assume is typical of most men, so I sometimes fall prey to misconceptions. I have learned to not avoid recipes just because they have a long list of ingredients. Many of these are likely to be seasonings which only require measuring. An investment in a well-stocked spice rack has saved me a great deal of time and effort.

MAIL ORDER SUPPLIERS OF NATURAL FOODS

The ingredients for the recipes in this book are generally available at well-stocked supermarkets and natural food stores. If you are unable to purchase the ingredients you need locally, the following mail order sources should be of great assistance. Call to inquire about price information or to request a catalog.

American Spoon Foods
411 East Lake Street
Petosky, MI 47770
1-800-222-5886
No-sugar-added fruit spreads.

Ariël Vineyards
Napa, CA 94558
1-800-456-9472
An impressive selection of premium de-alcoholized wine

Arrowhead Mills, Inc.
P.O. Box 2059
Hereford, TX 79045
1-800-858-4308
Organic whole grains, beans, seeds, flours, oils, peanut butter, and stupendous tahini.

Diamond Organics
Freedom, CA 95019
1-800-922-2396
Huge, year round assortment of stunning organic greens, vegetables, fresh and dried fruits, and nuts.

Frankferd Farms
717 Saxonburg Boulevard
Saxonburg, PA 16056
1-412-352-9500
Wide selection of organic grains, flours, nuts, seeds, dried fruits, pastas, non-dairy milks, and macrobiotic foods.

Gold Mine Natural Food Co.
1947 30th Street
San Diego, CA 92102-1105
1-800-475-3663
A wide variety of macrobiotic items including umeboshi plum paste, brown rice vinegar, misos, oils, nuts, seeds, organic grains and beans, and non-caffeinated grain beverages.

Herb and Spice Collection
(div. of Frontier Cooperative Herbs)
3021 78th Street
P.O. Box 299
Norway, IA 52318
1-800-786-1388
Non-irradiated herbs, spices, extracts, and flavorings along with related accessories. A good source for herbal seasonings, all-natural, vegan bacon bits, and vegetable oils. Many products are available in bulk.

The Mail Order Catalog
P.O. Box 180
Summertown, TN 38483
1-800-695-2241
Textured vegetable protein, nutritional yeast flakes, tempeh starter, and instant gluten flour (vital wheat gluten) for making seitan.

The Mountain Ark Trader
P.O. Box 3170
Fayetteville, AR 72702
1-800-643-8909
Macrobiotic items and equipment. A good source for umeboshi plum paste, toasted sesame oil, brown rice vinegar, and misos.

Vermont Country Maple, Inc.
P.O. Box 53
Jericho Center, VT 05465
1-802-864-7519
Pure maple syrup and granulated Maple Sprinkles.

Walnut Acres Organic Farms
Penns Creek, PA 17862
1-800-433-3998
Organic produce, fruits, flours, peanut butter, and canned beans.

KID-PLEASING RECIPES

These recipes were given the official stamp of approval from the kids who tested them. I hope these are a hit with the special children in your life.

Potatoes
Aunt Shayna's Potato Cakes, p. 143
Favorite Mashed Potatoes, p. 141
Hash Browns, p. 139
Old Country Potatoes, p. 142-43
Oven "Fried" Potatoes, p. 137
Pierogies in a Pot, p. 144-45
Twice-Baked Potatoes, p. 138

Grains
Bean & Bulgar Pilaf, p. 152
Brown Rice Croquettes, p. 144

Pasta
Baked Macaroni & Vegetable Casseroles,
p. 148
Cabbage & Pasta Bake, p. 149
Cheezy Macaroni, p. 151
Macaroni Skillet Dinner, p. 145
Pasta & Dogs, p. 150
Peanut Butter Noodles, p. 147
Pierogies in a Pot, p. 144-45

Tofu, Tempeh, Seitan & Beans
Chili Bean Topping for Grains or Pasta, p. 170-71
Country-Style Scrambled Tofu, p. 161
Crispy Tofu Sticks, p. 158
Easy Baked Beans, p. 171
Italian Beans & Bows, p. 174
Kraut, Dogs & Dumplings, p. 163
Rayaya's Tofu Cutlets, p. 159
Red Flannel Hash, p. 172
Saucy Beans & Franks, p. 170
Shepherd's Pie, p. 164-65

SUPER DUPER QUICK & EASY RECIPES

These recipes require an absolute minimum of preparation and cooking time for those days when you really, really, really don't feel like doing too much in the kitchen.

Sandwiches, Dips & Spreads
Bean Burritos, p. 101
Best Bean Burgers, p. 105
Carrot-Tofu Salad Sandwiches, p. 96
Cheeze Pizza for Two, p. 103
Cheeze Sandwiches - Toasted or Grilled, p. 93
Chili Rolls, p. 95
Deviled Tofu, p. 96
Green Pea Spread, p. 107
Open-face Seitan Sandwiches with Gravy, p. 99
P.B. & Broccoli Sandwiches, p. 94
P.L.T.s, p. 97
Ranch-Style Spread & Dip, p. 109
Simple Bean Spread & Dip, p. 107
Simple Grain Spread, p. 108
Tempeh Salad, p. 100
Tempeh Sloppy Joes, p. 100
Tofu Salad, p. 95

Soups
Breakfast Noodle Soup, p. 77
Mushroom Barley Chowder, p. 85
Old-Fashioned Tomato Rice Soup, p. 85
Pan Handle Chili, p. 79
Squash, Cabbage & White Bean Soup, p. 83

Salads
Cabbage & Apple Slaw with Caraway Vinaigrette, p. 66
Carrot-Sunflower Salad, p. 68
Waldorf Salad, p. 69

Vegetable Ideas
Stir-Fries Tonight!, p. 118

Grains, Potatoes & Pasta
Cheezy Macaroni, p. 151
Instant Mashed Potatoes, p. 142
Macaroni Skillet Dinner, p. 145
Peanut Butter Noodles, p. 147

Tofu, Tempeh, Seitan & Beans
Bean & Bulgur Pilaf, p. 152
Chili Bean Topping for Grains or Pasta, p. 170-71
Country-Style Scrambled Tofu, p. 161
Crispy Tofu Sticks, p. 158
Easy Baked Beans, p. 171
Italian Beans & Bows, p. 174
New Orleans Peasant-Style Red Beans, p. 173
Rayaya's Tofu Cutlets, p. 159
Saucy Beans & Franks, p. 170

The following menus offer a few ideas to get you started. If you are able to plan a full week (or several days' worth) of menus in advance, you can consolidate several shopping trips into one. Of course, you'll need to check on what is in your pantry, refrigerator, and freezer. Then make a list of everything you'll need to purchase.

If these menus do not suit your taste, meet your calorie requirements, or offer enough fresh fruits and vegetables for your liking, feel free to adjust them wherever you see fit. They are merely suggestions which may be followed precisely or mixed and matched as *you* deem appropriate.

Week One Menus

DAY 1

Breakfast:
Hot Oatmeal, p. 51,
with sliced bananas

Lunch:
Tempeh Sloppy Joes, p. 100
Celery and carrot sticks
Apple

Dinner:
"Fried" Tomatoes, p. 121
Brown rice
Steamed greens
Almond Fudge Cookies, p. 179

DAY 2

Breakfast:
Cinnamon Applesauce Muffins,
p. 41
Fresh fruit or fruit juice

Lunch:
P.L.T.s, p. 97
Almond Fudge Cookies
(from Day 1)

Dinner:
Bean & Bulgur Pilaf, p. 152
Steamed broccoli

DAY 3

Breakfast:
Karen's Kalewiches, p. 49

Lunch:
Cornucopia Oat Burgers, p. 104
on whole grain buns
with ketchup
Orange

Dinner:
Lentil, Mushroom
& Macaroni Stew, p. 88
Raw carrot sticks

DAY 4

Breakfast:
Cinnamon Applesauce Muffins
(from Day 2)
Fresh fruit or fruit juice

Lunch:
White Bean Hummus, p. 106
Whole wheat pita bread
Raw vegetable sticks

Dinner:
Cheezy Macaroni, p. 151
Steamed broccoli
or green beans and squash
Sliced fresh tomatoes

DAY 5

Breakfast:
Peanut Butter Banana
Pancakes, p. 34
with Extended Maple Syrup,
p. 55

Lunch:
Leftover Lentil Mushroom &
Macaroni Stew (from Day 3)
Orange & Carrot Salad, p. 69

Dinner:
Stuffed Sweet Potatoes, p. 140
Sliced beets
Steamed greens

DAY 6

Breakfast:
Breakfast Burritos, p. 48

Lunch:
Simple Grain Spread, p. 108,
on bagels
Fresh fruit

Dinner:
Red Flannel Hash, p. 172
with ketchup or gravy
Steamed broccoli

DAY 7

Breakfast:
French Toast, p. 32, with Hot Peach Topping, p. 54

Lunch:
Corn & Potato Chowder, p. 81, with whole grain crackers
Fresh fruit

Dinner:
Garbanzo & Vegetable Dinner Salad, p. 59
Sunflower Cookies, p. 181

Week Two Menus

DAY 1

Breakfast:
Quick Brown Rice Porridge, p. 51,

Lunch:
Deviled Tofu, p. 96, on bagels
Apple

Dinner:
Warm Dutch Potato Salad, p. 61
Leftover Sunflower Cookies,
(from Week 1, Day 7)

DAY 2

Breakfast:
Grapefruit halves
Yankee Corn Muffins, p. 39
Apple butter

Lunch:
Creamy-Crunchy Garbanzo
Salad, p. 60
Pear

Dinner:
Stir-Fries Tonight!, p. 118
Brown rice, p. 132-33

DAY 3

Breakfast:
Bear Mush, p. 52

Lunch:
P.B. & Broccoli Sandwiches, p. 94
Apple

Dinner:
Spicy Soy Crumble, p. 175
Favorite Mashed Potatoes, p. 141
Steamed green beans

DAY 4

Breakfast:
Fresh fruit or fruit juice
Yankee Corn Muffins
(from Day 2)

Lunch:
Old-Fashioned Tomato Rice
Soup, p. 85
Cheeze Sandwiches, p. 93

Dinner:
Bean Burritos, p. 101

DAY 5

Breakfast:
Apple Cobbler, p. 44

Lunch:
Tempeh Salad, p. 100
Whole grain crackers
Raw vegetable sticks
Banana

Dinner:
Aunt Shayna's Potato Cakes, p. 143
Sliced fresh tomatoes
Steamed kale

DAY 6

Breakfast:
Open-face Carrot Tofu Salad
Sandwiches, p. 99

Lunch:
Mushroom Barley Chowder, p. 85,
Leftover Sunflower Cookies
(from Day 1)
Orange

Dinner:
Saucy Beans & Franks, p. 170
Creamy Picnic Coleslaw, p. 65
Applesauce

DAY 7

Breakfast:
Fresh fruit or fruit juice
Glazed Cinnamon Buns, p. 46-47

Lunch:
Rayaya's Tofu Cutlets, p. 159,
on whole grain buns, with lettuce and tomato
Pear

Dinner:
Panhandle Chili, p. 79
Cornmeal Biscuits, p. 43
Cabbage & Apple Slaw with Caraway Vinaigrette, p. 66

BREAKFAST FARE & BREADS

Morning dispositions encompass everything from frazzled and harried to leisurely and relaxed. In order to accommodate your particular needs, I have created a range of recipes for those days when cold cereal just won't cut the mustard. These breakfast recipes take anywhere from 5 minutes to 30 minutes of preparation and baking or cooking time (some of the yeasted bread recipes, however, will take considerably longer due to the obligatory rising time). Some will be better suited to your weekday mornings while others will be preferable for casual weekends or brunch. Most of them are on the sweeter side without being overpowering, but you'll find a few savory surprises as well.

Breakfast is the perfect time to establish the mood and pace for the rest of your day. If you set your alarm clock just a half hour earlier, you'll be amazed at how much can be accomplished in that time. If you use that extra thirty minutes to make a special meal and then take the time to relax and enjoy it, the rest of your day can take on a brighter hue and perspective.

Additional Breakfast Ideas

If you prefer a breakfast on the sweeter side, also try the following:

Baked Apple Slices, p. 183
Carrot-Tofu Salad Sandwiches, p. 96
Rice, p. 132-33, topped with Hot Peach
    Topping, p. 54, or Hot Cinnamon
    Apple Topping, p. 54

In addition to the many breakfast recipes listed in this section, you may wish to try some other delectable dishes which lean toward the savory side of the palate. Even if the thought of having a savory breakfast holds little intrigue, I urge you to give it a try. Once Michael and I sampled savory morning meals, they rapidly became a part of our standard daily repertoire. The following are a few savory recipes which make great breakfast meals. They can be found in this section or in other sections throughout the book:

Breakfast Noodle Soup, p. 77
Karen's Kalewiches, p. 49
P.B. & Broccoli Sandwiches, p. 94
Stewed Winter Vegetables, p. 76

French Toast

This egg- and dairy-free French toast is so delicious it's hard to believe how easy it is to make. Try it with Hot Cinnamon Apple Topping, p. 54.

2/3 cup low-fat, non-dairy milk
4 teaspoons whole wheat pastry flour
1 1/2 teaspoons nutritional yeast flakes
pinch of salt (optional)

4 slices whole grain bread or whole grain sourdough bread

1. Place the milk, flour, nutritional yeast flakes, and salt in a small mixing bowl, and beat them together with a wire whisk to make a smooth, thin batter. Pour the batter into a wide, shallow bowl.

2. Dip the bread slices, one at a time, into the batter, making sure that each slice is well saturated.

3. Mist a 9-inch or 10-inch skillet with nonstick cooking spray, or coat it with a thin layer of canola oil. Place the skillet over medium-high heat. When the skillet is hot, add the soaked bread slices in a single layer. If all four slices will not fit in the skillet comfortably, cook just two slices at a time.

4. When the bottoms of the bread slices are well browned, carefully turn each slice over using a metal spatula. Cook the other sides until they are a deep golden brown. Serve hot.

Yield: 2 servings

Per serving: Calories: 183, Protein: 7 gm., Fat: 2 gm., Carbohydrate: 33 gm.

The Cook's Secrets:

If you need to cook the French Toast in two batches, a few drops of canola oil should be added to the skillet between each batch to help keep the French Toast from sticking to the pan.

Keep the first batch of French Toast warm by placing the cooked slices on a small, nonstick baking sheet in a 300°F oven while the second batch is cooking. If you do not have a nonstick baking sheet, use a regular baking sheet misted with nonstick cooking spray.

Whole Wheat Apple Pancakes

No need to set the alarm clock when these marvelous pancakes are on the menu. Moist and hefty, the aroma alone is a terrific wake-up call. Top them with a just touch of pure maple syrup.

3/4 cup whole wheat pastry flour
1 teaspoon non-aluminum baking powder (such as Rumford)
1/2 teaspoon ground cinnamon

1/2 cup low-fat, non-dairy milk
1 teaspoon vanilla extract

1 Granny Smith apple, peeled and grated (about 3/4 cup lightly packed)
3 Tablespoons raisins (optional)

1. Place the flour, baking powder, and cinnamon in a medium mixing bowl, and stir them together until they are thoroughly combined.

2. Pour the milk and vanilla extract into the dry ingredients, and stir them together with a wooden spoon to mix well. Stir in the grated apple. Then stir in the raisins, if using.

3. Mist a 9-inch or 10-inch skillet with nonstick cooking spray, and place it over medium-high heat. When the skillet is hot, spoon in the batter using 2 level tablespoonfuls for each pancake. Spread out each pancake using the back of a spoon.

4. You will need to cook the pancakes in several batches depending upon the size of your skillet. Cook the pancakes until the bottoms are brown, adjusting the heat as necessary. Carefully loosen the pancakes, and turn them over using a metal spatula. Cook the second side briefly, just until golden.

Yield: 2 servings (4 small pancakes per serving)

Per serving: Calories: 213, Protein: 7 gm., Fat: 1 gm., Carbohydrate: 43 gm.

The Cook's Secrets:
A nonstick skillet will work best. If you do not have a nonstick skillet, a few drops of canola oil should be added to the skillet between each batch to help keep the pancakes from sticking to the pan.

Keep the first batch of pancakes warm by placing them on a small, nonstick baking sheet in a 300°F oven while the remainder cook. If you do not have a nonstick baking sheet, use a regular baking sheet misted with nonstick cooking spray.

Peanut Butter Banana Pancakes

Kids love 'em with pure maple syrup, but fresh fruit or a fruit sauce is just as delightful.

3/4 cup whole wheat pastry flour
1 teaspoon non-aluminum baking powder (such as Rumford)

1 small, ripe banana, mashed (about 1/3 cup)
2 teaspoons smooth peanut butter
1/2 cup low-fat, non-dairy milk
1 teaspoon vanilla extract

1. Place the flour and baking powder in a medium mixing bowl, and stir them together until they are thoroughly combined.

2. Place the banana in a separate medium mixing bowl, and mash it well using a fork or your hands.

3. Add the peanut butter to the mashed banana, and cream them together. Stir in the milk and vanilla extract.

4. Pour the liquid mixture (from step #3) into the dry ingredients (from step #1), and stir them together until they are well combined.

5. Mist a 9-inch or 10-inch skillet with nonstick cooking spray, and place it over medium-high heat. When the skillet is hot, spoon in the batter using 2 level tablespoonfuls for each pancake. Spread out each pancake using the back of a spoon.

6. You will need to cook the pancakes in several batches depending upon the size of your skillet. Cook the pancakes until the bottoms are brown, adjusting the heat as necessary. Carefully loosen the pancakes, and turn them over using a metal spatula. Cook the second side briefly, just until golden.

Yield: 2 servings (4 to 5 pancakes per serving)

Per serving: Calories: 256, Protein: 8 gm., Fat: 4 gm., Carbohydrate: 47 gm.

The Cook's Secrets:
A nonstick skillet will work best. If you do not have a nonstick skillet, a few drops of canola oil should be added to the skillet between each batch to help keep the pancakes from sticking to the pan.

Keep the first batch of pancakes warm by placing them on a small, nonstick baking sheet in a 300°F oven while the remainder cook. If you do not have a nonstick baking sheet, use a regular baking sheet misted with nonstick cooking spray.

Banana Blueberry Pancakes

Plump, fresh blueberries dot the landscape of these spring and summer breakfast favorites.

2/3 cup whole wheat pastry flour
1/3 cup quick-cooking rolled oats (not instant)
1 teaspoon non-aluminum baking powder (such as Rumford)

1/2 cup ripe banana, mashed
1/2 cup low-fat, non-dairy milk
1/2 teaspoon vanilla extract

1/2 cup fresh blueberries

1. Place the flour, rolled oats, and baking powder in a medium mixing bowl, and stir them together until they are thoroughly combined.

2. Place the banana in a separate medium mixing bowl, and mash it well using a fork or your hands. Measure out 1/2 cup, set any remaining banana aside, and return the 1/2 cup to the bowl.

3. Stir the milk and vanilla extract into the banana, and pour this mixture into the dry ingredients (from step #1). Mix well. Then fold in the blueberries.

4. Mist a 9-inch or 10-inch skillet with nonstick cooking spray, and place it over medium-high heat. When the skillet is hot, spoon in the batter using 2 level tablespoonfuls for each pancake.

5. You will need to cook the pancakes in several batches depending on the size of your skillet. Cook the pancakes until the bottoms are well browned, adjusting the heat as necessary. Carefully loosen the pancakes, and turn them over using a metal spatula. Cook the second side briefly, just until golden.

Yield: 2 to 3 servings (makes 10 pancakes)

Per serving: Calories: 119, Protein: 7 gm., Fat: 2 gm., Carbohydrate: 45 gm.

The Cook's Secrets:
A nonstick skillet will work best. If you do not have a nonstick skillet, a few drops of canola oil should be added to the skillet between each batch to help keep the pancakes from sticking to the pan.

Keep the first batch of pancakes warm by placing them on a small, nonstick baking sheet in a 300°F oven while the remainder cook. If you do not have a nonstick baking sheet, use a regular baking sheet misted with nonstick cooking spray.

Whole Wheat Muffins

These lightly sweetened muffins are great for breakfast, but they also make a delightful accompaniment to soups, salads, and dinner entrées. The straightforward flavor lends itself to creative adaptation, so feel free to experiment by adding herbs, spices, flavoring extracts, or chopped dried fruits to make sweet or savory muffins. Many options are presented in Muffin Magic, p. 37.

1 1/3 cups whole wheat pastry flour
1/2 teaspoon non-aluminum baking powder (such as Rumford)
1/2 teaspoon baking soda
1/4 teaspoon salt

1/2 cup low-fat, non-dairy milk or water
3 Tablespoons apple juice concentrate
1 Tablespoon canola oil
1/2 to 1 teaspoon vanilla extract (optional for sweet muffins; do not use in savory muffins)

1. Preheat the oven to 350°F. Coat a 6-cup muffin tin with nonstick cooking spray, and set it aside.

2. Place the flour, baking powder, baking soda, and salt in a medium mixing bowl, and stir them together.

3. Place the remaining ingredients in a separate small mixing bowl or measuring cup, and stir until they are well combined. Pour this liquid mixture into the dry ingredients (from step #2), and stir them together to form a smooth, thick batter.

4. Immediately spoon the batter equally into the prepared muffin cups. Bake the muffins for 18 to 20 minutes.

5. Gently loosen the muffins and turn them on their sides in the muffin tin. Cover them with a clean kitchen towel, and let them rest for 5 minutes. This will keep them from developing a hard crust.

6. Transfer the muffins to a cooling rack, and serve them warm or at room temperature.

Yield: 6 muffins

Per muffin: Calories: 129, Protein: 4 gm., Fat: 2 gm., Carbohydrate: 22 gm.

The Cook's Secrets:
• Always preheat the oven and prepare the muffin tin before you mix the batter.
• Stir the batter just enough to combine the ingredients. Overbeating can make muffins heavy or tough.
• Work quickly since baking powder will loose its effectiveness if it is allowed to sit too long.
• Distribute the batter equally among the muffin cups so all the muffins will turn out to be approximately the same size.
• Always bake muffins on the center rack of the oven.
• For the best results, do not open the oven to peek at the muffins until the end of the recommended baking time.
• Egg-free, dairy-free, low-fat muffins may be slightly gummy when very hot. For the best results, allow your muffins to cool a bit before serving them.
• These muffins will keep for 2 to 3 days at room temperature in a sealed container. Cool the muffins thoroughly before storing them.
• Leftover muffins can be cut in half horizontally and toasted, split side up, in a toaster oven.

Muffin Magic

Plain whole wheat muffins are chameleon-like in their ability to adapt to any occasion—from breakfast to dessert. Start with the basic Whole Wheat Muffin recipe, p. 36, then adapt it as directed below.

Crunchy Nut or Seed Muffins: Stir into the batter 2 tablespoons of poppy seeds or sesame seeds, or up to 1/4 cup sunflower seeds or coarsely chopped walnuts, pecans, filberts or pumpkin seeds—raw or lightly toasted.

Dried Fruit Muffins: Stir into the batter 1/4 cup of raisins, currants, snipped prunes, or chopped dates. Other dried fruits such as chopped apricots, apples, and pears may be used as well. If the fruit is very hard, place it in a heatproof bowl, and cover it with boiling water. Let the fruit rest for 10 to 20 minutes. Drain the fruit in a colander or wire mesh strainer, and squeeze out the excess moisture. Chop the fruit and add it to the batter.

Fruit Juice Muffins: Use a sweet juice (such as apple or apricot) or a savory juice (such as tomato) in place of some or all of the milk or water. Depending upon the juice you select, the muffins may end up having an unusual (albeit interesting) color. For instance, purple grape juice will make purple colored muffins; tomato juice will turn them pink.

Zesty Muffins: Stir into the wet ingredients 1 to 3 teaspoons of organic lemon, lime, or orange zest. This is an especially good combination with Crunchy Nut or Seed Muffins.

Carob Muffins: Reduce the flour to 1 1/4 cups. Stir into the dry ingredients 1 1/2 tablespoons of unsweetened roasted carob powder. Nuts and/or dried fruits are a nice complement to this flavoring. These muffins are especially appealing to children and are also very good as cupcakes for dessert.

Sweet Tooth Muffins: Omit 2 tablespoons of the apple juice concentrate, and stir 2 tablespoons of your favorite liquid sweetener into the wet ingredients. Try light molasses, rice syrup, pure maple syrup, other fruit concentrates, or whatever else you prefer.

Alternately, omit 1 tablespoon of the apple juice concentrate, and add 2 tablespoons of your favorite granulated sweetener (i.e unbleached granulated sugar cane juice such as Sucanat, turbinado sugar, or granulated maple syrup) to the dry ingredients.

Surprise Muffins: Fill each muffin cup 1/2 full with batter. Make a small indentation in the center of the batter with your finger or a spoon, and fill the cavity with 1/2 teaspoon of fruit-sweetened jam, jelly, or fruit conserves. Cover the jelly with the remaining batter, and bake the muffins as directed.

Banana Nut Muffins

These dense, flavorful muffins are sweetened only with a little fruit juice concentrate and the rich, natural sweetness of ripe bananas. They are a great way to use up bananas that are getting a tad too ripe.

1 cup + 2 Tablespoons whole wheat pastry flour
1 teaspoon non-aluminum baking powder (such as Rumford)
1/2 teaspoon baking soda

2/3 cup ripe banana, mashed well (about 2 medium bananas)
3 Tablespoons apple juice concentrate
2 teaspoons canola oil
1 teaspoon vanilla extract

2 to 3 Tablespoons walnuts, finely broken or chopped
2 to 3 Tablespoons raisins or currants (optional)

1. Preheat the oven to 350°F. Coat a 6-cup muffin tin with nonstick cooking spray, and set it aside.

2. Place the flour, baking powder, and baking soda in a medium mixing bowl, and stir them together.

3. In a separate small mixing bowl, place the banana, apple juice concentrate, oil, and vanilla. Stir them together until they are well combined. Pour this liquid mixture into the dry ingredients (from step #2), and stir them together to form a thick batter. Stir in the walnuts and raisins or currants, if using.

4. Immediately spoon the batter equally into the prepared muffin cups. Bake the muffins for 18 to 22 minutes.

5. Gently loosen the muffins and turn them on their sides in the muffin tin. Cover the muffins with a clean kitchen towel, and let them rest for 5 minutes. This will keep them from developing a hard crust.

6. Transfer the muffins to a cooling rack, and serve them warm or at room temperature.

Yield: 6 muffins

Per muffin: Calories: 146, Protein: 3 gm., Fat: 3 gm., Carbohydrate: 24 gm.

The Cook's Secrets:
Review The Cook's Secrets for Whole Wheat Muffins, p. 36.

Yankee Corn Muffins

Slightly sweet and very adaptable, these muffins are a great breakfast treat. If you add a few savory seasonings, however, you can transform them into a very special dinner or soup accompaniment.

1/4 pound fat-reduced, firm regular tofu, rinsed, patted dry, and crumbled
1/4 cup apple juice concentrate
1/4 cup water
1 Tablespoon canola oil

1/2 cup whole wheat pastry flour
1/3 cup yellow cornmeal
1 teaspoon non-aluminum baking powder (such as Rumford)
1/2 teaspoon baking soda
1/4 teaspoon salt

1. Preheat the oven to 350°F. Coat a 6-cup muffin tin with nonstick cooking spray, and set it aside.

2. Place the tofu, juice concentrate, water, and oil in a food processor or blender, and process into a smooth, creamy emulsion. Set aside.

3. Place the remaining ingredients in a medium mixing bowl, and stir them together until they are well combined.

4. Pour the blended mixture (from step #2) into the dry ingredients (from step #3), and mix just until the dry ingredients are moistened. The batter will be very stiff and dry looking.

5. Immediately spoon the batter equally into the prepared muffin cups. Bake for 20 to 22 minutes.

6. Gently loosen the muffins and turn them on their sides in the muffin tin. Cover the muffins with a clean kitchen towel, and let them rest for 5 minutes. This will keep them from developing a hard crust.

7. Transfer the muffins to a cooling rack, and serve them warm or at room temperature.

Yield: 6 muffins

Per muffin: Calories: 119, Protein: 4 gm., Fat: 2 gm., Carbohydrate: 18 gm.

The Cook's Secrets:
Review The Cook's Secrets for Whole Wheat Muffins, p. 36.

Blueberry Corn Muffins: Fold 1/2 cup fresh blueberries, rinsed and patted dry, into the batter.

Spicy Corn Muffins: Stir 1/4 cup sliced scallions, 2 tablespoons chopped green chilies, and 1/2 teaspoon ground cumin into the batter.

Cheezy Corn Muffins: Stir 1 tablespoon nutritional yeast flakes into the dry ingredients.

Smoky Corn Muffins: Stir 1 tablespoon vegetarian bacon bits into the batter.

Extra Corny Muffins: Stir 1/2 cup whole corn kernels into the batter.

Peanut Butter & Jelly Muffins

Every kid's favorite—regardless of age!

1 1/3 cups whole wheat pastry flour
1 teaspoon non-aluminum baking powder (such
   as Rumford)
1/2 teaspoon baking soda

4 Tablespoons crunchy peanut butter
1/3 cup low-fat, non-dairy milk
1/3 cup apple juice concentrate
1 1/2 teaspoons canola oil

2 Tablespoons strawberry, raspberry, apricot, or
   blackberry jelly

1. Preheat the oven to 350°F. Coat a 6-cup muffin tin with nonstick cooking spray, and set it aside.

2. Place the flour, baking powder, and baking soda in a medium mixing bowl, and stir them together.

3. Place the peanut butter in a small mixing bowl or measuring cup. Gradually stir in the milk, creaming it well with the peanut butter. Then gradually stir in the apple juice concentrate and the oil. Mix thoroughly.

4. Pour the liquid mixture (from step #3) into the dry ingredients (from step #2), and stir until they are well combined. The batter will be fairly thick.

5. Immediately spoon some of the batter into the prepared muffin cups, filling the cups just halfway.

6. With your finger or a spoon, make a small indentation in the center of the batter in the cups. Fill each cavity with 1 teaspoon of the jelly. Cover the jelly with the remainder of the batter, smoothing out the tops. *Do not overfill the muffin cups!* Bake the muffins for 22 to 25 minutes.

7. Gently loosen the muffins and turn them on their sides in the muffin tin. Cover the muffins with a clean kitchen towel, and let them rest for 5 minutes. This will keep them from developing a hard crust.

8. Transfer the muffins to a cooling rack, and serve them warm or at room temperature.

Yield: 6 large muffins

Per muffin: Calories: 209, Protein: 6 gm., Fat: 6 gm., Carbohydrate: 31 gm.

The Cook's Secrets:
Use a jelly that is firm, not runny, and a thick, unsweetened natural peanut butter for the best results.

Review The Cook's Secrets for Whole Wheat Muffins, p. 36.

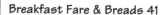

Cinnamon Applesauce Muffins

Moist and sweet, these muffins are chock-full of raisins and brimming with home-style flavor.

1 cup whole wheat pastry flour
1 teaspoon non-aluminum baking powder (such as Rumford)
1/2 teaspoon baking soda
1/2 teaspoon ground cinnamon

1/2 cup applesauce
1/4 cup low-fat, non-dairy milk or water
2 Tablespoons pure maple syrup
1 Tablespoon canola oil
1 1/2 teaspoons fresh lemon juice
1 teaspoon vanilla extract

1/2 cup currants or raisins

1. Preheat the oven to 350°F. Coat a 6-cup muffin tin with nonstick cooking spray, and set it aside.

2. Place the flour, baking powder, baking soda, and cinnamon in a medium mixing bowl, and stir them together.

3. Place the remaining ingredients *except the currants or raisins* in a small mixing bowl, and stir them together well. Pour this liquid mixture into the dry ingredients (from step #2), and mix until they are well combined. Then stir in the currants or raisins. The batter will be fairly thick.

4. Immediately spoon the batter equally into the prepared muffin cups. Bake the muffins for 18 to 20 minutes.

5. Gently loosen the muffins and turn them on their sides in the muffin tin. Cover the muffins with a clean kitchen towel, and let them rest for 5 minutes. This will keep them from developing a hard crust.

6. Transfer the muffins to a cooling rack, and serve them warm or at room temperature.

Yield: 6 muffins

Per muffin: Calories: 150, Protein: 3 gm., Fat: 2 gm., Carbohydrate: 28 gm.

The Cook's Secrets:
Review The Cook's Secrets for Whole Wheat Muffins, p. 36.

Whole Wheat Biscuits

These biscuits are amazingly light and flaky. And, because they are "dropped" rather than rolled, they are incredibly quick and easy. Biscuits are great as a base under plain gravy, stroganoffs, or vegetable stews. Personally, I have always thought of chili and biscuits as culinary soulmates. Of course, they are also great breakfast fare served with fruit-sweetened jam or apple butter.

1 cup whole wheat pastry flour
2 teaspoons non-aluminum baking powder (such as Rumford)
heaping 1/4 teaspoon salt

1/2 cup low-fat, non-dairy milk or water
1 1/2 Tablespoons canola oil

1. Preheat the oven to 425°F. Mist a baking sheet with nonstick cooking spray, and set it aside.

2. Place the flour, baking powder, and salt in a medium mixing bowl, and stir them together.

3. Place the milk or water and oil in a small measuring cup or mixing bowl. Then pour this liquid into the flour mixture, and stir just until the dough clings together and is evenly moistened.

4. Drop the dough by large, rounded spoonfuls into 6 mounds on the prepared baking sheet.

5. Bake the biscuits for 10 to 12 minutes, or until they are golden brown. Transfer them to a cooling rack using a metal spatula. Serve warm.

Yield: 6 biscuits

Per biscuit: Calories: 108, Protein: 3 gm., Fat: 3 gm., Carbohydrate: 15 gm.

The Cook's Secrets:
Don't overmix the dough as this will produce tough, mealy biscuits.

Cool leftovers completely and store them in an airtight container for up to 2 days. To reheat leftover biscuits, wrap them loosely in foil, and heat them in a 300°F oven or toaster oven for 15 to 18 minutes.

Cinnamon Raisin Biscuits: Place 1/4 cup raisins in a heatproof bowl. Pour boiling water over the raisins to cover them. Let them soak for 5 minutes; then drain well. Set the raisins aside. Prepare the biscuits as directed except add 1/2 teaspoon ground cinnamon to the flour mixture. Stir in the soaked and drained raisins after pouring in the milk or water.

Garden Biscuits: Add 2 tablespoons finely shredded carrot, 1 tablespoon minced fresh parsley, and 1 tablespoon finely chopped scallions to the flour mixture when pouring in the milk or water.

Green Onion & Basil Biscuits: Add 1 tablespoon finely chopped scallions and 1/2 teaspoon dried basil leaves to the flour mixture when pouring in the milk or water.

Also try the variations listed for Cornmeal Biscuits on the next page.

Cornmeal Biscuits

Slightly crunchier than plain, whole wheat biscuits, this cornmeal version is a perfect match with everything from soup to nuts.

3/4 cup whole wheat pastry flour
1/2 cup yellow cornmeal
2 teaspoons non-aluminum baking powder (such as Rumford)
heaping 1/4 teaspoon salt

1/2 cup low-fat, non-dairy milk or water
1 1/2 Tablespoons canola oil

1. Preheat the oven to 425°F. Mist a baking sheet with nonstick cooking spray, and set it aside.

2. Place the flour, cornmeal, baking powder, and salt in a medium mixing bowl, and stir them together.

3. Place the milk or water and oil in a small measuring cup or mixing bowl. Then pour this liquid into the flour mixture, and stir just until the dough clings together and is evenly moistened.

4. Drop the dough by large, rounded spoonfuls into 6 mounds on the prepared baking sheet.

5. Bake the biscuits for 10 to 12 minutes, or until they are golden brown. Transfer them to a cooling rack using a metal spatula. Serve warm.

Yield: 6 biscuits

Per biscuit: Calories: 133, Protein: 3 gm., Fat: 3 gm., Carbohydrate: 20 gm.

The Cook's Secrets:
Don't overmix the dough as this will produce tough, mealy biscuits.

Cool leftovers completely and store them in an airtight container for up to 2 days. To reheat leftover biscuits, wrap them loosely in foil, and heat them in a 300°F oven or toaster oven for 15 to 18 minutes.

Chili Biscuits: Prepare the biscuits as directed except add 2 tablespoons chopped, canned, mild green chilies to the flour mixture when pouring in the milk or water.

Spicy Biscuits: Prepare the biscuits as directed except add 1/4 to 1/2 teaspoon chili powder or 1/8 teaspoon of cayenne pepper to the dry flour mixture.

Also try the variations listed for Whole Wheat Biscuits on the previous page.

Apple Cobbler

Individual fruit tarts make a sweet breakfast or a satisfying dessert.

TOPPING:
1/3 cup whole wheat pastry flour
1/3 cup quick-cooking rolled oats (not instant)
1/4 teaspoon non-aluminum baking powder (such as Rumford)

2 Tablespoons apple juice concentrate
1 teaspoon canola oil

FILLING:
2 medium baking apples (Granny Smith, Jonathan, Rome Beauty, Cortland, Northern Spy, York Imperial, etc.), peeled and sliced
2 to 4 Tablespoons raisins or currants
2 teaspoons fresh lemon juice

1 Tablespoon whole wheat pastry flour
2 Tablespoons apple juice concentrate
1/4 teaspoon ground cinnamon

1. Preheat the oven to 350°F. Mist two 15-ounce or 16-ounce individual casserole dishes with nonstick cooking spray, and set them aside.

2. For the topping, place the flour, oats, and baking powder in a medium mixing bowl, and stir them together. Set aside.

3. Place the apple juice concentrate and oil in a small measuring cup, and whisk them together. Pour this liquid into the oat-flour mixture, and cut it in using a pastry blender or a fork until it is crumbly. Set aside.

4. For the filling, place the apple slices and raisins in a medium mixing bowl. Sprinkle the lemon juice over the fruit, and toss them together until they are evenly coated.

5. Place the flour, juice concentrate, and cinnamon in a small measuring cup, and beat them together using a wire whisk or a fork until the mixture is very smooth. Pour this mixture over the fruit, and toss them together until the fruit is evenly coated.

6. Distribute the fruit and any liquid remaining in the bowl between the prepared casserole dishes. Crumble half of the reserved topping (from step #2) over each casserole.

7. Bake the cobblers for 30 minutes, or until the tops are golden brown and the apples are fork tender. Serve hot, warm, room temperature, or chilled.

Yield: 2 servings

Per serving: Calories: 334, Protein: 6 gm., Fat: 4 gm., Carbohydrate: 68 gm.

The Cook's Secrets:
For variety, use a combination of two different apples such as Granny Smith and Jonathan.

For dessert, serve the Cobbler or Buckle with a small scoop of vanilla non-dairy frozen dessert on top. It's decadently delightful.

Peach Cobbler: Substitute 2 fresh peaches, peeled and sliced, for the apples.

Blueberry Buckle: Substitute 2 cups fresh blueberries for the apples, and omit the raisins and lemon juice.

Pear Pandowdy

Fresh pears with a sweet biscuit topping are sure to tempt sleepy tastebuds. Pear Pandowdy also makes a scrumptious, filling dessert after a light meal.

FILLING:
2 large pears, peeled and diced
2 teaspoons fresh lemon juice
2 to 4 Tablespoons raisins or currants

BISCUIT TOPPING:
3/4 cup whole wheat pastry flour
1/4 teaspoon non-aluminum baking powder (such as Rumford)

4 Tablespoons apple juice concentrate
3 Tablespoons low-fat, non-dairy milk or water
1 teaspoon canola oil

1. Preheat the oven to 350°F. Mist two 15-ounce or 16-ounce individual casserole dishes with nonstick cooking spray, and set them aside.

2. Place the diced pears in a medium mixing bowl, and toss them with the lemon juice. Add the raisins or currants, and toss again.

3. Distribute the fruit and any liquid in the bowl between the prepared casserole dishes.

4. For the biscuit topping, place the flour and baking powder in a medium mixing bowl, and stir them together.

5. Place the apple juice concentrate, milk or water, and oil in a small measuring cup, and stir them together well. Pour this liquid into the flour mixture (from step #4), and mix well to make a smooth batter. Spoon the batter equally over the fruit in the casserole dishes, spreading it out to cover the fruit as best as possible.

6. Bake the pandowdy for 30 minutes.

7. Remove the casserole dishes from the oven using oven mitts or pot holders, and place them on a cooling rack. Allow the pandowdy to cool slightly before serving, about 5 to 10 minutes, if time permits. Serve the pandowdy warm, room temperature, or chilled.

Yield: 2 servings

Per serving: Calories: 376, Protein: 7 gm., Fat: 3 gm., Carbohydrate: 78 gm.

Glazed Cinnamon Buns

With just the right balance of cinnamon and sweetness, this luscious recipe has been part of my "private stock" for years. It makes a large quantity for a small household, but one bun per person never seems to suffice. Besides, once the neighbors catch a whiff of the intoxicating aroma, you'll never have a moment's peace until they get a taste.

2/3 cup low-fat, non-dairy milk
4 Tablespoons apple juice concentrate

1 1/2 teaspoons active dry yeast
1 Tablespoon canola oil
1/4 teaspoon salt

approx. 2 cups whole wheat pastry flour (more or less, as needed)
approx. 1/2 cup additional whole wheat pastry flour for kneading

CINNAMON SWIRL FILLING:
1 1/2 Tablespoons tahini
5 Tablespoons apple butter (unsweetened and unspiced)
1 teaspoon ground cinnamon

1 recipe Apple Glaze, p. 47

1. Place the milk in a 1-quart saucepan, and scald it (see Basic Cooking Terms, p. 15). Remove the saucepan from the heat, and pour the milk into a large mixing bowl. Stir in the juice concentrate. The mixture should now be lukewarm.

2. Stir the yeast, oil, and salt into the lukewarm mixture.

3. Then gradually beat in the 2 cups of flour with a wooden spoon, adding only 1/2 cup at a time, until the mixture forms a soft but kneadable dough.

4. Turn the dough out onto a floured board, and knead it for 5 minutes, until it is smooth and elastic. Alternately, knead the dough directly in the mixing bowl. It is necessary to knead in the additional 1/2 cup of flour (more or less as needed) in order to work the dough properly and achieve a smooth and elastic consistency.

5. Transfer the dough to a clean, large, lightly oiled bowl, turning it once to coat the top. Cover the bowl with a clean, damp cloth, and let the dough rise in a warm place (see The Cook's Secrets p. 47) for 30 to 60 minutes, or until doubled in size.

6. Mist a baking sheet with nonstick cooking spray, and set it aside.

7. While the dough is rising, prepare the filling. Place the tahini in a small mixing bowl. Vigorously stir in the apple butter, one tablespoon at a time, until it is all incorporated. Then stir in the cinnamon. Cover the bowl and set it aside.

8. Punch the dough straight down into the center with your fist. Then punch it in about 8 places. Turn the dough out onto a very lightly floured board, and knead it for a minute or two.

9. Flour the board and roll the dough out into a rectangle, approximately 8 inches by 15 inches. Spread the reserved filling (from step #7) evenly over the dough, to within 1/2 inch of the edge. Roll the dough up into a log starting with one of

the shorter sides. Pinch the end seam closed with lightly water-dampened fingers.

10. Slice the log into 8 to 10 equal slices, and place the pieces swirl side up on the prepared baking sheet. Arrange the buns so they are not touching. Cover the buns with a clean, damp cloth or kitchen towel, and let them rest for 10 minutes.

11. Preheat the oven to 350°F while the buns are resting.

12. Bake the buns for 20 to 22 minutes, or until they are lightly golden brown. Transfer the buns to a cooling rack.

13. While the buns are baking, prepare the Apple Glaze (recipe follows). Set it aside.

14. While the buns are still warm (not hot), spread 1 teaspoon of the Apple Glaze over the top of the buns and partway down the sides using a table knife.

Yield: 8 to 10 cinnamon buns

Per bun (with Apple Glaze): Calories: 179, Protein: 5 gm., Fat: 2 gm., Carbohydrate: 32 gm.

The Cook's Secrets:
Do not substitute applesauce for the apple butter. Apple butter, which has a particular color, texture, and flavor, is the secret ingredient in this recipe.

I have found the best "warm place" (about 85°F to 100°F) to let dough rise is in a gas oven with a pilot light (do not turn the oven on) or in an electric oven heated at 200°F *for one or two minutes only* and then turned off. (Place the covered bowl of bread dough in the oven *after* you have turned off the heat.)

Apple Glaze

1 Tablespoon cold water
2 teaspoons cornstarch

4 Tablespoons apple juice concentrate

1. Place the water in a 1-quart saucepan. Add the cornstarch and stir until it is completely dissolved.

2. Gradually stir in the apple juice concentrate, mixing well.

3. Place the saucepan over medium-high heat, and cook the mixture, stirring constantly, until it is very thick, smooth, and clear. Remove the saucepan from the heat.

4. Using a table knife, spread 1 teaspoon of the glaze over the top and partway down the sides of each bun.

Yield: enough glaze for 8 to 10 buns using 1 teaspoon per roll

Per teaspoon: Calories: 15, Protein: 0 gm., Fat: 0 gm., Carbohydrate: 4 gm.

Breakfast Burritos

A favorite with the young ones, these banana roll-ups make a substantial morning meal.

2 whole wheat flour tortillas (lard-free)

2 Tablespoons peanut butter (smooth or
   crunchy)
4 to 6 teaspoons fruit-sweetened jam or jelly, or
   to taste
2 very small, thin bananas, or 1 medium banana
   cut in half (lengthwise or widthwise)

1. Warm the tortillas before assembling the burritos. To do this, place the tortillas, one at a time, in a dry 9-inch or 10-inch skillet. Place the skillet over medium heat for about 1 minute, or just until the tortilla is heated. Immediately remove the tortilla from the skillet, and lay it on a flat surface. Warm the remaining tortilla in the same fashion.

2. When the tortillas have been warmed, spread one side of each tortilla evenly with the peanut butter. Then spread the jam or jelly over the peanut butter.

3. Place the banana on the edge of each tortilla on top of the jelly, and roll the tortilla around the banana to enclose it. Serve at once.

Yield: 2 servings

Per serving: Calories: 370, Protein: 8 gm., Fat: 13 gm., Carbohydrate: 54 gm.

The Cook's Secrets:
To spread the peanut butter with ease, have it at room temperature before assembling the burritos.

Karen's Kalewiches

Kale for breakfast? My friend Karen Bernard, who devised this recipe, and her young daughter Rachel love it. It is certainly a welcome switch from sweeter fare and is a chewy, pleasant way to start the day. Additionally, kale is a nutrition powerhouse and is loaded with iron and bone-building calcium. Karen's secret for the magnificent taste of these open-face sandwiches is to use the very finest olive oil available. Although any good whole grain bread will suffice, Karen strongly recommends a tasty sourdough.

4 cups fresh kale leaves, lightly packed

1 to 2 teaspoons olive oil (optional)
pinch of salt, to taste

2 slices whole grain bread, toasted

1. Rinse the kale well, taking care to wash off any sand or grit. Remove the thick center ribs, and coarsely tear the leaves.

2. Place the kale in a steamer basket or steamer insert in a large saucepan filled with an inch of water. Bring the water to a boil. Cover the saucepan with a lid, and reduce the heat to medium. Steam the kale until it is wilted and very tender, about 10 to 12 minutes.

3. Place half of the kale on each slice of toast. Drizzle 1/2 to 1 teaspoon of olive oil over each serving, if desired, and sprinkle with a little salt to taste. Serve at once with a knife and fork.

Yield: 2 servings

Per serving: Calories: 118, Protein: 5 gm., Fat: 1 gm., Carbohydrate: 21 gm.

The Cook's Secrets:

For Greenwiches, replace the kale with an equal amount of mustard greens, collard greens, turnip greens, or a combination of two or more different kinds of greens. Steam as directed above.

If you prefer, use a splash of fresh lemon juice and/or soy sauce in place of or in addition to the salt.

A Note From Anne & Matt:
One of the best purchases we've made is a bread machine. It is certainly not the same as bread made by hand, but it is very convenient and much better than all but the best bakery bread (and always cheaper). It adds a lot to our meals to have a warm loaf of bread.

Crunchy Fruit Crisps

Both children and adults love making and eating these crunchy delights. They work triple duty—as a quick breakfast, a healthful snack, or a not-too-sweet dessert.

1 crisp eating apple, cored and sliced into rings
1 pear, cut into four wedges
1 small banana, sliced lengthwise and cut in half widthwise (to make four pieces)

2 to 4 Tablespoons peanut butter or almond butter (crunchy or smooth)

about 1/2 cup crisped rice cereal, or as needed

1. Spread a thin layer of peanut butter or almond butter on one side of each apple ring, on one of the cut sides of each pear wedge, and on the sliced side of each banana piece.

2. Place the cereal in a small mixing bowl. Press the nut-buttered side of the fruit firmly into the cereal. Divide the fruit equally between two plates. Serve at once.

Yield: 2 servings

Per serving: Calories: 297, Protein: 6 gm., Fat: 10 gm., Carbohydrate: 41 gm.

The Cook's Secrets:
For smaller appetites, use only 2 fruits, 2 tablespoons of nut butter, and about 1/3 cup of cereal.

Apples & Tahini

This is a fun breakfast or snack, especially for young children. They love dipping the apple slices into the tahini. We greatly enjoy and appreciate this breakfast whenever we're exceptionally rushed. It's finger food at its finest!

2 crisp eating apples, cored and sliced into 8 wedges each
2 Tablespoons tahini

1. Divide the apple slices equally between two plates.

2. Spoon half the tahini onto one side of each of the plates, and serve.

Yield: 2 servings

Per serving: Calories: 176, Protein: 3 gm., Fat: 7 gm., Carbohydrate: 23 gm.

A Note From Karen:
Here's a fun food that my young daughter Rachel really enjoys. I slice bananas into wheels and spread one side of each wheel with a little peanut butter or almond butter. Then I arrange the pieces on a plate in a flower pattern and put the end piece of the banana in the center. If you like, you can also put a raisin on top of the nut butter in the center of each banana wheel. Rachel likes to eat these using a fork or a toothpick.

Oatmeal

This recipe makes the perfect quantity for two bowls of creamy, hot oatmeal—a satisfying way to jump-start your day. Using quick-cooking rolled oats makes it easy to have oatmeal, even if you're in a hurry.

Oatmeal is a super match with sliced banana, peaches, or fresh berries. For a special treat, try it topped with Hot Peach Topping, p. 54, or Hot Cinnamon Apple Topping, p. 54.

1 1/4 cups cold water
3/4 cup quick-cooking rolled oats (not instant)

2 to 4 teaspoons sweetener of your choice, or
  to taste (optional)

1 cup low-fat, non-dairy milk, or as needed
  (optional)

1. Place the cold water and rolled oats in a 1-quart saucepan. Bring the water to a boil. Reduce the heat to low, and cook the oatmeal uncovered, stirring constantly, for 2 minutes.

2. Remove the saucepan from the heat, and cover it with a lid. Let the oatmeal rest for 3 to 5 minutes.

3. Stir the oatmeal and spoon it equally into two cereal bowls. Top each serving with some of the sweetener and milk, if desired. Serve at once.

Yield: 2 servings

Per serving: Calories: 125, Protein: 6 gm., Fat: 2 gm., Carbohydrate: 20 gm.

Quick Brown Rice Porridge

This delicately sweetened, creamy grain dish—somewhere between a pudding and a hot cereal—makes a fantastic morning eye-opener. Serve it warm or chilled.

3/4 cup quick-cooking brown rice (not instant)
1 cup low-fat, non-dairy milk, or 1 cup water +
  1 Tablespoon tahini
6 Tablespoons apple juice concentrate
1/4 cup raisins
1/2 teaspoon ground cinnamon
1/2 teaspoon vanilla extract
2 Tablespoons slivered almonds (optional)

1. Place all the ingredients in a 1-quart saucepan, and stir them together until they are well combined. Bring the mixture to a boil, then immediately reduce the heat to medium.

2. Simmer the porridge uncovered, stirring occasionally, for 12 to 15 minutes, or until the mixture begins to thicken and the rice is tender. Remove the saucepan from the heat.

3. Serve the porridge warm, or transfer it to a storage container, and allow to cool. Then cover the container with a tight fitting lid, and chill the porridge in the refrigerator for several hours or overnight.

Yield: 2 servings

Per serving: Calories: 311, Protein: 6 gm., Fat: 1 gm., Carbohydrate: 68 gm.

Bear Mush

Warming and surprisingly chewy, this mixture of bulgur wheat and quinoa makes a hearty morning meal.

1 1/3 cups apple juice, orange juice, or cold water (see The Cook's Secrets at right)

3 Tablespoons bulgur (medium or fine ground) or cracked wheat

3 Tablespoons quinoa (be sure to rinse the quinoa thoroughly before using it in order to remove its bitter tasting, protective coating called "saponin")

1 to 2 teaspoons sweetener of your choice, or to taste (optional)

2/3 cup low-fat, non-dairy milk or fruit juice, or as needed (optional)

1. Place the juice or cold water, bulgur, and quinoa in a 1-quart saucepan, and bring the mixture to a boil. Reduce the heat to low, cover the saucepan with a lid, and simmer the porridge for 15 minutes.

2. Remove the lid and simmer the mixture for 7 to 10 minutes longer, stirring occasionally, until the grain is cooked and the porridge is thick.

3. Spoon the porridge into two cereal bowls, and top each serving with some of the sweetener and/or milk or juice, if desired. Serve at once.

Yield: 2 servings

Per serving: Calories: 283, Protein: 8 gm., Fat: 2 gm., Carbohydrate: 57 gm.

The Cook's Secrets:

If you do not have apple juice or orange juice on hand, you can make the exact amount you need by using 1/3 cup frozen juice concentrate mixed with 1 cup water.

A sprinkle of cinnamon and/or 1/4 cup of raisins may be added before, during or after cooking, if desired.

Bread Pudding

What a sweet way to use up slightly stale bread! Of course, fresh bread works just fine as well. This delicious pudding is a delightful breakfast or dessert. The luscious aroma that emerges as it bakes will arouse even the sleepiest taste buds.

3 Tablespoons currants

1 1/2 cups whole grain bread cubes, very firmly packed (remove crusts, if desired)
3 Tablespoons walnuts, coarsely chopped

1/2 of a 10.5-ounce package fat-reduced, firm silken tofu (about 3/4 cup), crumbled (see The Cook's Secrets at right)
1/2 cup apple juice concentrate
1/4 cup water
1/2 teaspoon vanilla extract
1/8 teaspoon ground nutmeg

ground cinnamon, as needed

1. Preheat the oven to 350°F. Mist two 15-ounce or 16-ounce individual casserole dishes with nonstick cooking spray, and set them aside.

2. Place the currants in a heatproof bowl, and cover them with boiling water. Let them soak for 10 minutes, or until they are softened. Then drain them well in a wire mesh strainer.

3. Place the bread, softened currants, and walnuts in a medium mixing bowl, and toss them together. Set aside.

4. Place the tofu, apple juice concentrate, water, vanilla, and nutmeg in a food processor or blender, and process them into a smooth cream.

5. Pour the blended mixture over the bread cubes, currants, and walnuts (from step #3). Mix thoroughly but gently, making sure that all of the bread cubes are evenly moistened but not crumbled.

6. Spoon the mixture into the prepared casserole dishes. Be sure to divide the liquid and solid portions evenly between them. Sprinkle the tops lightly with ground cinnamon.

7. Bake for 25 to 30 minutes. Serve warm.

Yield: 2 servings

Per serving: Calories: 376, Protein: 13 gm., Fat: 11 gm., Carbohydrate: 54 gm.

The Cook's Secrets:
Use the remainder of the package of tofu to make half a recipe of Tofu Sour Cream, p. 73, or Low-Fat, Egg-Free Mayonnaise, p. 110. Raisins, dried cherries, or chopped dried apricots may be substituted for the currants, if desired.

Hot Peach Topping

What a luscious topping for pancakes, French Toast, p. 32, or porridge.

1 cup frozen, unsweetened peach slices, or
   1 large, fresh peach, peeled and sliced
1/3 cup water
2 Tablespoons raisins
1 Tablespoon pineapple juice concentrate
1 teaspoon vanilla extract

1 Tablespoon cornstarch
4 Tablespoons apple juice concentrate

1. Place the peach slices, water, raisins, juice concentrate, and vanilla extract in a 1-quart saucepan. Bring the mixture to a boil. Immediately reduce the heat to medium, and cook the topping, stirring occasionally, until the raisins are soft.

2. Meanwhile, place the cornstarch in a small measuring cup. Using a fork, stir the juice concentrate into the cornstarch until the mixture is completely smooth.

3. When the raisins are soft, stir the cornstarch mixture (from step #2) into the hot fruit. Cook, stirring constantly over medium heat, until the sauce is clear and thickened. Remove the saucepan from the heat. Serve the topping hot or warm.

Yield: 2 servings

Per serving: Calories: 136, Protein: 1 gm., Fat: 0 gm., Carbohydrate: 33 gm.

Hot Cinnamon Apple Topping

This chunky sauce makes a tempting topping for pancakes, French Toast, p. 32, Oatmeal, p. 51, or vanilla non-dairy frozen dessert. The sauce has a gentle sweetness that is mellow but not cloying.

1 Granny Smith apple, peeled, cored, and cut
   into 12 equal slices
2/3 cup apple juice concentrate
2 Tablespoons raisins or chopped dates
1 teaspoon fresh lemon juice
1/4 teaspoon ground cinnamon

1. Place all of the ingredients in a 1-quart saucepan, and bring the mixture to a boil. Reduce the heat to medium-low, and simmer, stirring occasionally, until the apple is soft but not mushy. Serve hot or warm.

Yield: 2 servings

Per serving: Calories: 221, Protein: 1 gm., Fat: 0 gm., Carbohydrate: 53 gm.

Extended Maple Syrup

Pure maple syrup is unquestionably delicious, but it can also be quite expensive. To keep costs down as well as to temper its powerful sweetness, maple syrup may be diluted with water and a pinch of thickening starch. This extended syrup still has a tantalizing maple flavor, but has half the calories and less of a "sugar rush."

1/3 cup water
1 1/2 teaspoons cornstarch
1/3 cup pure maple syrup

1. Place the water and cornstarch in a 1-quart saucepan, and stir until the cornstarch is completely dissolved. Stir in the maple syrup, and bring the mixture to a boil stirring constantly.

2. Reduce the heat to low, and cook, stirring constantly, until the mixture is clear and slightly thickened. Watch very closely so the syrup does not boil over the pan.

Yield: 2/3 cup

Per 1/4 cup serving: Calories: 132, Protein: 0 gm., Fat: 0 gm., Carbohydrate: 33 gm.

The Cook's Secrets:
This syrup tastes best when it is warm, but leftovers may be stored in the refrigerator for up to a week. It will still be delicious served cold or reheated.

Only cornstarch must be used in this recipe. Do not substitute arrowroot or any other thickening starch, as the syrup will become gummy.

MAIN DISH SALADS, SIDE DISH SALADS & DRESSINGS

Salads are among my favorite foods because they are so easily adapted to changing seasons, weather conditions, moods, and appetites, plus they are brimming with life and freshness. There are several different kinds of salads: raw vegetable, cooked vegetable, lettuce, fruit, grain, bean, pasta, potato, side dish, and main course salads. Sometimes these delineations overlap, forming yet another category— the eclectic salad.

Although I have included several recipes for various two-serving salads, it is very easy to invent your own. If you are new to cooking, the art of salad preparation is a great place to learn the craft. You can be a "master," a "finger painter," or something in between, and every creation will be greeted with applause.

The main thing to consider when creating a salad is what your "canvas" or foundation ingredient will be. It could be lettuce (or several varieties of lettuce), fruit, spinach, tender baby greens, raw cabbage or other raw vegetables, cooked vegetables, tomatoes, beans, cooked rice or other cooked grains, pasta, or potatoes. Once you have decided on your "main" ingredient, place it in your salad bowl (or any large mixing bowl), and layer on any other ingredients you desire. You can serve your salad directly from the salad bowl, keeping the layers intact, or you can toss the salad and create a little intrigue.

If you like your dressing simple, try a tiny bit of oil and vinegar. Always use the finest oil you can afford. I highly recommend extra virgin olive oil for its exquisite flavor and quality. There are a broad variety of vinegars on the market, and it is fun to try different ones—herb-flavored vinegar, fruity vinegar, red wine vinegar, balsamic vinegar, rice vinegar, apple cider vinegar, umeboshi plum vinegar, etc. These are available at major supermarkets, gourmet food shops, specialty markets, and natural food stores. If you prefer not to use a vinegar, try a citrus juice instead. Lemon juice, orange juice, and lime juice add a delicious zing to salads.

Of course, low-fat, bottled dressings are widely available. I have also supplied several different recipes in this book for speedy, low-fat, homemade dressings that are very easy to prepare. In addition, there are special dressings included with many of the salad recipes that would be superb on other salads as well.

The following salad ingredients can add the crowning touch to your "masterpiece." Try incorporating one or several of them:

Artichoke hearts (whole or quartered)
Beets (sliced, diced, or julienned)
Bell pepper (chopped, sliced, or diced)
Carrot (shredded, sliced, or chopped)
Celery (sliced or diced)
Cherry tomatoes (whole or halved)
Cooked beans (any kind)
Cooked vegetables (chunked, chopped, or
    sliced)
Croutons
Cucumber (sliced or diced)
Fruit (fresh or dried)
Herbs (fresh), snipped
Jerusalem artichokes (sliced)
Jicama (julienned, chopped, or sliced)
Kohlrabi (julienned or sliced)
Lettuce (any kind, torn)
Mushrooms (whole, sliced, or chopped)
Nuts or seeds (chopped or whole)
Olives (whole or sliced)
Onion (chopped or sliced)
Parsley and/or other fresh herbs
Pasta (hot or cold; experiment with a variety
    of sizes and shapes; cut any long
    strands into bite-size pieces)
Potato (chunked or cubed)
Radishes (sliced)
Radicchio
Raisins
Scallions (sliced)
Spinach (torn)
Spring greens
Summer squash (julienned, sliced, or diced)
Tomato (sliced or chunked)
Water chestnuts (sliced)
Watercress

As you can see, the possibilities are endless. So, put on your "artist's smock" (apron), and prepare to create your magnum opus.

Cleaning Salad Greens

Salad greens must be washed thoroughly under cold water prior to using them in order to remove any soil, dirt, or grit. Rub your fingers along the center rib of the leaves where dirt and grit accumulate, and rinse the entire leaf completely. Salad greens should then be dried. This will keep the greens from becoming soggy and will help the salad dressing cling better. Drying can be done by patting the leaves gently with a clean kitchen towel or spinning them in a salad spinner, one the most inventive and practical kitchen gadgets available. Place the leaves in the spinner, and rotate it rapidly. Centrifugal force will propel the water from the leaves and deposit it in the bottom bowl of the spinner.

A Note From Billy:
At the end of a long day it's hard to gather up the motivation to cook. Salads are one of my mainstays for dinner. I buy only organic vegetables, so they do not need to be peeled. I scrub several different vegetables at a time and store them in the refrigerator. This way, in the evening when I'm tired, all I have to do is a little chopping and dinner is ready.

Mexican Black Bean Salad

A refreshing main dish salad with authentic "south of the border" flavor. For added crunch, serve it with baked corn tortilla chips, or crumble a few chips on top of the salad as a garnish.

BEAN SALAD:
1 15-ounce can black beans, rinsed well and drained

1 8-ounce can whole kernel corn, drained (about 1 cup)
1 cup jicama, peeled and diced (see The Cook's Secrets at right)
2 ripe, medium tomatoes, seeded, and chopped (see The Cook's Secrets at right)
2 scallions, sliced
2 to 4 Tablespoons fresh cilantro leaves, chopped
3 Tablespoons black olives, sliced (optional)

CHILI LIME DRESSING:
2 Tablespoons fresh lime juice
1 teaspoon olive oil
1/2 teaspoon ground cumin
1/4 teaspoon chili powder
1/8 teaspoon garlic granules

2 cups fresh spinach leaves (stems removed), coarsely chopped

1. Place all the ingredients for the bean salad in a large mixing bowl, and toss them together gently.

2. Place the ingredients for the dressing in a small mixing bowl or small measuring cup, and stir them together until they are well combined.

3. Pour the dressing over the salad, and mix gently but thoroughly.

4. To serve, line two serving plates with the spinach, and mound half of the salad in the center of each plate.

Yield: 2 main dish servings

Per serving: Calories: 358, Protein: 14 gm., Fat: 3 gm., Carbohydrate: 68 gm.

The Cook's Secrets:
Jicama (pronounced HEE-kah-mah), also called the Mexican potato, is a round tuber which is used extensively in Mexican cooking. It has tan skin and crisp, white flesh that is similar in texture to a water chestnut or crisp apple. It is delicious served raw whenever crunchiness and a slightly sweet flavor are desired.

Jicama can also be added to steamed or stir-fried vegetables near the end of the cooking time. Simply peel off the skin, and slice or dice the flesh. Look for a tuber that is unblemished (no damp or soft spots) and heavy. Store the jicama at room temperature until you are ready to use it. Then loosely cover any leftover jicama with plastic wrap, and store it in the vegetable crisper section of the refrigerator where it will keep for several days.

To seed a tomato, cut the tomato in half crosswise, and gently squeeze out the seeds.

Garbanzo & Vegetable Dinner Salad

An array of humble ingredients is transformed into a magnificent main dish salad.

CREAMY DRESSING:
2/3 cup Low-fat, Egg-free Mayonnaise, p. 110, or
    your favorite egg- and dairy-free mayonnaise
1 Tablespoon fresh parsley, minced
1 to 2 teaspoons sweetener of your choice

SALAD:
1 15-ounce can garbanzo beans, rinsed well and
    drained (about 1 1/2 cups)
1 cup fresh mushrooms, sliced
1 cup celery, sliced
1 cup carrot, pared and sliced
1/4 cup mild red onion, finely chopped
1 to 2 Tablespoons sunflower seeds (optional)

2 cups fresh spinach leaves (stems removed),
    torn

2 Tablespoons vegetarian bacon bits (optional)

1. For the dressing, place the mayonnaise, parsley, and sweetener in a small mixing bowl or measuring cup, and stir to combine.

2. For the salad, place the remaining ingredients *except the spinach leaves and bacon bits* in a large mixing bowl. Add the reserved dressing and toss well to combine thoroughly.

3. To serve, divide the spinach leaves between two large dinner plates, and spoon the salad mixture on top. Sprinkle the tops of the salads with the bacon bits, if using. Serve at once.

Yield: 2 main dish servings

Per serving: Calories: 386, Protein: 17 gm., Fat: 12 gm., Carbohydrate: 52 gm.

Creamy-Crunchy Garbanzo Salad

Yield: 2 main dish servings

Per serving: Calories: 336, Protein: 18 gm., Fat: 10 gm., Carbohydrate: 43 gm.

This makes a lovely lunch or dinner entrée. It is presented on a base of fresh lettuce or spinach leaves.

1 15-ounce can garbanzo beans, rinsed well and
   drained (about 1 1/2 cups)
4 radishes, halved and sliced
2 scallions, sliced
1 small red or green bell pepper, chopped
1/4 cup fresh parsley, finely chopped

1 recipe Creamy Vinaigrette, p. 73

salt and ground black pepper, to taste

4 cups lettuce leaves or fresh spinach leaves
   (stems removed), torn

1. Place the garbanzo beans, radishes, scallions, bell pepper, and parsley in a large mixing bowl. Toss them together well.

2. Pour the dressing over the bean and vegetable mixture, and toss again until everything is evenly coated.

3. Season the bean salad with salt and pepper, to taste, and toss once more.

4. Divide the lettuce or spinach between two large salad bowls or dinner plates. Top the greens with the bean salad, and serve.

A Note From Anne & Matt:
Be flexible and creative. Experiment, try new things. Don't be afraid of failure!

Develop a core of favorite vegan-friendly restaurants and treat yourself once in awhile. When you don't have the time or energy to cook, don't "battle with the kitchen" as this will only make for an unhappy relationship with cooking. Cooking is not a chore, it is a joy!

Warm Dutch Potato Salad

A delectable, warm salad with a smoky, sweet-sour dressing.

2 cups fresh kale leaves, torn and lightly packed

1 pound new potatoes or small red potatoes, cut into bite-size chunks (about 2 1/2 cups)
1/2 pound fresh green beans, trimmed and cut into 1-inch pieces

1 recipe Sweet & Sour Dressing, p. 70

salt and ground black pepper, to taste

2 Tablespoons vegetarian bacon bits

1. Rinse the kale well, taking care to wash off any sand or grit. Remove the thick center ribs, and coarsely tear the leaves.

2. Place the kale in a steamer basket or steamer insert in a large saucepan filled with an inch of water. Bring the water to a boil. Cover the saucepan with a lid, and reduce the heat to medium. Steam the kale until it is wilted and very tender, about 10 to 12 minutes.

3. Cool the kale to room temperature. Then transfer the kale to a wire mesh strainer and, using your hands, squeeze out as much liquid as possible. Set the kale aside.

4. Place the potatoes and green beans in a steamer basket or steamer insert in a large saucepan filled with an inch of water. (Use the same steamer and saucepan from step #2.) Bring the water to a boil. Cover the saucepan with a lid, and reduce the heat to medium. Steam the vegetables for 15 to 20 minutes, or until the potatoes are done and the green beans are tender-crisp.

5. Transfer the cooked potatoes and green beans to a large mixing bowl. Pour the dressing over the vegetables, and toss gently to coat them evenly. Season with additional salt and pepper, if desired, and toss gently again.

6. Divide the kale between two large salad bowls or dinner plates. Top the kale with the potato and green bean mixture. Sprinkle the top of each salad with half of the vegetarian bacon bits. Serve at once.

Yield: 2 main dish servings

Per serving: Calories: 341, Protein: 9 gm., Fat: 1 gm., Carbohydrate: 72 gm.

Marinated Vegetable Salad

This colorful main dish salad is a festive addition to picnics as well as to everyday fare.

HAVE READY:
1/2 cup Italian Dressing, p. 71

1/2 cup broccoli, cut into bite-size florets
1/2 cup cauliflower, cut into bite-size florets
1/2 cup carrots, pared and sliced

1/2 cup celery, sliced
1/2 cup red or green bell pepper, chopped
1/2 cup canned kidney beans, rinsed well and
  drained
1/2 cup canned garbanzo beans, rinsed well and
  drained
4 or 5 very thin slices red onion, cut in half and
  separated into crescents
6 pitted black olives, sliced

1. Fill a 2-quart saucepan halfway with water, and bring the water to a boil. Carefully drop in the broccoli florets, cauliflower florets, and the carrots. Blanch them for 5 minutes.

2. Drain the broccoli, cauliflower, and carrots in a colander, and place them in a large mixing bowl.

3. Add the remaining ingredients to the vegetables in the bowl, and stir in the prepared salad dressing. Toss well until the ingredients are evenly distributed and well coated with the dressing.

4. Cover and refrigerate the salad at least 3 hours or overnight to fully develop the flavors, stirring occasionally. Serve with a slotted spoon.

Yield: 2 main dish servings

Per serving: Calories: 234, Protein: 8 gm., Fat: 3 gm., Carbohydrate: 42 gm.

Warm Salad of Seitan & Black-Eyed Peas

Seitan is low in fat, high in protein, and extremely versatile. Combining seitan with canned beans and fresh salad ingredients creates a fiber-rich, satisfying meal.

HAVE READY:
1 recipe Italian Dressing, p. 71

3/4 cup canned black-eyed peas, rinsed well and drained
1/2 cup fresh mushrooms, sliced
1/4 cup scallions, thinly sliced
1/4 cup celery, sliced
1/4 cup red bell pepper, chopped
6 to 8 pitted black olives, sliced

1 cup seitan, sliced into strips

3 to 4 cups fresh spinach leaves (stems removed), lightly packed and torn

1. Place the black-eyed peas, mushrooms, scallions, celery, bell pepper, and olives in a medium mixing bowl. Add the Italian Dressing, toss gently, and set aside.

2. Mist a 9-inch or 10-inch skillet with nonstick cooking spray, or coat the skillet with a thin layer of canola oil. Place the skillet over medium-high heat. When the skillet is hot, add the seitan strips in a single layer, and brown them well on both sides, turning them once with a fork.

3. Remove the skillet from the heat. Pour the reserved vegetable mixture (from step #1) over the seitan, and toss gently but thoroughly.

4. Divide the spinach between two large salad bowls or dinner plates. Spoon the seitan mixture over the spinach. Serve immediately.

Yield: 2 main dish servings

Per serving: Calories: 290, Protein: 30 gm., Fat: 2 gm., Carbohydrate: 35 gm.

Spicy Black-Eyed Pea Salad

This quick, tangy salad makes an exciting main course. It can be served immediately or prepared a full day ahead. This is one dish that appreciates a little extra time to marinate.

HAVE READY:
1 recipe Italian Dressing, p. 71
2 teaspoons Dijon mustard

1 16-ounce can black-eyed peas, rinsed well and drained
1 cup whole kernel corn, frozen (thawed under hot tap water and drained) or 1 8-ounce can whole kernel corn, drained
1 large, ripe tomato, seeded and chopped (see The Cook's Secrets at right)
1 medium green bell pepper, chopped
1 to 2 Tablespoons fresh parsley or cilantro, minced
1 teaspoon ground cumin
1/4 teaspoon Tabasco sauce, or to taste

4 large romaine lettuce leaves

1. Prepare the dressing according to the directions. Then whisk in the Dijon mustard. Chill the dressing until you are ready to assemble the salad.

2. Place the black-eyed peas, corn, tomato, green pepper, parsley or cilantro, cumin, Tabasco sauce, and reserved dressing (from step #1) in a medium mixing bowl. Toss to thoroughly combine.

3. Serve the salad at once, or cover the bowl tightly and chill the salad in the refrigerator for up to 24 hours. When you are ready to serve the salad, line two large salad bowls or dinner plates with the lettuce leaves, and spoon the salad on top.

Yield: 2 main dish servings

Per serving: Calories: 443, Protein: 19 gm., Fat: 2 gm., Carbohydrate: 85 gm.

The Cook's Secrets:
To thaw frozen corn, measure it and then transfer it to a wire mesh strainer. Place the corn under hot tap water, stirring with a spoon until it is defrosted, letting the water drain through the strainer. Measure the corn again and add more, if necessary.

To seed a tomato, cut the tomato in half crosswise, and gently squeeze out the seeds.

Creamy Picnic Coleslaw

The Cook's Secrets:
A food processor fitted with the appropriate metal blade or shredding disc will greatly speed the work of preparing the cabbage and carrot.

Coleslaw seems to be everybody's favorite salad, and with this delicious version it's easy to understand why.

SALAD:
1 1/2 cups green cabbage, finely chopped
1/2 cup red cabbage, finely chopped
1 medium carrot, pared and shredded (about 1/2 cup)

CREAMY COLESLAW DRESSING:
1/4 cup Low-Fat, Egg-Free Mayonnaise, p. 110, or your favorite egg- and dairy-free mayonnaise
2 teaspoons apple juice concentrate
2 teaspoons water
1/2 to 1 teaspoon whole celery seeds, caraway seeds, or poppy seeds

salt and ground black pepper, to taste

A Note from Mary:
One of our favorite meals is salad. But, when I say salad, I mean SALAD. Ray and I like our salads HUGE. We get very creative with our ingredients, so they are not only big, they are beautiful and fun to prepare. We serve our salads with a good, hearty bread for a healthful and delicious feast.

1. Place the cabbage and carrot in a medium mixing bowl, and toss them together. Set aside.

2. Place the dressing ingredients *except the salt and pepper* in a small mixing bowl, and beat them together with a wire whisk.

3. Pour the dressing over the cabbage mixture, and toss to mix thoroughly. Season the salad with salt and pepper, to taste, and toss once more.

Yield: about 2 cups (2 to 4 side dish servings)

Per 2/3 cup serving: Calories: 52, Protein: 2 gm., Fat: 3 gm., Carbohydrate: 6 gm.

Cabbage & Apple Slaw with Caraway Vinaigrette

This special coleslaw can be made quite quickly. It is a delicious side dish salad and an attractive escort alongside chili, soups, or burgers.

SALAD:
2 1/2 cups green cabbage, shredded
1 medium carrot, pared and shredded (about 1/2 cup)
1 crisp red apple, coarsely chopped

CARAWAY VINAIGRETTE:
2 Tablespoons apple cider vinegar
2 Tablespoons apple juice (or 2 teaspoons apple juice concentrate mixed with 4 teaspoons water)
2 teaspoons brown rice syrup or other liquid sweetener of your choice
1 teaspoon Dijon mustard
1/2 teaspoon whole caraway seeds, or 1/4 teaspoon ground caraway seeds
several drops liquid smoke (optional)

1. Place the cabbage, carrot, and apple in a medium mixing bowl. Toss them together and set aside.

2. Place the dressing ingredients in a 1-quart saucepan, and whisk them together. Bring the mixture to a boil. As soon as the dressing starts to bubble, pour it over the vegetable-apple mixture. Toss to mix thoroughly. Serve at once.

Yield: **2 side dish servings**

Per serving: Calories: 131, Protein: 1 gm., Fat: 0 gm., Carbohydrate: 30 gm.

The Cook's Secrets:
A food processor fitted with the appropriate metal blade or shredding disc will greatly speed the work of preparing the cabbage and carrot.

Wax Bean & Tomato Salad

Yellow string beans (known as wax beans), tomatoes, and fresh herbs are featured in this delicious and colorful salad.

1 very small, mild onion, minced
1 large, ripe tomato, seeded and chopped (see The Cook's Secrets at right)
2 teaspoons balsamic vinegar

3/4 pound fresh wax beans, trimmed

1/4 cup of your favorite fresh herb, chopped (try one or a combination of several: basil, cilantro, dill, marjoram, oregano, parsley, rosemary, tarragon, thyme, or watercress)

1. Place the onion, tomato, and vinegar in a medium glass or ceramic mixing bowl. Toss them together well, then set them aside to marinate while you prepare the beans.

2. Place the beans in a stainless steel steamer basket or steamer insert in a large saucepan filled with an inch of water. Bring the water to a boil. Cover the saucepan with a lid, and reduce the heat to medium. Steam the beans until they are tender-crisp, about 12 to 18 minutes.

3. Refresh the beans under cold water to stop the cooking and cool the beans. Drain the beans well, then place them in the bowl with the onion and tomato.

4. Add the fresh herbs of your choice to the salad, and toss well.

5. Serve the salad at once, or cover the bowl and allow the vegetables to marinate in the refrigerator for several hours before serving.

Yield: 2 side dish servings

Per serving: Calories: 45, Protein: 2 gm., Fat: 0 gm., Carbohydrate: 9 gm.

The Cook's Secrets:
If you prefer, fresh green beans may be substituted for the wax beans.

It is essential to use only fresh herbs in this recipe, even if parsley is the only one you have available. Dried herbs will simply not produce good results.

To seed a tomato, cut the tomato in half crosswise, and gently squeeze out the seeds.

If the salad has been chilled in the refrigerator, allow it to come to room temperature before serving it.

Creamy Cucumber Salad

This is a refreshing side dish salad with intriguing, Indian-style seasonings.

1 1/2 cups cucumber, diced (peel if waxed and
    remove seeds if they are very large)

3/4 cup Tofu Sour Cream, p. 73
1/4 cup fresh cilantro leaves, chopped
2 teaspoons fresh gingerroot, minced or grated
several grains cayenne pepper, to taste

1. Place the diced cucumber in a medium mixing bowl, and set it aside.

2. Place the remaining ingredients in a small mixing bowl, and stir them together until they are well combined. Pour this dressing over the cucumber, and mix thoroughly.

3. Serve the salad at once, or cover the bowl and chill the salad in the refrigerator.

Yield: 2 side dish servings

Per serving: Calories: 138, Protein: 9 gm., Fat: 6 gm., Carbohydrate: 10 gm.

Carrot-Sunflower Salad

This crunchy, naturally sweet salad has special appeal for kids.

1 cup carrots, pared and grated
3 Tablespoons raisins
2 Tablespoons Low-Fat, Egg-Free Mayonnaise,
    p. 110, or your favorite egg- and dairy-free
    mayonnaise
2 Tablespoons raw (not roasted) sunflower
    seeds

salt, to taste

1. Place all the ingredients *except the salt* in a small mixing bowl, and stir to combine thoroughly.

2. Season the salad with salt to taste.

3. Serve at once or cover the bowl and chill the salad in the refrigerator.

Yield: 2 side dish servings

Per serving: Calories: 138, Protein: 3 gm., Fat: 7 gm., Carbohydrate: 17 gm.

Waldorf Salad

The original version of this wonderful salad, created at New York's Waldorf-Astoria Hotel in the 1890s, contained only apples, celery, and mayonnaise. Chopped walnuts later became an integral part of the dish. Here I include grapes as an optional addition. Waldorf Salad makes a wonderful side dish or even a great stuffing for baked winter squash. (Fill the center cavity with the salad just before serving.) It's worth tracking down organic apples, raisins, and grapes for this salad as their flavors are incomparable.

1 crisp, red eating apple, diced (peel if waxed)
1 teaspoon fresh lemon juice

1/4 cup celery, finely chopped
1/4 cup seedless grapes, halved (optional)
3 Tablespoons raisins or chopped dates
3 Tablespoons walnuts, coarsely chopped

2 to 3 Tablespoons Low-Fat, Egg-Free
    Mayonnaise, p. 110, or your favorite egg- and
    dairy-free mayonnaise
tiny pinch of ground nutmeg

a few leaves of leaf lettuce or romaine lettuce,
    as needed (optional)

1. Place the diced apple in a medium mixing bowl, and toss it with the lemon juice.

2. Add the celery, grapes (if using), raisins or dates, and nuts, and toss them together with the apple.

3. Fold the mayonnaise into the apple mixture. Sprinkle in a tiny bit of ground nutmeg, and mix gently.

4. Serve immediately or cover the bowl and chill the salad for up to 10 hours. If desired, spoon the salad onto two lettuce-lined salad plates for an attractive presentation.

Yield: 2 side dish servings

Per serving: Calories: 181, Protein: 3 gm., Fat: 9 gm., Carbohydrate: 22 gm.

Orange & Carrot Salad

This light fruit and vegetable salad makes a pleasant luncheon dish, appetizer, side salad, or not-too-sweet dessert.

1 navel orange, peeled and sectioned

2 medium carrots, pared and finely shredded or
    grated
3 Tablespoons fresh lemon juice
scant 1/2 teaspoon ground cinnamon

1. Slice each section of the navel orange into four pieces, and place the pieces and any juice in a small mixing bowl.

2. Add the remaining ingredients to the orange pieces in the bowl, and stir them together to mix well.

3. Serve at once or cover the bowl and chill the salad in the refrigerator.

Yield: 2 side dish servings

Per serving: Calories: 70, Protein: 1 gm., Fat: 0 gm., Carbohydrate: 16 gm.

Sweet & Sour Dressing

A fat-free dressing with a splendid, sweet-sour flavor. In addition to salads, it is enchanting on hot or cold grains.

1/2 cup cold water
1 1/2 teaspoons cornstarch
1/4 teaspoon garlic granules
1/4 teaspoon dry mustard

1/4 cup apple cider vinegar
2 Tablespoons pineapple juice concentrate or apple juice concentrate
1 teaspoon soy sauce
pinch of salt, to taste

1. Place the water in a 1-quart saucepan, and in it dissolve the cornstarch, garlic granules, and dry mustard using a wire whisk.

2. Place the saucepan over medium-high heat, and cook the cornstarch mixture, stirring constantly, until it is thickened.

3. Remove the saucepan from the heat, and stir in the remaining ingredients using a wire whisk.

4. Serve the dressing warm or allow it to cool. Then transfer the dressing to a storage container, and chill it in the refrigerator. The dressing will thicken slightly when chilled. Stir it well before serving.

Yield: about 2/3 cup

Per Tablespoon: Calories: 9, Protein: 0 gm., Fat: 0 gm., Carbohydrate: 2 gm.

Catalina French Dressing

Moderately sweet, this dressing is always well received. It is great with everything from artichokes to zucchini.

1/2 cup cold water
1 1/2 teaspoons cornstarch
1/4 teaspoon garlic granules
1/4 teaspoon onion granules

2 Tablespoons ketchup
2 Tablespoons apple cider vinegar
2 Tablespoons apple juice concentrate
1/4 teaspoon paprika

1. Place the water in a 1-quart saucepan, and in it dissolve the cornstarch, garlic granules, and onion granules using a wire whisk.

2. Place the saucepan over medium-high heat, and cook the cornstarch mixture, stirring constantly, until it is thickened.

3. Remove the saucepan from the heat, and stir in the remaining ingredients using a wire whisk.

4. Serve the dressing warm or allow it to cool. Then transfer the dressing to a storage container, and chill it in the refrigerator. The dressing will thicken slightly when chilled. Stir it well before serving.

Yield: about 2/3 cup

Per Tablespoon: Calories: 11, Protein: 0 gm., Fat: 0 gm., Carbohydrate: 2 gm.

Italian Dressing

Not too overpowering, this light Italian dressing is simply delicious.

1/2 cup cold water
1 1/2 teaspoons cornstarch
1/4 teaspoon garlic granules
1/4 teaspoon onion granules

1/4 cup red wine vinegar
2 Tablespoons apple juice concentrate
1/2 teaspoon dried oregano leaves
1/4 teaspoon dried basil leaves
pinch of salt, or to taste

1. Place the water in a 1-quart saucepan, and in it dissolve the cornstarch, garlic granules, and onion granules using a wire whisk.

2. Place the saucepan over medium-high heat, and cook the cornstarch mixture, stirring constantly, until it is thickened.

3. Remove the saucepan from the heat, and stir in the remaining ingredients using a wire whisk.

4. Serve the dressing warm or allow it to cool. Then transfer the dressing to a storage container, and chill it in the refrigerator. The dressing will thicken slightly when chilled. Stir it well before serving.

Yield: about 2/3 cup

Per Tablespoon: Calories: 8, Protein: 0 gm., Fat: 0 gm, Carbohydrate: 2 gm..

French-Style Vinaigrette

This dressing is tart and direct with barely a hint of sweetness.

1/2 cup cold water
1 1/2 teaspoons cornstarch
1/4 teaspoon garlic granules

1 Tablespoon red wine vinegar
1 Tablespoon fresh lemon juice
1 Tablespoon apple juice concentrate
1 teaspoon Dijon mustard
1/8 teaspoon salt, or to taste
dash of ground black pepper

1. Place the water in a 1-quart saucepan, and in it dissolve the cornstarch and garlic granules using a wire whisk.

2. Place the saucepan over medium-high heat, and cook the cornstarch mixture, stirring constantly, until it is thickened.

3. Remove the saucepan from the heat, and stir in the remaining ingredients using a wire whisk.

4. Serve the dressing warm or allow it to cool. Then transfer the dressing to a storage container, and chill it in the refrigerator. The dressing will thicken slightly when chilled. Stir it well before serving.

Yield: about 1/2 cup

Per Tablespoon: Calories: 7, Protein: 0 gm., Fat: 0 gm., Carbohydrate: 2 gm.

Creamy Dijon Dressing

If you like Dijon mustard, you'll love this dressing. Balsamic vinegar lends a distinct but mellow tone. It's great on steamed vegetables, especially broccoli and cabbage.

1/2 cup cold water
1 1/2 teaspoons cornstarch

2 Tablespoons Dijon mustard
2 Tablespoons balsamic vinegar (see The Cook's Secrets above right)
1/8 teaspoon salt, or to taste
pinch of ground black pepper, to taste

1. Place the water in a 1-quart saucepan, and in it dissolve the cornstarch using a wire whisk.

2. Place the saucepan over medium-high heat, and cook the cornstarch mixture, stirring constantly, until it is thickened.

3. Remove the saucepan from the heat, and stir in the remaining ingredients using a wire whisk.

4. Serve the dressing warm, or allow it to cool. Then transfer the dressing to a storage container, and chill it in the refrigerator. The dressing will thicken slightly when chilled. Stir it well before serving.

Yield: about 2/3 cup

Per Tablespoon: Calories: 7, Protein: 0 gm., Fat: 0 gm., Carbohydrate: 0 gm.

The Cook's Secrets:
Balsamic vinegar is the key to the gentle flavor of this dressing. It is a dark brown vinegar with a delicate sweet taste. Balsamic vinegar is made from the juice of a very sweet white grape and is aged in wooden barrels for a minimum of ten years. It is available in most supermarkets, Italian markets, and gourmet food stores.

Thousand Island Dressing

Rich and creamy, this is a great topping for vegetarian burgers or baked potatoes as well as hearty salads.

1/4 cup Low-Fat, Egg-Free Mayonnaise, p. 110, or your favorite egg- and dairy-free mayonnaise
2 Tablespoons ketchup
1 1/2 Tablespoons pickle relish (sweet or dill), lightly drained
slightly heaping 1/4 teaspoon onion granules
1/8 teaspoon salt, or to taste

1. Place all the ingredients in a measuring cup or small mixing bowl, and stir them together to combine them thoroughly.

2. Serve the dressing at once, or transfer it to a storage container, and chill it in the refrigerator.

Yield: about 1/3 cup

Per Tablespoon: Calories: 27, Protein: 1 gm., Fat: 2 gm., Carbohydrate: 3 gm.

Creamy Vinaigrette

This creamy, piquant dressing is especially tasty on vegetables, lettuce, potatoes or beans.

1/2 of a 10.5-ounce package fat-reduced, firm silken tofu, drained and crumbled (about 3/4 cup)
4 teaspoons fresh lemon juice
4 teaspoons red wine vinegar
1 1/2 teaspoons Dijon mustard
1 1/2 teaspoons olive oil
1 small clove garlic, minced or pressed

1. Place all the ingredients in a blender or food processor, and process until the mixture is very smooth and creamy.

2. Serve the dressing at once, or transfer it to a storage container, and chill it in the refrigerator.

Yield: about 3/4 cup

Per Tablespoon: Calories: 12, Protein: 1 gm., Fat: 0 gm., Carbohydrate: 1 gm.

Tofu Sour Cream

Appropriately tart, creamy, and delicious, Tofu Sour Cream is the ideal non-dairy replacement for its dairy counterpart.

1 10.5-ounce package fat-reduced, firm silken tofu, crumbled
1 Tablespoon canola oil or olive oil
2 teaspoons fresh lemon juice
2 teaspoons apple cider vinegar
1/2 teaspoon sweetener of your choice
1/2 teaspoon salt

1. Place all the ingredients in a food processor fitted with a metal blade or in a blender. Process several minutes until the mixture is very smooth and creamy.

2. Transfer the mixture to a storage container, and store it in the refrigerator. It will keep for about 5 days.

Yield: about 1 1/4 cups

Per 1/4 cup serving: Calories: 40, Protein: 2 gm., Fat: 3 gm., Carbohydrate: 2 gm.

The Cook's Secrets:
The secret to the ultra-creamy consistency of this Tofu Sour Cream is processing it for several minutes. This is necessary to pulverize the tofu thoroughly and eliminate any graininess. After the long processing time, the texture will be miraculously transformed.

SOUPS, STEWS & CHOWDERS

Soup is fun to make and soothing to eat. Generally speaking, soup is a liquid that can be served either hot or cold as a first course, entrée, or even dessert. Soups can be thick or thin, clear or creamy, smooth or chunky. Thin soups work best as a first course, especially when the main dish is creamy or rich. Thick soups can enrich a light meal or stand on their own as the main course.

If you are serving soup as a first course, avoid repeating ingredients or flavors that will be used in the other courses. If the soup is to be served as the main dish, round out the meal with a crisp salad and whole grain rolls, bread, or crackers.

To thicken a thin soup without adding fat, purée some of the soup's cooked vegetables, and then return the purée to the soup. Cornstarch and flour (dissolved first in a cool liquid), instant potato flakes, and puréed cooked beans also work well as thickeners.

If you are inventive, you can easily create your own unique soup at the spur of the moment. Here's the formula:

Blender Soup

Sauté some chopped onion and/or garlic in a small amount of vegetable oil or water. Place the cooked onion or garlic in a blender with other cooked vegetables or beans (this is a terrific way to use up leftovers!). Good vegetable choices are potatoes or sweet potatoes, winter or summer squash, carrots, broccoli, and steamed greens. Add about 1/3 to 1/2 cup of water or vegetable broth for each cup of vegetables or beans. Purée the soup until it is smooth. Then season it to taste with salt, pepper, dried or fresh herbs, and any other seasonings you choose. Transfer the soup to a saucepan, and heat it over a medium flame.

Fresh Vegetable Broth

If you prefer to use vegetable broth in your recipes instead of water and would rather not use vegetable bouillon cubes or mixes, here are two handy techniques for creating fresh broth without much effort.

1. Don't throw out vegetable scraps, peelings, garlic and onion skins, carrot tops, parsley and spinach stems, etc.; store them in a covered container in the refrigerator or freezer. Then, when you have some spare time, place them in a 4 1/2-quart saucepan or Dutch oven. Cover them with approximately 2 parts water to 1 part vegetables, and bring the water to a boil.

Reduce the heat to medium-low, cover the saucepan with a lid, and let the mixture simmer for about an hour. Strain the mixture by pouring it through a wire mesh strainer placed over a large bowl. Use the broth immediately or store it in the refrigerator. The broth can also be frozen in 1-quart containers or even in ice cube trays for easy retrieval.

2. Save the water from steamed vegetables, potatoes, pasta, home-cooked beans, or the simmering broth from homemade seitan. All of these will make a light, tasty, vegetarian broth.

Each of the following recipes makes enough soup for three to four servings. Because the flavor of soup improves when it is stored for a day or two, leftovers are usually welcome. Leftover soup makes a savory breakfast, quick lunch, light supper, or satisfying midday snack. The larger quantity also gives you the option of serving the soup as a first course or as a main dish.

Several of the soups will require blending into a smooth purée. This must be done in several small batches, depending on the capacity of your blender container. Be sure to take this into consideration when processing the soups. **Don't overfill your blender jar!** This is important because the mixture will temporarily "expand" with air during processing, and without sufficient space the contents of the blender jar will not be able to move freely.

Keep in mind that hot soups release a surprising amount of steam when puréed. This can force the lid of the blender jar to pop off or propel a spray of hot mixture out from under the lid rim. As a standard precautionary measure, **fill the blender container no more than halfway when puréeing soups**, and use a kitchen towel to hold the lid slightly ajar to allow some of the steam to escape.

To purée or blend soup in batches, transfer a small portion of the mixture to a blender. Process until the mixture is completely smooth. Pour the blended mixture into a large bowl, and process the remaining soup in the same manner. To purée soup safely, you may need to blend it in two to four batches. When all the soup has been puréed, transfer the blended mixture back to the cooking vessel, and proceed with the recipe as directed.

A Note From Paula:

My husband David and I like to have soup throughout the week, so we make one big pot of soup on the weekend and keep it in the refrigerator. Once the soup is made, it's very easy to just transfer the amount we want to reheat to a small saucepan. We get a lot of quick lunches and dinners out of one soup recipe. All we need to do to complete the meal is slice our favorite bread which, of course, is essential to dunk into the soup!

Stewed Winter Vegetables

This is the vegetarian answer to chicken soup! Karen Bernard gave me a broad concept for this soothing, healing stew. Then I formalized the quantities and nailed down the cooking time to get the precise result. The flavor is sweet and mild, and the texture is thick and juicy.

This stew makes a fabulous meal—whether it's served for breakfast, lunch, or dinner. The key to thoroughly enjoying this stew is to serve it with plenty of whole grain bread to dip into the broth throughout your meal.

6 to 8 cups winter vegetables (choose a mix of yams, rutabaga, turnips, parsnips, potatoes, and carrots), peeled and cut into equal size chunks

1 large onion, cut into wedges

6 to 8 cloves garlic, whole, halved, sliced or coarsely chopped

water, as needed

2 cups greens (kale, collard greens, turnip greens, or mustard greens), torn into small pieces or chopped, or 1/2 to 1 cup fresh parsley, chopped

1 to 2 teaspoons olive oil (optional)

salt or soy sauce, to taste

1. Place the yams, rutabaga, turnips, parsnips, potatoes, carrots, onion, and garlic in a 4 1/2-quart saucepan or Dutch oven. Fill the saucepan with enough water to more than cover the vegetables. The more water you use, the more broth you will have. (However, do not fill the saucepan more than two-thirds full with vegetables and water. This will help to prevent the contents from boiling over as the soup cooks.)

2. Bring the water to a boil, then reduce the heat to medium-low. Cover the saucepan with a lid, and simmer the soup for 30 minutes.

3. Stir in the greens or parsley, cover the saucepan again, and continue to cook for 10 to 15 minutes longer, or until everything is very tender and the root vegetables are starting to break apart.

4. Ladle some of the stew into 2 large soup bowls. Drizzle 1/2 to 1 teaspoon olive oil over each serving, if desired, and sprinkle lightly with salt or soy sauce, to taste.

Yield: about 4 servings

Per serving: Calories: 191, Protein: 3 gm., Fat: 0 gm., Carbohydrate: 43 gm.

The Cook's Secrets:
To prevent the yams from discoloring after they have been peeled and chunked, place them in a bowl of water to which a little lemon juice has been added. When the remaining vegetables have been prepared, place the yams in a colander, and rinse off the lemon water thoroughly before proceeding with the recipe.

Breakfast Noodle Soup

This elegant combination of simple ingredients is delightful any time of day, but we find it especially energizing in the morning. If you want to try a savory breakfast for a change, give this recipe a try. It's speedy and delicious.

1/8 to 1/4 pound (2 to 4 ounces) soba noodles (see The Cook's Secrets at right)

2 cups water or vegetable broth
2 cloves garlic, minced or pressed
1 medium carrot, pared and thinly sliced on the diagonal
1 cup broccoli, cut into bite-size florets

2 Tablespoons sweet white miso or other light miso

soy sauce, to taste (optional)

1. Fill a 4 1/2-quart saucepan or Dutch oven two-thirds full with water. Bring the water to a rolling boil. Add the noodles and cook them until they are al dente. Drain the noodles well. Then divide them between two large soup bowls.

2. Meanwhile, place the water and garlic in a 2-quart saucepan, and bring the water to a boil. Carefully drop in the carrots, and cook them for 1 minute. Then stir the broccoli florets in with the carrots. Cover the saucepan with a lid, and reduce the heat to medium. Simmer the soup for 5 to 8 minutes, or until the vegetables are tender.

3. Remove the saucepan from the heat. Stir the miso into the broth, mixing well until it is thoroughly dissolved.

4. Ladle the vegetables and the broth over the noodles in the soup bowls. Drizzle a little soy sauce over each serving, if desired. Serve the soup at once with a spoon and a fork or chopsticks to scoop up the noodles.

Yield: 2 servings

Per serving: Calories: 124, Protein: 5 gm., Fat: 1 gm., Carbohydrate: 22 gm.

The Cook's Secrets:
Soba noodles are an Asian pasta made from buckwheat flour or a combination of buckwheat and whole wheat flours. They are very thin like spaghetti. (If you want to make this recipe but are fresh out of soba noodles, thin spaghetti may be substituted.) Soba noodles are absolutely delicious and are a good replacement for almost any refined pasta. They are available in Asian markets and natural food stores. Cook them in boiling water until al dente, just as you would other pastas. I highly recommend using mugwort soba noodles in this recipe. They are green in color with a distinct but very mild flavor.

For a heartier meal, 1/2 to 1 cup of firm tofu (regular or silken), cut into small cubes, may be added to the soup along with the broccoli.

Old World Cabbage Soup

This is very chunky vegetable soup with a light tomato broth. If you want to make this recipe even more stew-like, a cup of seitan chunks may be added near the end of the cooking time. I like to garnish each serving with a healthy dab of Tofu Sour Cream, p. 73.

4 cups water
3 1/2 cups green cabbage, shredded
1 14.5-ounce can whole tomatoes, with juice
1 cup carrots, pared, cut in half lengthwise and
    sliced into half-moons
1 cup onion, chopped
1/2 cup celery, chopped
1/2 cup tomato paste
2 Tablespoons fresh parsley, minced
2 Tablespoons sweetener of your choice (optional)
2 Tablespoons soy sauce, or to taste
1 1/2 teaspoons dried basil leaves

salt and ground black pepper, to taste

1 cup seitan, cut into chunks (optional)

Tofu Sour Cream, p. 73, for garnish (optional)

1. Place all the ingredients *except the seitan and Tofu Sour Cream* in a 4 1/2-quart saucepan or Dutch oven. Break the tomatoes apart with your hands or the side of a wooden spoon.

2. Bring the mixture to a boil, then reduce the heat to medium-low. Cover the saucepan with a lid, and simmer the soup for 1 hour, or until the cabbage is tender. If desired, seitan chunks may be added about 5 minutes before the soup has finished cooking.

3. Season the soup with salt and pepper, to taste.

4. For an attractive finish, place a large dollop of Tofu Sour Cream in the center of each serving. Serve the soup hot.

Yield: about 1 1/2 quarts (3 to 4 servings)

Per serving: Calories: 105, Protein: 4 gm., Fat: 0 gm., Carbohydrate: 21 gm.

Pan Handle Chili

Nothing satisfies quite like a "steaming bowl of red." The bulgur in this recipe adds a "meaty" chewiness that complements the soft, rich texture of the beans. Don't be daunted by the lengthy list of ingredients—it primarily consists of seasonings. This recipe is nothing less than simple and delicious, and it will win you raves every time. Serve it with Yankee Corn Muffins, p. 39, baked corn chips, or my personal favorites, Whole Wheat Biscuits, p. 42, or Cornmeal Biscuits, p. 43.

2 teaspoons olive oil
1 cup onion, finely chopped
1/2 cup celery, finely chopped
2 cloves garlic, minced or pressed

2 ripe, medium tomatoes, peeled, seeded, and
    coarsely chopped (see The Cook's Secrets at
    right)
1 15-ounce can red kidney beans, pinto beans, or
    black beans, rinsed well and drained
1 8-ounce can tomato sauce (1 cup), or 1/3 cup
    tomato paste mixed with 2/3 cup water
1 cup water
1/3 cup bulgur (medium ground)
2 Tablespoons tomato paste
1 Tablespoon sweetener of your choice
1 Tablespoon chili powder
1/2 teaspoon dried oregano leaves
1/4 teaspoon ground black pepper
1/4 teaspoon ground cumin
1/8 teaspoon allspice
pinch of cayenne pepper, to taste

salt to taste

1. Place the olive oil in a 4 1/2-quart saucepan or Dutch oven, and heat it over medium-high. When the oil is hot, add the onion, celery, and garlic. Reduce the heat to medium, and cook, stirring occasionally, for 10 to 15 minutes, or until the onion is tender.

2. When the onion is tender, stir in the remaining ingredients *except the salt*, and bring the mixture to a boil. Reduce the heat to low, cover the saucepan with a lid, and simmer the chili for 20 minutes, stirring occasionally.

3. Season the chili with salt, to taste. Serve hot.

Yield: about 1 quart (3 to 4 servings)

Per serving: Calories: 301, Protein: 12 gm., Fat: 3 gm., Carbohydrate: 55 gm.

The Cook's Secrets:
To peel a tomato, first use a sharp knife to cut a small cross in the bottom of the tomato. Turn the tomato over and cut out the core. Immerse the tomato in a pot of boiling water for about 10 to 15 seconds. Remove the tomato from the pot using a slotted spoon, and transfer it to a bowl of cold water. Let it rest for one minute. Remove the tomato from the cold water, and peel off the skin using your fingers—it should peel away easily.

To seed a tomato, cut the tomato in half crosswise, and gently squeeze out the seeds.

If you prefer a milder chili, go easy on the black pepper and cayenne, or eliminate them completely.

For added sweetness and texture, stir in one grated carrot and/or a few raisins before bringing the mixture to a boil in step #2.

Red Onion & Beet Soup

This is borscht the way my grandmother (from Russia) and husband's grandmother (from Poland) used to make it. It's interesting that, despite their widely divergent backgrounds, both families had very similar recipes. For an authentic "old country" meal, serve this soup with plenty of dark pumpernickel bread or peasant-style black bread.

HAVE READY:
1/4 to 1/2 cup Tofu Sour Cream, p. 73

2 small potatoes, peeled and cut into 2-inch
    chunks

1 1/2 teaspoons olive oil
1 large red onion, cut in half and thinly sliced
2 cloves garlic, minced or pressed

1 15-ounce can sliced beets, undrained
water or vegetable broth, as needed
1 Tablespoon apple juice concentrate
1 Tablespoon fresh lemon juice

salt and ground black pepper, to taste

1. Place the potatoes in a steamer basket or steamer insert in a large saucepan filled with an inch of water. Bring the water to a boil. Cover the saucepan with a lid, and reduce the heat to medium. Steam the potatoes until they are fork-tender, about 20 to 25 minutes. Set aside.

2. Meanwhile, place the olive oil in a 4 1/2-quart saucepan or Dutch oven, and heat it over medium-high. When the oil is hot, add the onion and garlic. Reduce the heat to medium, and sauté them for about 20 minutes, or until the onion is very soft and tender.

3. While the onions are cooking, drain the beets *but reserve the liquid*. Add enough water or vegetable broth to the liquid to equal 4 cups. Set aside.

4. Slice the beets into thin strips. When the onions have finished cooking, stir the beets, reserved liquid (from step #3), apple juice concentrate, and lemon juice into the saucepan containing the onions.

5. Warm the soup over medium, until it is heated through. Season it with salt and pepper, to taste.

6. Ladle some of the soup into two large soup bowls. Top each serving with several chunks of warm potatoes and 2 heaping tablespoons of Tofu Sour Cream.

Yield: about 5 cups (3 to 4 servings)

Per serving: Calories: 176, Protein: 5 gm., Fat: 3 gm., Carbohydrate: 30 gm.

The Cook's Secrets
This soup may be prepared in advance and chilled. It is delicious when served cold along with the hot potatoes and cold Tofu Sour Cream which provide interesting contrasts in temperatures.

Corn & Potato Chowder

This warming chowder is "comfort food" at its finest.

3 medium potatoes, peeled and diced
1 1/2 cups water

1 teaspoon canola oil
1 small onion, chopped
1 stalk celery, diced
1 medium carrot, pared and chopped
1 small red bell pepper, finely chopped
1/2 teaspoon dried thyme leaves or dried
    oregano leaves

2/3 cup low-fat, non-dairy milk

1 cup fresh corn kernels or 1 cup frozen corn ker-
    nels, thawed, or 1 8-ounce can whole kernel
    corn, drained

salt and ground black pepper, to taste

1. Place the potatoes and water in a 4 1/2-quart saucepan or Dutch oven, and bring the water to a boil. Reduce the heat to low, cover the saucepan with a lid, and simmer the potatoes for 20 minutes.

2. Meanwhile, place the oil in a 9-inch or 10-inch skillet, and heat it over medium-high. When the oil is hot, add the onion, celery, carrot, red bell pepper, and thyme or oregano leaves. Cook, stirring constantly, until the vegetables are just tender, about 5 to 8 minutes. Remove the skillet from the heat, and set aside.

3. When the potatoes are tender, remove the saucepan from the heat. Using a slotted spoon, transfer 1 1/2 cups of the potatoes to a blender. Add the milk to the blender, and process until the mixture is smooth.

4. Pour the blended mixture into the saucepan containing the remaining potatoes and their cooking liquid. Stir in the corn and the reserved cooked vegetables (from step #2).

5. Place the saucepan over medium heat, and warm the soup through before serving it, about 5 to 10 minutes. Serve hot.

Yield: about 1 1/2 quarts (3 to 4 servings)

Per serving: Calories: 188, Protein: 3 gm., Fat: 2 gm., Carbohydrate: 39 gm.

The Cook's Secrets:
If you have fresh herbs available, use 2 teaspoons chopped fresh herbs in place of the dry herbs, and add them along with the corn.

Cream of Cauliflower & Lima Bean Soup

This is a creamy, blended soup with a few whole lima beans added for extra bite. I like to use only fordhook lima beans because they are large, sweet, and meaty.

This soup is delicious as an entrée, and leftovers taste wonderful. Nevertheless, this recipe makes a fairly large quantity for a small household. If this seems like too much soup for your needs, feel free to halve the ingredients. The directions would be the same. Alternately, you can freeze the leftovers.

1 16-ounce package of frozen fordhook lima
  beans

2 teaspoons olive oil
1 medium onion, chopped
2 to 3 cloves garlic, chopped
2 teaspoons whole caraway seeds

1 medium head cauliflower, cut into small florets
5 cups water or vegetable broth

salt and ground black pepper, to taste

fresh parsley, chopped, for garnish (optional)

1. Place the lima beans in a 2-quart saucepan, and cover them completely with water. Bring the water to a boil. Reduce the heat to medium-low, cover the saucepan with a lid, and simmer the lima beans for 10 to 12 minutes, or until they are tender.

2. Drain the beans well in a colander or wire mesh strainer. Then divide them into two equal portions, placing each portion in a separate small bowl. Set the beans aside.

3. Place the oil in a 4 1/2-quart saucepan or Dutch oven, and heat it over medium-high. When the oil is hot, add the onion, garlic, and caraway seeds. Cook them, stirring often, over medium heat for 10 minutes, or until the onion is soft.

4. When the onion is soft, add the cauliflower and water or broth to the saucepan. Bring the soup to a boil. Reduce the heat to medium, cover the saucepan with a lid, and simmer the soup for 10 to 12 minutes, or until the cauliflower is very tender.

5. Purée the soup in batches. To do this, transfer a small portion of the vegetables, some of the cooking water, and some of the lima beans (use the beans from only one of the bowls from step #2) to a blender. Process until the mixture is completely smooth. Pour the blended soup into a large mixing bowl. Continue processing the rest of the soup in a similar fashion, using up the remainder of the lima beans from the one bowl only. (For more information on batch blending, see p. 75.)

6. Return the blended soup to the 4 1/2-quart saucepan, and stir in the reserved whole lima beans from the second bowl (from step #2).

7. Season the soup with salt and pepper, to taste. Heat the soup over medium-low until the beans are heated through and the soup is very hot. Garnish each serving with a little chopped parsley, if desired.

Yield: about 2 quarts (5 servings)

Per serving: Calories: 138, Protein: 6 gm., Fat: 1 gm., Carbohydrate: 23 gm.

The Cook's Secrets

Keep a close eye on the lima beans during cooking. Lima beans create a lot of foam which can be forced out from under the lid of the saucepan. To keep foam to a minimum, you can try one of the following techniques: 1) stir the lima beans often, 2) lift the lid occasionally, 3) cook the lima beans with the lid slightly ajar, or 4) add a teaspoon of oil to the cooking water.

Squash, Cabbage & White Bean Soup

The sophisticated flavor of this delightful soup belies its ease of preparation.

2 teaspoons olive oil
1 medium onion, finely chopped
2 large cloves garlic, minced or pressed

4 cups water or vegetable broth
2 cups green cabbage, finely shredded
1 16-ounce can white beans (great northern beans, navy pea beans, etc.), rinsed well and drained
1 12-ounce package frozen cooked winter squash
1/2 teaspoon dried thyme leaves, finely crushed

1/2 teaspoon salt, or to taste
ground black pepper, to taste

1. Place the olive oil in a 4 1/2-quart saucepan or Dutch oven, and heat it over medium-high. When the oil is hot, add the onion and garlic, and sauté them until the onion is golden brown, about 10 minutes.

2. Add the remaining ingredients *except the salt and pepper,* and bring the mixture to a boil, stirring constantly to help defrost the squash.

3. Once the mixture has come to a boil, reduce the heat to low, cover the saucepan with a lid, and cook the soup for about 10 minutes, or until the cabbage is tender but not mushy.

4. Season the soup with salt and pepper to taste. Serve hot.

Yield: about 1 1/2 quarts (3 to 4 servings)

Per serving: Calories: 268, Protein: 12 gm., Fat: 4 gm., Carbohydrate: 47 gm.

Cheddar Cheeze Soup

This soup was a childhood favorite, so of course I was compelled to create a dairy-free version that was as creamy and rich-tasting as the one I remember. Although the basic, "plain" rendering below is delicious in its own right, the variations which follow are even more exciting and are a tasty way to tempt young ones to eat vegetables they might otherwise shun. Herbs may also be added to these variations; dill weed is particularly nice with green peas, thyme or oregano is a good match with mixed vegetables, and basil is a pleasant complement to broccoli.

1 medium potato, peeled and coarsely chopped
1 medium carrot, pared and coarsely chopped
1 medium onion, coarsely chopped
1 cup water

1 10.5-ounce package fat-reduced, firm silken
    tofu, crumbled
1/2 cup nutritional yeast flakes
2 Tablespoons fresh lemon juice
1 1/4 teaspoons salt
1 teaspoon onion granules
1/4 teaspoon garlic granules

1 cup low-fat, non-dairy milk

1. Place the potato, carrot, onion, and water in a 2-quart saucepan, and bring the water to a boil. Reduce the heat to medium, cover the saucepan with a lid, and simmer the vegetables, stirring once or twice, for 10 minutes or until they are tender.

2. Purée the soup in batches. To do this, transfer a small portion of the cooked vegetables, some of the cooking water, and a small of amount of each of the remaining ingredients *except the milk* to a blender. Process each batch until the mixture is completely smooth. Pour the blended soup into a large mixing bowl. Continue processing the rest of the vegetables, the cooking water, and the remaining ingredients in a similar fashion. (For more information on batch blending, see p. 75.)

3. Return the blended soup to the saucepan, and stir in the milk. Place the saucepan over low heat, and warm the soup, stirring often, until it is hot.

Yield: 5 cups (3 to 4 servings)

Per serving: Calories: 178, Protein: 15 gm., Fat: 1 gm., Carbohydrate: 26 gm.

Broccoli Cheeze Soup or Cauliflower Cheeze Soup: Prepare the recipe as directed above. Add 1 1/2 cups broccoli or cauliflower, cut or broken into small florets, and steamed until tender.

Cheezy Vegetable Soup: Prepare the recipe as directed above. Add 1 10-ounce package of frozen vegetables, cooked according to the package directions, and drained.

Green Peas & Cheeze Soup: Prepare the recipe as directed above. Add 1 1/2 cups frozen loose-pack green peas, cooked according to the package directions, and drained.

Herbed Cheddar Cheeze Soup: Prepare the recipe as directed above. Add up to 1 1/2 teaspoons of your favorite dried herb or 4 teaspoons of your favorite chopped fresh herb.

Old-Fashioned Tomato Rice Soup

This staple recipe creates homemade flavor in record time by incorporating a few handy shortcuts. The secret to this soup's wonderful flavor is cooking the onions until they are very brown and tender.

2 teaspoons olive oil or canola oil
1 cup onions, finely chopped

1 6-ounce can (2/3 cup) tomato paste
3 1/2 cups water
2/3 cup quick-cooking rice (not instant)
2 Tablespoons sweetener of your choice
1/2 teaspoon garlic granules

salt and ground black pepper, to taste

1. Place the oil in a 4 1/2-quart saucepan or Dutch oven, and heat it over medium-high. When the oil is hot, add the onions and sauté them until they are very dark brown and tender, about 15 minutes.

2. Stir in the tomato paste, water, rice, sweetener, and garlic granules, mixing well until the tomato paste is thoroughly incorporated. Bring the soup to a boil. Reduce the heat to low, cover the saucepan with a lid, and simmer the soup for 12 to 15 minutes, or until the rice is tender.

3. Season the soup with salt and pepper, to taste. Serve hot.

Yield: about 1 quart (3 servings)

Per serving: Calories: 185, Protein: 3 gm., Fat: 3 gm., Carbohydrate: 35 gm.

Mushroom Barley Chowder

Quick-cooking barley and canned cream-style corn are the secrets to making this quick, hearty soup taste like it simmered all day.

2 8.5-ounce cans cream-style corn (dairy-free)
2 cups fresh mushrooms, sliced
2 cups water or vegetable broth
1/2 cup scallions, sliced
1/2 cup quick-cooking barley
1 teaspoon dried basil leaves
1/8 teaspoon ground black pepper

salt, to taste

1. Place all the ingredients *except the salt* in a 4 1/2-quart saucepan or Dutch oven, and bring the soup to a boil. Reduce the heat to low, cover the saucepan with a lid, and simmer the soup for 10 minutes.

2. Season the soup with salt, to taste. Serve hot.

Yield: 1 quart (3 servings)

Per serving: Calories: 202, Protein: 5 gm., Fat: 0 gm., Carbohydrate: 44 gm.

Navy Bean Soup

Typically, robust and flavorful bean soups turn out to be all-day cooking affairs. By using a few convenient shortcuts, however, you can ladle this one out in under 30 minutes!

2 15-ounce cans navy beans, rinsed well and
   drained
3 1/2 cups water or vegetable broth
1 8-ounce can tomato sauce (1 cup), or 1/3 cup
   tomato paste combined with 2/3 cup water
1 medium onion, chopped
2 medium carrots, pared and thinly sliced or
   diced
2 cloves garlic, minced or pressed
1 stalk celery, sliced
1 medium potato, peeled and diced
1 whole bay leaf
1/4 teaspoon dried thyme leaves
1/8 teaspoon ground black pepper

1 Tablespoon fresh parsley, minced (optional)
salt, to taste

1. Place *half of the beans* and the remaining ingredients, *except the parsley and salt*, in a 4 1/2-quart saucepan or Dutch oven. Set the remaining beans aside.

2. Bring the mixture to a boil. Reduce the heat to medium-low, cover the saucepan with a lid, and simmer the soup for 20 minutes, or until the vegetables are tender.

3. Place 1 cup of the soup broth in a blender along with the reserved beans (from step #1). Process until the mixture is very smooth.

4. Return the blended mixture to the remaining soup in the saucepan, and heat it through for about 5 minutes.

5. Stir in the parsley, if using, and season the soup with salt, to taste.

6. Remove the bay leaf before serving. Serve hot.

Yield: about 1 1/2 quarts (3 to 4 servings)

Per serving: Calories: 437, Protein: 20 gm., Fat: 1 gm., Carbohydrate: 85 gm.

A Note From Scott:
Some thick soups and stews, especially those with beans, will thicken even more after refrigeration. The leftovers make great "pot pie" fillings. If you like, stir in some additional seasonings to vary the taste, and put it in a crust or a casserole dish. Top the filling with mashed potatoes, and bake the pot pie until the potatoes are golden brown and the filling is hot.

Lentil-Couscous Stew

A perennial favorite—hearty, thick, and flavorful. Garnish each serving with finely chopped, fresh basil leaves or parsley.

4 cups water or vegetable broth
1 cup dry lentils, picked over, rinsed well and
   drained
1 14.5-ounce can whole tomatoes, with juice
1 medium carrot or parsnip, pared and chopped
1/2 cup onion, chopped
6 Tablespoons tomato paste
4 cloves garlic, minced or pressed
1 stalk celery, chopped
2 to 3 teaspoons olive oil (optional)
1 1/2 teaspoons dried basil leaves
1/2 teaspoon dried oregano leaves

1/2 cup couscous (whole-wheat or regular)

salt and ground black pepper, to taste

fresh basil leaves or fresh parsley, finely chopped
   for garnish (optional)

1. Place all the ingredients *except the couscous, salt, pepper, and garnish* in a 4 1/2-quart saucepan or Dutch oven.

2. Break the tomatoes apart with your hands or with the side of a wooden spoon.

3. Bring the stew to a boil. Reduce the heat to low, cover the saucepan with a lid, and simmer the stew, stirring occasionally, for 50 minutes.

4. Stir in the couscous, replace the cover, and cook the stew for 10 minutes longer.

5. Season the stew with salt and pepper, to taste.

6. Garnish each serving with finely chopped fresh basil leaves or parsley, if desired.

Yield: 1 1/2 quarts (3 to 4 main dish servings)

Per serving: Calories: 262, Protein: 13 gm., Fat: 0 gm., Carbohydrate: 51 gm.

The Cook's Secrets:
Although this stew is delicious when it is served immediately, the flavor will improve somewhat if it has an opportunity to cool and then rest in the refrigerator (in a covered container) several hours or overnight. This permits the seasonings to blend.

To reheat the stew, transfer the amount you need to a small saucepan. Place the saucepan over low heat, and warm the stew, stirring often, until it is hot and bubbly. Use a *flame tamer* to keep the stew from sticking to the bottom of the saucepan. If the stew becomes too thick for your liking, thin it with a small amount of tomato juice until you achieve the desired consistency.

Lentil, Mushroom & Macaroni Stew

This power-packed stew is terrific on cool days when hot, substantial fare is just the ticket. To round out your meal, serve the stew with whole grain bread or rolls and a colorful vegetable salad.

3 1/2 cups water or vegetable broth
1 cup dry lentils, picked over, rinsed well and drained
1 cup mushrooms, thickly sliced
1 medium onion, chopped
1 small stalk celery, chopped
2 cloves garlic, minced or pressed
1/2 teaspoon dried thyme leaves, well crumbled
1 whole bay leaf

1/2 cup elbow macaroni (uncooked)

3 Tablespoons light molasses or sorghum syrup, to taste
4 teaspoons red wine vinegar
1 teaspoon salt, or to taste
ground black pepper, to taste

1. Place all the ingredients *except the maca-roni, molasses, vinegar, salt, and pepper* in a 4 1/2-quart saucepan or Dutch oven, and bring the mixture to a boil. Reduce the heat to low. Cover the saucepan with a lid, and simmer the stew, stirring occasionally, for 1 hour or until the lentils are very tender.

2. Meanwhile, fill a 2-quart saucepan halfway with water, and bring the water to a boil. Carefully drop in the pasta, and cook it until it is al dente. Drain the pasta in a colander, and set it aside.

3. Remove the bay leaf from the stew, and stir in the molasses and vinegar. Season the stew with salt and pepper, to taste. Mix well.

4. Then stir in the reserved cooked macaroni (from step #2). Heat the stew through, if neces-sary, and serve hot.

Yield: 5 cups (3 to 4 main dish servings)

Per serving: Calories: 261, Protein: 11 gm., Fat: 0 gm., Carbohydrate: 53 gm.

The Cook's Secrets:
As an option, in place of (or in addition to) the mush-rooms, stir in 1/2 to 1 cup of seitan strips or chunks along with the cooked macaroni.

Brunswick Seitan Stew

This dish originated in Brunswick County, Virginia, where it was first made with (horrors!) squirrel!! This revised version is made with seitan which makes a practical and compassionate substitute.

2 teaspoons olive oil
1 large onion, cut in half and sliced
1 medium green bell pepper, diced
2 cloves garlic, minced or pressed

1 1/2 cups water or vegetable broth
1 14.5-ounce can whole tomatoes, with juice
1 cup frozen fordhook lima beans
1 cup whole kernel corn (fresh, canned, or defrosted frozen)
2 Tablespoons fresh parsley, chopped
1 Tablespoon anchovy-free Worcestershire sauce or soy sauce
1 teaspoon paprika
1/2 teaspoon Tabasco sauce, or more to taste

1/2 to 3/4 cup seitan, cut into chunks
1/3 cup instant potato flakes

salt and ground black pepper, to taste

1. Place the olive oil in a 4 1/2-quart saucepan or Dutch oven, and heat it over medium-high. When the oil is hot, stir in the onion, bell pepper, and garlic, and sauté them for 10 to 15 minutes, or until the onion is browned and tender.

2. Stir in the water, tomatoes and their juice, lima beans, corn, parsley, Worcestershire sauce, paprika, and Tabasco sauce. Break the tomatoes apart with your hands or the side of a wooden spoon.

3. Bring the mixture to a boil. Reduce the heat to medium-low, cover the saucepan with a lid, and simmer the stew for 20 minutes, or until the lima beans are tender.

4. Stir in the seitan and the potato flakes, mixing thoroughly. The broth will thicken. Reduce the heat to low, and cook, stirring constantly, for 5 minutes longer. Season with salt and pepper to taste. Serve hot.

Yield: 2 to 3 main dish servings

Per serving: Calories: 375, Protein: 21 gm., Fat: 5 gm., Carbohydrate: 62 gm.

The Cook's Secrets:
To thaw frozen corn, measure it and then transfer it to a wire mesh strainer. Place the corn under hot running tap water, stirring it with a spoon until it is defrosted, letting the water drain through the strainer. Measure the corn again and, if necessary, add more.

Chuckwagon Stew

Plenty of herbs and seasonings make a sensational broth for this stew. Bread for dipping into the gravy is absolutely essential. Come and get it!

1 1/2 cups water or vegetable broth
4 ounces (1/4 pound) tempeh, cut into 1/2-inch cubes (for more information about tempeh, see p. 18)
1 medium or 2 small potatoes, peeled and cut into bite-size chunks
2 medium carrots, pared and sliced
1 medium onion, cut into wedges
1/4 cup ketchup
2 Tablespoons soy sauce
1 to 2 teaspoons olive oil (optional)
1/2 teaspoon garlic granules
1/2 teaspoon dried tarragon leaves
1/8 teaspoon ground black pepper

5 teaspoons whole wheat pastry flour
1/4 cup cold water

salt, to taste

1 to 2 teaspoons fresh parsley, minced, for garnish (optional)

1. Place the first 11 ingredients in a 4 1/2-quart saucepan or Dutch oven. Bring the stew to a boil. Reduce the heat to medium-low, and cover the saucepan with a lid. Simmer the stew until the vegetables are tender, about 30 minutes, stirring occasionally.

2. Place the flour in a small mixing bowl or measuring cup. Gradually stir in the water, beating vigorously with a fork until the mixture is smooth.

3. Stir the flour-water mixture into the stew. Cook, stirring constantly, until the gravy is thickened and bubbly. Season with salt, to taste.

4. To serve, ladle the stew into large soup bowls. Garnish each serving with the parsley, if desired.

Yield: 2 main dish servings

Per serving: Calories: 291, Protein: 14 gm., Fat: 4 gm., Carbohydrate: 49 gm.

SANDWICHES, SPREADS, BURGERS & PIZZA

Sandwiches are a modern-day staple. In fact, it's a rare week when most of us don't have at least one meal consisting of a sandwich. There are numerous meat analogs (substitutes) available in addition to veggie burgers, seasoned tofu, tempeh, flavored seitan, and tofu frankfurters (all obtainable at natural food stores and many supermarkets) which make vegetarian sandwich preparation a breeze. Nevertheless, it takes just a modicum of time and creativity to devise a truly spectacular sandwich filling on your own.

Here are a few ideas for unique spreads and fillings to hoist your sandwiches from ho-hum to sensational. Serve them on whole grain bread, sourdough bread, or rice cakes, or stuff them into whole grain pita pockets:

- Thick, leftover bean soup or split pea soup.

- Leftover grains mixed with grated or finely chopped raw vegetables and moistened with a dab of low-fat, egg-free mayonnaise or nut or seed butter.

- Canned beans, drained, mashed, and mixed with your choice of ketchup, salsa, tomato sauce, garlic granules, pickle relish, horseradish, mustard, nut butter, tahini, vegetable broth, low-fat, egg-free mayonnaise, anchovy-free Worcestershire sauce, Tabasco sauce, and/or other seasonings of your choice.

- Leftover, well-cooked vegetables, mashed and thickened with leftover grains or fresh (or dry) bread crumbs.

- Salad sandwiches made of finely chopped raw vegetables and torn lettuce leaves tossed with a light dressing. (If you are packing this as a lunch, don't add tomatoes or the dressing until you're ready to eat. This way the bread won't become soggy.)

- Grilled vegetables or leftover, slow-roasted vegetables, served plain, with a sauce, or with a splash of fresh lemon juice or brown rice vinegar.

- Steamed greens, drained well. Squeeze out any extra moisture with your hands. Spread the bread with mustard, ketchup, or barbecue sauce, and/or a thin layer of tahini or low-fat, egg-free mayonnaise. Add thin slices of onion, if you like.

- Steamed kale and well-drained sauerkraut on bread spread with a thin layer of tahini or mustard.

- Marinated tofu, tempeh, or seitan (see p. 154), sautéed or grilled, if desired, with lettuce and tomato slices.

- Marinated tofu, tempeh, or seitan (see p. 154), sautéed or grilled, if desired, with sauerkraut, raw or sautéed onion, and mustard.

- Tempeh sautéed with sliced mushrooms and layered with steamed kale.

- Leftovers of any kind (casseroles, stews, whatever) blended with a small amount of liquid (vegetable broth, tomato juice, water, etc.), tomato sauce, ketchup, or low-fat, egg-free mayonnaise until the consistency is thick and spreadable.

• Make "Montage Spread" by puréeing a whole range of leftovers (for example, cooked beans, steamed broccoli, cooked millet, and tomato sauce).

• A thin layer of nut or seed butter (peanut butter, almond butter, sunflower butter, tahini, etc.) topped with grated raw carrot or zucchini, sliced tomato, minced steamed vegetables (such as broccoli or cauliflower), and/or thinly sliced onion, seasoned with a splash of soy sauce.

• A thin layer of tahini topped with mustard, finely chopped scallion, and sauerkraut.

• A thin layer of nut or seed butter (peanut butter, almond butter, sunflower butter, tahini, etc.) topped with fruit butter and/or fresh fruits such as apple, banana, mango, or orange. Raisins or other dried fruits are also a nice addition.

• Perk up any humdrum sandwich filling by spreading the bread with an exciting condiment such as an exotic mustard, favorite barbecue sauce, or thick salad dressing.

Sandwich preparation is one area of cooking that has absolutely no rules and begs for creativity. It's a good place to test out your culinary aesthetics because absolutely anything goes!

The following are a few additional sandwich recipes found elsewhere in this book:
Breakfast Burritos, p. 48
Karen's Kalewiches, p. 49

A Note From Susan:
I'm a single mother of a teenage son and also have a very demanding, full-time job, so I rarely have the time, motivation, or desire to further "work" in the kitchen. I depend mostly on pasta and grains for meals. My one regular mainstay is tortillas. I fill them with cooked grains, raw and sautéed veggies, and maybe a protein food like beans or tofu. I'll add a few seasonings and sometimes a little salsa. Stuffed tortillas are easy to make, fun to eat, and suit my hectic schedule.

Toasted or Grilled Cheeze Sandwiches

This perennial kid-pleaser still has all the goo and glory that made it so outrageously popular, but now it's low-fat and dairy-free! We like to serve these with a dab of grainy mustard spread on top.

MELTY CHEEZE:
1/3 cup water
4 teaspoons nutritional yeast flakes
1 Tablespoon oat flour (see The Cook's Secrets below right)
1 Tablespoon fresh lemon juice
1 Tablespoon tahini
2 teaspoons tomato paste
1 teaspoon cornstarch
1/2 teaspoon onion granules
1/8 teaspoon each garlic granules, turmeric, dry mustard, and salt

4 slices whole grain bread

1. To make the melty cheeze, place all the ingredients *except the bread* in a 1-quart saucepan, and whisk them together until the mixture is smooth. Bring the mixture to a boil, stirring constantly with a wire whisk. Reduce the heat to low, and continue to cook, stirring constantly, until the melty cheeze is very thick and smooth.

2. Remove the saucepan from the heat. Place two of the bread slices on a plate. Cover one side of each of the bread slices evenly with the melty cheeze. Top with the remaining two bread slices, and follow the directions below for either Toasted Cheeze Sandwiches or Grilled Cheeze Sandwiches.

3. *For Toasted Cheeze Sandwiches:*
Place the sandwiches on a dry, broiler-proof baking sheet, and slip under the broiler for just a few minutes only or until the top slice of bread is lightly browned. Carefully turn the sandwiches over using a metal spatula, and broil them another minute or two until the other slice of bread is lightly browned, *watching closely so the sandwiches don't burn.* Remove the baking sheet from the oven.

3. *For Grilled Cheeze Sandwiches:*
Mist a 9-inch or 10-inch skillet with nonstick cooking spray, or coat it with a thin layer of canola oil. Place the skillet over medium-high heat. When the skillet is hot, add the sandwiches and brown them well on each side, carefully turning them over once with a metal spatula. (If both sandwiches do not fit comfortably in the skillet at the same time, grill them separately.)

4. Transfer the sandwiches to serving plates using the metal spatula. Slice the sandwiches in half diagonally, and serve them at once.

Yield: 2 sandwiches

Per sandwich: Calories: 196, Protein: 8 gm., Fat: 6 gm., Carbohydrate: 26 gm.

The Cook's Secrets:
If you do not have oat flour, you can make it yourself from rolled oats. Just put 3/4 cup of rolled oats in a blender, and whirl them around for a minute or two, or until they are finely ground. This will yield about 1/2 cup of oat flour.

P.B. & Broccoli Sandwiches

Most people think of jelly as the definitive complement to peanut butter, but once you try it with broccoli you may never view peanut butter in quite the same light. My friend Karen Bernard innovated this sandwich. It's a very palatable way to add colorful green vegetables to a child's often monochrome repertoire and makes a delicious meal for grownups as well.

1 1/2 cups broccoli, cut into bite-size pieces (cut off the tough woody portion of the stem; if you are using the stem as well as the florets, be sure to pare it well to remove the fibrous outer portions)

2 to 4 Tablespoons peanut butter (if you store your peanut butter in the refrigerator, bring it to room temperature first so it will spread easily)

4 slices whole grain bread, toasted

soy sauce, to taste

1. Place the broccoli in a steamer basket or insert over a saucepan filled with an inch of water. Bring the water to a boil. Cover the saucepan with a lid, and reduce the heat to medium. Steam the broccoli until it is bright green and tender to your liking.

2. Place the toast on a flat surface, and spread one side of each piece with some of the peanut butter. (If you are watching your fat consumption, use the smaller quantity only.)

3. Divide the broccoli equally between two of the pieces of toast, placing it on top of the peanut butter.

4. Sprinkle the broccoli with the soy sauce.

5. Top the broccoli with the remaining toast slices, peanut-buttered side in. Slice the sandwiches in half, and serve.

Yield: 2 sandwiches

Per sandwich: Calories: 259, Protein: 10 gm., Fat: 12 gm., Carbohydrate: 24 gm.

The Cook's Secrets:
If you have leftover broccoli in the refrigerator, this is a great way to use it up! These sandwiches are terrific for breakfast and dinner as well as for lunch.

For a less hefty sandwich, use only 2 slices of toasted bread (one per sandwich) and 1 to 2 tablespoons of peanut butter. Serve the sandwiches open-face with a knife and fork.

If you prefer, almond butter, sunflower seed butter, or tahini may be substituted for the peanut butter.

Chili Rolls

These simple sandwiches make a quick and satisfying lunch. Serve them with pickle spears on the side, if you like.

4 ounces (1/4 pound) tempeh, steamed for 20 minutes and cooled until easily handled (see p. 18)

2 Tablespoons tomato paste
2 Tablespoons water
1/2 teaspoon dried oregano leaves
1/2 teaspoon chili powder
1/2 teaspoon anchovy-free Worcestershire sauce or soy sauce
1/4 teaspoon salt
several drops Tabasco sauce, to taste (optional)

2 whole grain buns, split in half

1. Grate the tempeh on the coarse side of a grater, and place it in a medium mixing bowl. Stir in the remaining ingredients *except the buns,* and mix well.

2. Place the buns on a dry baking sheet, cut side up. Spread the tops evenly with the tempeh mixture, spreading it to the edge of each bun. (This will help to keep the edges of the bun from burning.)

3. Place the sandwiches under the broiler for 4 to 5 minutes. Watch closely so the sandwiches do not burn.

4. Serve the sandwiches hot. They may be eaten by picking them up with your hands, or you can use a knife and fork.

Yield: 2 servings

Per serving: Calories: 242, Protein: 14 gm., Fat: 5 gm., Carbohydrate: 35 gm.

Tofu Salad

This is a great sandwich filling that's a snap to prepare whenever the age-old question arises "what's for lunch?" For an attractive finishing touch, tuck a few lettuce leaves into each sandwich.

1/2 pound fat-reduced, firm regular tofu, rinsed, patted dry, and well mashed
1/4 cup celery, diced
1/4 cup Low-Fat, Egg-Free Mayonnaise, p. 110, or your favorite egg- and dairy-free mayonnaise
2 Tablespoons fresh parsley, minced (optional)
2 teaspoons sweet or dill pickle relish, drained
1/2 teaspoon onion granules
1/8 teaspoon turmeric
salt and ground black pepper, to taste

1. Place all the ingredients in a medium mixing bowl. Stir well until they are thoroughly combined.

2. Serve the salad at once, or transfer it to a storage container, and chill it in the refrigerator.

Yield: about 1 1/4 cups (2 servings)

Per serving: Calories: 162, Protein: 15 gm., Fat: 9 gm., Carbohydrate: 7 gm.

Carrot-Tofu Salad Sandwiches

The carrots and raisins in this spread create a delicious, mildly sweet breakfast sandwich as well as an enjoyable luncheon meal.

1 Tablespoon tahini
2 Tablespoons fresh lemon juice
1/4 teaspoon ground cinnamon

1/4 pound fat-reduced, firm regular tofu, rinsed, patted dry, and mashed
1/2 cup carrots, pared and grated
3 to 4 Tablespoons raisins
salt, to taste

4 slices whole grain bread

1. Place the tahini in a small mixing bowl. Gradually stir in the lemon juice and cinnamon to form a smooth, thick paste.

2. Stir the mashed tofu and grated carrots into the tahini-lemon mixture, mixing until they are well combined. Then stir in the raisins.

3. Season the salad with salt, to taste.

4. To assemble the sandwiches, divide the spread evenly between two slices of the bread. Cover the salad with the remaining slices of bread. Cut the sandwiches in half, and serve.

Yield: 2 sandwiches

Per sandwich: Calories: 267, Protein: 12 gm., Fat: 8 gm., Carbohydrate: 35 gm.

The Cook's Secrets:
For breakfast sandwiches or for a lighter meal, use only two slices of bread, and serve the sandwiches open-face with a knife and fork.

Deviled Tofu

A tangy, sprightly, dazzling yellow spread that is sublime on crackers or bread. Garnish it with a light dusting of paprika for an eye-catching finish.

1/2 pound fat-reduced, firm regular tofu, rinsed, patted dry and well mashed
1 Tablespoon onion, finely minced
2 teaspoons prepared yellow mustard
2 teaspoons anchovy-free Worcestershire sauce
1/4 teaspoon salt, or to taste
1/8 teaspoon turmeric
pinch of cayenne pepper, to taste

1. Place all the ingredients in a medium mixing bowl. Mix thoroughly until they are well combined.

2. Serve the spread at once, or transfer it to a storage container, and chill it in the refrigerator.

Yield: 1 cup (2 servings)

Per serving: Calories: 127, Protein: 13 gm., Fat: 6 gm., Carbohydrate: 6 gm.

P.L.T.s

A healthful and delicious alternative to an ever-popular classic.

4 slices whole grain bread, toasted if desired

2 to 4 Tablespoons Low-Fat, Egg-Free Mayonnaise, p. 110, or 1 to 2 Tablespoons tahini

2 medium dill pickles, patted dry and thinly sliced lengthwise
salt and ground black pepper, to taste
1 ripe, medium tomato, thickly sliced
2 very thin slices of mild onion (optional)
2 large leaves leaf lettuce or romaine lettuce

1. Place the bread on a flat surface, and spread one side of each slice with some of the mayonnaise or tahini.

2. Place the pickle slices on top of the mayonnaise or tahini on two slices of the bread. Sprinkle the pickle slices lightly with pepper, to taste.

3. Lay the tomato slices over the pickle. Sprinkle them with salt and pepper, to taste.

4. Place the onion slices, if using, over the tomato. Cover them with the lettuce leaves.

5. Place the remaining bread slices over the lettuce, with the mayonnaise or tahini side facing in. Slice the sandwiches in half, and serve.

Yield: 2 sandwiches

Per sandwich: Calories: 140, Protein: 6 gm., Fat: 5 gm., Carbohydrate: 20 gm.

Banana Dogs

Peanut butter and banana sandwiches always receive top ratings from kids of all ages.

2 whole grain frankfurter (hot dog) buns

2 to 4 Tablespoons peanut butter (if you store your peanut butter in the refrigerator, bring it to room temperature first so it will spread easily)
2 Tablespoons raisins

2 very small, thin bananas or 1 large banana split in half lengthwise

1. Split the buns by slicing them lengthwise two-thirds of the way through.

2. Spread the cut sides with the peanut butter. Then sprinkle the raisins over the peanut butter, pressing them in lightly.

3. Place a banana (or banana half) on each bun, and serve.

Yield: 2 servings

Per serving: Calories: 387, Protein: 10 gm., Fat: 13 gm., Carbohydrate: 57 gm.

Slow-Roasted
Broccoli Hoagies
with Mustard-Dill Sauce

When you want something truly special, this heavenly sandwich will fit the bill. Slow-roasting brings out the deep, rich flavor of the vegetables. It may take a little time to do the roasting, but it certainly doesn't take much effort.

4 cups broccoli, cut into bite-size pieces (trim the stalk to remove the tough, woody portion, and peel it to expose its tender center part)
1 1/2 cups mushrooms, halved (if small) or quartered (if large)
4 to 6 large cloves garlic, coarsely chopped or sliced
1 large onion, cut in half and thinly sliced into half-moons

4 to 6 large black olives, sliced (optional)

3 Tablespoons water
1 1/2 teaspoons olive oil

salt and ground black pepper, to taste

MUSTARD-DILL SAUCE:
3 Tablespoons Low-Fat, Egg-Free Mayonnaise, p. 110, or your favorite egg- and dairy-free mayonnaise
1 Tablespoon Dijon mustard
1 1/2 teaspoons dried dill weed

2 Kaiser rolls, hoagie rolls, large Italian rolls, or other crusty rolls, split

1. Move one of the oven racks to the lowest level. Preheat the oven to 400°F.

2. Place the water in the bottom of a deep 4-quart or 6-quart casserole dish. Layer all the vegetables *except the olives* into the casserole. Drizzle the oil over the top of the vegetables. Cover the casserole with a lid, and place it in the oven, on the lowest rack, for 20 minutes.

3. Remove the casserole from the oven. Remove the lid, stir the vegetables, and finish roasting them uncovered for 20 minutes longer.

4. Remove the casserole from the oven, and stir in the olives, if using. Season the vegetables with salt and pepper, to taste. Stir the vegetables again, and set the casserole aside.

5. While the vegetables are roasting, prepare the Mustard-Dill Sauce by placing the mayonnaise, mustard, and dill weed in a small mixing bowl or measuring cup. Stir them together well to make a smooth sauce. Set aside.

6. Slice the rolls and spread each cut side generously with the Mustard-Dill Sauce. Pile the roasted vegetables on the bottom half of each roll. Cover the vegetables with the top half of each roll, and serve.

Yield: 2 sandwiches

Per sandwich: Calories: 302, Protein: 11 gm., Fat: 10 gm., Carbohydrate: 44 gm.

The Cook's Secrets:
This will appear to be a large quantity of vegetables. However, once the vegetables are roasted they will reduce considerably. If the quantity is too much for

you and your dining partner to consume in one sitting, place the leftovers in a covered container in the refrigerator to be eaten within the next day or two. The leftovers will make a delicious cold salad.

For extra flavor, mix the vegetables with a little Italian Dressing, p. 71, or other low-fat dressing of your choice while they are still warm, prior to storing them in the refrigerator.

Open-face Seitan Sandwiches
with Gravy

For a lovely luncheon, garnish these popular diner-style sandwiches with fresh tomato slices on the side to add a colorful contrast. For dinner, serve them with mashed potatoes or whipped yams along with peas, green beans, or asparagus.

1 Tablespoon cornstarch
1 1/2 Tablespoons soy sauce

2/3 cup cold water or vegetable broth
1/4 teaspoon garlic granules

1 Tablespoon tahini

1 cup seitan, thinly sliced
ground black pepper, to taste

2 large slices whole grain bread, toasted, if
   desired

1. To make the gravy, place the cornstarch and soy sauce in a 1-quart saucepan, and stir them together well to make a thin paste.

2. Gradually whisk the water or vegetable broth and garlic granules into the cornstarch mixture.

3. Place the saucepan over medium-high heat, and cook the mixture, stirring constantly with a wire whisk, until the gravy thickens and comes to a boil. Remove the saucepan from the heat, and beat in the tahini using the wire whisk.

4. Stir the seitan into the gravy, and season it with pepper, to taste.

5. Place the saucepan over low heat, and warm the mixture, stirring occasionally, just until the seitan is heated through.

6. To assemble the sandwiches, place one slice of bread or toast on each of two serving plates, and spoon the seitan and gravy equally over each slice. Serve the sandwich open-face with a knife and fork.

Yield: 2 sandwiches

Per sandwich: Calories: 229, Protein: 27 gm., Fat: 6 gm., Carbohydrate: 18 gm.

Tempeh Sloppy Joes

A choice standby made even better because now it's vegetarian.

4 ounces (1/4 pound) tempeh, cut into 1/4-inch cubes (for information about tempeh, see p. 18)
1 8-ounce can tomato sauce (1 cup)
1/4 cup onion, finely chopped
1/4 cup red or green bell pepper, finely chopped
1 small carrot, pared and shredded (about 1/4 cup)
2 teaspoons soy sauce
1 clove garlic, minced or pressed
1/4 teaspoon chili powder
1/4 teaspoon ground cumin

2 burger buns or hard rolls, split and toasted, if desired

1. Place all the ingredients *except the buns* in a 2-quart saucepan. Bring the mixture to a boil. Reduce the heat to medium, and cover the saucepan with a lid. Simmer the mixture, stirring occasionally, for 20 to 25 minutes, or until the onion and pepper are tender.

2. Place the bottom half of the buns on two serving plates, and spoon the hot tempeh mixture equally over them. Top the tempeh mixture with the remaining bun halves, and serve.

Yield: 2 sandwiches

Per sandwich: Calories 283, Protein: 15 gm., Fat: 5 gm., Carbohydrate: 43 gm.

Tempeh Salad

This chewy salad is great on crackers or in sandwiches. For an attractive luncheon, scoop the salad onto lettuce-lined palates, garnish it with a little paprika, and surround it with fresh tomato wedges.

4 ounces (1/4 pound) tempeh, steamed for 20 minutes and cooled until easily handled (see p. 18)

1/2 cup celery, diced, or 1/2 cup carrot, pared and grated (about 2 small)
1/4 cup Low-Fat, Egg-Free Mayonnaise, p. 110, or your favorite egg- and dairy-free mayonnaise
2 Tablespoons scallion, thinly sliced (optional)
1 to 2 Tablespoons fresh parsley, minced
1/8 teaspoon poultry seasoning, or 1/4 or 1/2 teaspoon curry powder, to taste (optional)
salt and ground black pepper, to taste

1. Cut the tempeh into 1/4-inch cubes, and place it in a medium mixing bowl.

2. Add the remaining ingredients to the tempeh, and mix them together gently but thoroughly.

3. Season the salad with salt and pepper, to taste.

4. Serve the salad at once, or transfer it to a storage container, and chill it in the refrigerator.

Yield: 2 servings

Per serving: Calories: 172, Protein: 12 gm., Fat: 8 gm., Carbohydrate: 13 gm.

Bean Burritos

Bean burritos are always fun to construct, and they make a satisfying lunch or dinner. Burritos are quick and easy to prepare, and kids enjoy them enormously.

4 whole wheat flour tortillas (lard-free)

BURRITO FILLING:
1 15-ounce can pinto beans, rinsed well and
    drained
1/2 cup tomato sauce, or 2 Tablespoons tomato
    paste mixed with 6 Tablespoons water
2 Tablespoons canned chopped green chilies,
    or 2 Tablespoons finely chopped red or green
    bell pepper
1 teaspoon chili powder
1/4 teaspoon garlic granules
1/4 teaspoon ground cumin
1/4 teaspoon dried oregano leaves
several drops Tabasco sauce, to taste

TOPPING OPTIONS (select one or more):
1/2 to 1 cup lettuce, shredded
1 ripe, medium tomato, chopped
1/2 of a small avocado, cut into chunks
1/4 cup carrot, pared and shredded
1/4 cup fresh cilantro leaves, chopped
1/4 cup black olives, sliced
1 to 2 scallions, sliced
2 to 3 Tablespoons Tofu Sour Cream, p. 73
2 Tablespoons onion, chopped

1. Warm the tortillas. To do this, place the tortillas, one at a time, in a dry 9-inch or 10-inch skillet. Place the skillet over medium heat for about 1 minute, or just until the tortilla is heated. Immediately remove the tortilla from the skillet, and lay it on a flat surface. Warm the remaining tortillas in the same fashion.

2. To make the filling, place all the filling ingredients in a 2-quart saucepan. Bring the mixture to a boil. Reduce the heat to medium, and simmer the mixture uncovered for 5 minutes, stirring occasionally. Remove the saucepan from the heat.

3. Mash the beans slightly with the back of a wooden spoon, a fork, or a potato masher.

4. Spoon 1/4 of the bean mixture onto each of the tortillas, placing it in a strip along one side, slightly off center. Add your favorite toppings, and roll the tortillas around the filling.

5. To eat, carefully pick up the burritos with your hands, or use a knife and fork.

Yield: 2 servings (2 burritos per person)

Per serving: Calories: 475, Protein: 20 gm., Fat: 5 gm., Carbohydrate: 88 gm.

Vegetable Pizza for Two

This pizza is quick and easy, especially if you have a good pizza sauce on hand. Even the crust is speedy to make, and it's just the right size for two.

HAVE READY:
4 to 5 Tablespoons Pizza Sauce, p. 126, Pizza Emergency Sauce, p. 127, or your favorite canned or jarred pizza sauce

VEGETABLE TOPPING:
1/2 cup broccoli, cut into bite-size florets
1/2 cup mushrooms, halved (if small) or quartered (if large)
1/4 cup onion, chopped or thinly sliced
1/2 small red bell pepper, cut into bite-size strips

CRUST:
1/4 cup warm water (between 125° to 130°)
1/2 teaspoon active dry yeast

1 teaspoon olive oil
1/4 teaspoon sweetener of your choice
pinch of salt
1/2 cup whole wheat pastry flour

1. Preheat the oven to 425°F. Spray a 10-inch glass pie plate with nonstick cooking spray, and set it aside.

2. Place the broccoli, mushrooms, onion, and bell pepper in a steamer basket or steamer insert in a large saucepan filled with an inch of water. Bring the water to a boil. Cover the saucepan with a lid, and reduce the heat to medium.

Steam the vegetables until they are tender. Remove the lid, and set the saucepan and vegetables aside.

3. Meanwhile, place the warm water in a small mixing bowl. Sprinkle the yeast over the water, and let it rest for 1 minute. Then stir in the oil, sweetener, and salt. Gradually stir in the flour, beating well to form a soft dough. Cover the bowl with a clean, damp kitchen towel, and let the dough rest in a warm place for 10 to 20 minutes.

4. Press or spread the dough into the prepared pie plate, patting it out into a circle using water-moistened fingers. Make sure there are no holes in the crust. Bake the crust for 10 minutes.

5. Remove crust from the oven and spread with the sauce. Then arrange the reserved steamed vegetables (from step #2) over the sauce.

6. Bake the pizza for 15 minutes. Slice it into 4 wedges. Serve hot.

Yield: 2 servings

Per serving: Calories: 162, Protein: 5 gm., Fat: 3 gm., Carbohydrate: 27 gm.

The Cook's Secrets:
Some additional vegetable choices which do not need to be steamed are grated carrot, sliced olives, or water-packed artichoke hearts cut into quarters.

Cheeze Pizza for Two

This uncomplicated blend of tofu and light miso creates a sharply flavored, white "cheese" that is absolutely delicious on pizza. The trick is to chill it for at least 30 minutes before using it, in order to allow the flavors to fully develop.

Prepare Vegetable Pizza For Two as directed on p. 102, but in addition to or instead of the vegetables, use the following topping:

PIZZA CHEEZE:
1/4 pound fat-reduced, firm regular tofu, rinsed, patted dry and crumbled
2 Tablespoons light miso (preferably sweet, white miso)

1. Place the tofu in a small mixing bowl. Add the miso, and mash it into the tofu with a fork. When the miso has been thoroughly incorporated, cover the bowl tightly and allow the Pizza Cheeze to rest in the refrigerator for at least 30 minutes.

2. When you are ready to use the Pizza Cheeze, crumble it evenly over the top of the pizza, and bake the pizza as directed on p. 102.

Yield: 2 servings

Per serving: Calories: 255, Protein: 14 gm., Fat: 7 gm., Carbohydrate: 35 gm.

The Cook's Secrets:
Pizza Cheeze may be prepared up to 5 days in advance, if desired, and stored in a covered container in the refrigerator.

English Muffin Cheeze Pizzas: Pizza Cheeze is also a terrific topping for English muffins. Just split and toast two English muffins. Place the toasted muffins on a dry baking sheet, and spread each muffin half with approximately 1 tablespoon of your favorite pizza sauce. Crumble some of the Pizza Cheeze on top of the sauce, and pop the pizzas under the broiler for just a few minutes, until the sauce bubbles and the "cheese" is golden brown. Watch closely so the pizzas don't burn. English Muffin Cheeze Pizzas make a great last minute lunch or dinner and are an easy, popular snack for teenagers.

Cornucopia Oat Burgers

Many years ago, a wonderful local vegetarian restaurant served these delicious burgers. My version of their memorable entrée has long been a staple in my household.

1 teaspoon canola oil
1/4 cup onion, chopped

1/4 cup walnuts, chopped
1/4 cup quick-cooking rolled oats (not instant)
1/4 cup fresh whole grain bread crumbs (see The Cook's Secrets at right)
1 Tablespoon whole wheat pastry flour
1/4 teaspoon dried sage, crumbled
1/8 teaspoon dried thyme leaves, crushed
1/8 teaspoon salt

1/3 cup boiling water

1. Place the oil in a 9-inch or 10-inch skillet, and heat it over medium-high. When the oil is hot, add the onion. Reduce the heat to medium, and sauté the onion until it is tender, about 10 to 15 minutes. Set aside.

2. Place the remaining ingredients *except the water* in a heatproof, medium mixing bowl, and stir to combine them thoroughly.

3. Pour the boiling water over the oat mixture, and stir it well. Then stir in the reserved onion (from step #1).

4. When the mixture is cool enough to handle, form it into 2 patties using lightly water-moistened hands.

5. Coat the skillet (used in step #1) with a thin layer of canola oil, or mist it with nonstick cooking spray. Place the skillet over medium heat. When the skillet is hot, add the patties, and brown them well on both sides, turning them once using a metal spatula.

Yield: 2 burgers

Per burger: Calories: 192, Protein: 5 gm., Fat: 12 gm., Carbohydrate: 16 gm.

The Cook's Secrets:
Fresh bread crumbs can be made by tearing one or two slices of whole grain bread into small pieces and whirling the pieces in a food processor fitted with a metal blade. Alternately, rub the slices of bread along the side of a box grater.

A Note From Scott:
Many recipes call for just 1/4 cup of onions or some other small amount. When this happens, I'm left with part of an onion that's either too big or not big enough to use in another recipe. So, I now buy dried chopped onions in bulk. This way I use only what I need, and it's fast and easy.

Just place 2 tablespoons of dried, chopped onion in a small, heatproof bowl, and cover the onion with hot water to rehydrate it. Wait five minutes. Drain the onion in a wire mesh strainer. You'll be left with 1/4 cup of onion. No slicing, no mess, no leftovers.

For soup, just add a little extra water, pour in the onions dry, and they will rehydrate as the soup cooks.

Best Bean Burgers

This simple, mainstay recipe can be adapted easily to suit a variety of tastes. Just use the herbs and seasonings you most prefer for a different flavor every time. These firm burgers are terrific served on buns topped with all your favorite trimmings—ketchup, mustard, pickle relish, onion, lettuce—the works!

1 8-ounce can of beans (about 3/4 cup), rinsed
   well, drained and mashed (see The Cook's
   Secrets at right)
1/4 cup quick-cooking rolled oats (not instant)
1/4 cup fresh whole grain bread crumbs (see The
   Cook's Secrets at right)

SEASONINGS (use one or more):
1 teaspoon nutritional yeast flakes
1/4 to 1/2 teaspoon of your favorite dried herbs,
   or 1 1/2 teaspoons chopped fresh herbs
1/4 teaspoon onion granules
1/4 teaspoon garlic granules
1/4 teaspoon chili powder
1/4 teaspoon curry powder
1/4 teaspoon paprika
1/4 teaspoon dry mustard
1/4 teaspoon ground ginger
1/4 teaspoon ground cumin
1/4 teaspoon ground coriander
1/4 teaspoon poultry seasoning
pinch of cayenne pepper, or several drops
   Tabasco sauce, to taste
salt and ground black pepper, to taste

1. Place all the ingredients, including the seasonings of your choice, in a medium mixing bowl, and mix them together until they are well combined. The mixture will be very stiff. The easiest way to combine everything thoroughly is to use your hands.

2. Form the mixture into 2 patties, pressing firmly with your hands.

3. Coat a 9-inch or 10-inch skillet with a thin layer of canola oil, or mist it with nonstick cooking spray. Place the skillet over medium heat. When the skillet is hot, add the patties, and brown them well on both sides, turning them once with a metal spatula.

Yield: 2 burgers

Per burger: Calories: 155, Protein: 9 gm., Fat: 0 gm., Carbohydrate: 27 gm.

The Cook's Secrets:
Use whatever beans you like to make these burgers —white, pink, black, or red. Each one will yield a slightly different taste and appearance.

To mash the beans, use a fork, potato masher, or your hands.

Fresh bread crumbs can be made by tearing one or two slices of whole grain bread into small pieces and whirling the pieces in a food processor fitted with a metal blade. Alternately, rub the slices of bread along the side of a box grater.

White Bean Hummus

Plenty of fresh herbs and unusual seasonings perk up this ever-popular, Middle-Eastern bean spread. Serve it as a dip with raw vegetables or pita triangles or as a sandwich filling with lettuce and tomato. Try great northern beans or other white beans instead of the traditional garbanzo beans for a slightly different twist. Paprika makes an attractive garnish.

1 15-ounce can garbanzo beans, Great Northern beans, or other white beans of your choice, rinsed well and drained
2 to 3 Tablespoons fresh lemon juice
2 Tablespoons fresh lime juice
2 Tablespoons tahini
1 clove garlic, minced or pressed
1/4 teaspoon ground cumin

3 to 4 Tablespoons fresh parsley, chopped
3 to 4 Tablespoons fresh mint leaves, fresh cilantro leaves, fresh basil leaves, or fresh dill weed, chopped
salt and ground black pepper, to taste

1. Place the beans, lemon juice, lime juice, tahini, garlic, and cumin in a food processor fitted with a metal blade, and process until the mixture is very smooth and well blended.

2. By hand, stir in the parsley and fresh mint leaves, cilantro, basil leaves, or dill weed. Alternately, add the herbs to the mixture in the food processor, and pulse until they are chopped and evenly distributed. Season with salt and pepper, to taste.

3. Serve at once, or transfer the spread to a storage container, and chill it in the refrigerator.

Yield: about 1 1/2 cups (3 servings)

Per serving: Calories: 326, Protein: 14 gm., Fat: 8 gm., Carbohydrate: 48 gm.

The Cook's Secrets:
Because Great Northern beans (and many other white beans) are considerably softer when cooked than garbanzo beans, you may need to use only 2 tablespoons of lemon juice instead of the 3 called for in the recipe. Start with 2 tablespoons of lemon juice, and add more gradually until you achieve the taste and consistency you like.

Fresh herbs are the secret to the special flavor of this hummus. If you're in a pinch, though, or if fresh herbs are unavailable, you can substitute 2 teaspoons dried parsley flakes for the fresh parsley and 2 teaspoons dried herb of your choice for the fresh herbs.

Simple Bean Spread & Dip

Quick and tasty, this sandwich filling is also great with rice cakes, crispbread, or crunchy raw vegetables. Only two ingredients—what could be simpler!

1 16-ounce can pinto beans or kidney beans, rinsed well and drained
1/3 cup fat-free barbecue sauce, chili sauce, or salsa

1. Place the beans and sauce in a food processor fitted with a metal blade, and process them until they are very smooth and well blended. Alternately, mash the beans well with a fork or a potato masher, and stir in the sauce.

2. Serve at once, or transfer the spread to a storage container, and chill it in the refrigerator.

Yield: 1 1/3 cups (4 servings)

Per serving: Calories: 163, Protein: 8 gm., Fat: 0 gm., Carbohydrate: 31 gm.

The Cook's Secrets:
Because the flavor of this spread is derived from the seasoning sauce you use, be sure to select one with a taste you particularly like.

Green Pea Spread

Frozen green peas make this creamy spread economical as well as convenient.

1 cup loose-pack, frozen green peas

1 Tablespoon Low-Fat, Egg-Free Mayonnaise, p. 110, or your favorite egg- and dairy-free mayonnaise
1/4 teaspoon dried thyme leaves, crushed
1/4 teaspoon ground cumin
salt and ground black pepper, to taste

1. Cook the peas according to the package directions. Transfer them to a wire mesh strainer, and drain them well.

2. Place the cooked peas along with the remaining ingredients in a food processor fitted with a metal blade. Process the mixture until it is very smooth and well blended.

3. Serve at once, or transfer the spread to a storage container, and chill it in the refrigerator.

Yield: 1/2 cup (2 servings)

Per serving: Calories: 77, Protein: 4 gm., Fat: 1 gm., Carbohydrate: 13 gm.

Simple Grain Spread

This is a great way to use up small amounts of left-overs, but we enjoy this recipe so much that we usually cook grain specifically for it. (Quick-cooking rice is ideal!) You can easily adapt the recipe to suit your particular tastes or mood.

1 to 1 1/2 cups cooked grain (rice, barley, bulgur, etc.)

1 to 2 Tablespoons peanut butter, almond butter, tahini, or egg- and dairy-free mayonnaise (more or less depending on the moistness of the grain)

1 small carrot, or 1/2 of a large carrot, pared and shredded

1 Tablespoon water (more or less depending on the moistness of the grain)

salt or soy sauce and ground black pepper, to taste

1. Place all the ingredients *except the salt or soy sauce and pepper* in a food processor fitted with a metal blade. Process until the grain is coarsely chopped but not puréed. Add just enough water to facilitate processing, if needed. The mixture should be very thick, not runny.

2. Season the spread with salt or soy sauce and pepper, to taste.

3. Serve at once, or transfer the spread to a storage container, and chill it in the refrigerator.

Yield: 1 to 1 1/2 cups (3 to 4 servings)

Per serving: Calories: 131, Protein: 3 gm., Fat: 4 gm., Carbohydrate: 21 gm.

The Cook's Secrets:

This spread begs for your creativity. Try adding small amounts of additional chopped vegetables such as bell pepper, onion, garlic, scallion, celery, or radish. When used as a sandwich filling, lettuce and tomato slices are pleasant, moist additions.

Try adding one or more of the following savory seasonings to the prepared spread:

- a pinch of chili powder or curry powder;
- up to 1/4 teaspoon of your favorite dried herbs or spices such as basil, dill weed, thyme, cumin, or paprika;
- 1 tablespoon of chopped fresh herbs such as basil, chives, cilantro, dill weed, mint, or parsley. After adding the seasoning, taste the spread and add more, if desired.

For a slightly sweet spread that particularly appeals to children, omit the soy sauce and pepper, and add a pinch of cinnamon and a tablespoon or more of raisins.

Ranch-Style Spread & Dip

A thick, creamy spread that can easily be made year-round, even at the last minute, using dried herbs. If you are lucky enough to have access to fresh herbs, however, this is a scrumptious opportunity to revel in their glory.

This recipe makes a delicious dip for raw vegetables, globe artichokes, and chips, as well as a tantalizing spread for crackers, crusty French bread, or chewy, toasted bagels. It's also a magnificent baked potato topper. For an amazing sandwich filling, try topping the spread with thick slices of fresh tomatoes when they are in peak season.

1 10.5-ounce package fat-reduced, firm silken
   tofu, drained and crumbled
1/3 cup fresh parsley, minced, or 2 Tablespoons
   dried parsley flakes
2 Tablespoons fresh onion, minced,
   or 2 to 4 Tablespoons scallions, chopped,
   or 4 teaspoons dried onion flakes
1 Tablespoon olive oil
1 Tablespoon fresh dill weed, or 1 teaspoon dried
   dill weed
1 Tablespoon fresh tarragon leaves, chopped,
   or 1 teaspoon dried tarragon leaves
1 to 2 cloves garlic, minced or pressed,
   or 1/2 teaspoon garlic granules
1/2 teaspoon salt
1/8 teaspoon ground black pepper

1. Place all the ingredients in a food processor fitted with a metal blade. Process until the mixture is creamy, smooth, and well blended.

2. Serve at once, or transfer the spread to a storage container, and chill it in the refrigerator.

Yield: about 1 1/2 cups (3 to 4 servings)

Per serving: Calories: 74, Protein: 6 gm., Fat: 5 gm., Carbohydrate: 2 gm.

The Cook's Secrets:
Other fresh herbs may be substituted if you prefer. Try basil, cilantro, rosemary, sage, thyme, or any other fresh herbs you have on hand.

Ranch-Style Dressing: Use the spread as is, or thin it with enough non-dairy milk to achieve the consistency you desire. Taste for salt and add more if necessary.

Low-Fat, Egg-Free Mayonnaise

Mayonnaise has a reputation for being delicious but high in fat and cholesterol. Try this tasty, low-fat, cholesterol-free version, and indulge to your heart's content.

1 10.5-ounce package fat-reduced, firm silken
  tofu, crumbled
1 1/2 to 2 Tablespoons olive oil
2 teaspoons fresh lemon juice
1 to 2 teaspoons sweetener of your choice
2 teaspoons apple cider vinegar
1/2 teaspoon prepared yellow mustard
1/2 teaspoon salt

1. Place all the ingredients in a food processor fitted with a metal blade or in a blender, and process several minutes until the mixture is very smooth and creamy.

2. Use at once, or transfer the mayonnaise to a storage container, and chill it in the refrigerator. It will keep for about a week.

Yield: about 1 1/3 cups

Per Tablespoon: Calories: 18, Protein: 1 gm., Fat: 1 gm., Carbohydrate: 0 gm.

The Cook's Secrets:
The secret to the ultra-creamy consistency of this low-fat, egg-free mayonnaise is processing it for several minutes. This is necessary to pulverize the tofu thoroughly and eliminate any graininess. After the long processing time, the texture will be miraculously transformed.

VEGETABLE ENTRÉES, SIDE DISHES, SAVORY TOPPINGS & SAUCES

Vegetables add brilliance, beauty, taste, and nutrition to meals. Their vast array of shapes, shades, textures, and flavors is mind boggling. A plate of greens, a vibrant squash, a scarlet tomato, a pristine cauliflower—these are nature's palette from which we color our meals.

Children who are positively introduced to vegetables at an early age grow into adults who continue to appreciate vegetables throughout their lives. As role models, how we regard our own food, and whether or not we practice what we preach by eating what we profess to be healthful, will determine how the children in our lives view what's on their plate.

Vegetables are absolutely essential for maintaining proper nutrition. Scientists and researchers are only beginning to discover the complexity and significance of micro-nutrients found in vegetables, some of which may be associated with the prevention or alleviation of certain illnesses. A vitamin pill is not a substitute for a balanced diet and should not be equated with the intricate network of nourishment—currently known or yet to be uncovered—which is contained in vegetables.

In my area of the country we are fortunate to have a few organic farms which offer Community Supported Agriculture programs (CSAs). This is an arrangement whereby non-farmers annually buy a "share" in the farm. For the farmer, part of the farm's budget is secured in advance. In return, the shareholder receives produce on a weekly basis that is organically grown and fresher than anything obtainable in a store. With a CSA, members have the opportunity to get to know who is growing their food, how it is grown, and where it comes from. If it is feasible, investigate joining a CSA in your area. You will gain a closer connection with your food and your community by participating in a CSA. It's almost like having your own personal organic farmer!

If you do not have a CSA near you, or if you prefer to shop at a retail outlet, seek out a retailer who carries certified organically grown produce. If the produce at the store is not labeled regarding how it is grown, inquire with your grocer to determine which produce is organic. Encourage the store to carry more organically grown foods and to identify them as such. The more pressure consumers place on their grocers to carry wholesome, pesticide-free, non-genetically engineered foods, the more they will meet our demand for them, and the safer our food supplies will be.

A Note From Karen:

I eat whole, organic, vegan foods because they make me feel healthy and alive. I also know that this is one of the many ways I can positively change the world. While it might seem like a small act to some, the way I see it, every bite of tofu adds up. The gradual change I've made from the traditional North American diet has had profound effects on my life and, in turn, has positively affected many others.

GUIDE TO COOKING COMMON FRESH VEGETABLES

The variety of vegetables available to us year-round is astounding. Vegetables are not only delicious and colorful, they are a vital part of our daily diet. As a group, vegetables are naturally low in calories and supply many essential nutrients including carbohydrates, vitamins A and C, minerals, and fiber.

In most cases, vegetables should simply be washed or scrubbed just before eating or cooking them and peeled if they have been exposed to pesticides or other agrichemicals. Trim off the stems, roots, and any bruised areas, if necessary. There are several ways to cook fresh vegetables including sautéing, steaming, baking, broiling, grilling, and slow-roasting. Cooking times will vary depending on the density and moisture content of the vegetable, how it is cut or sliced, whether or not it has been peeled, and its age.

Sautéing or Stir-Frying

Sautéing (also called stir-frying) is a fun, familiar way to cook vegetables, and, although the vegetables require almost constant tossing while they cook, the total cooking time is usually quite brief. Oil is commonly used to sauté vegetables since it keeps them from sticking to the skillet or wok. However, vegetables may also be sautéed fat-free using a small amount of liquid such as water, wine, or lemon juice to get the cooking started. If you use a nonstick skillet or a small amount of nonstick cooking spray, very little or possibly no oil or liquid may be needed. After the cooking begins, the vegetables will begin to release their juices, so you should not need to add any more liquid, unless the heat is turned up so high that the juices evaporate as soon as they emerge.

During sautéing it is important to keep as much of the vegetable flesh exposed to the cooking surface as possible. This helps to speed up the cooking process and ensures even tenderness. The best way to do this is to slice the vegetables on a diagonal, if appropriate, or cut them into long, thin slivers.

A light misting of nonstick vegetable cooking spray or one teaspoon of oil is generally sufficient to get the cooking started and prevent sticking. Be sure to use an oil with a high flash point, such as canola oil. If you prefer to use a fat-free liquid, you will need approximately 1/4 cup.

Heat the oil or liquid over medium-high. Add denser, longer-cooking vegetables to the hot pan first. As soon as they begin to soften, add the shorter-cooking vegetables to the pan. Stir and toss the vegetables constantly, steering them toward the center of the pan where the heat is more concentrated. Remove the vegetables from the cooking vessel as soon as they are tender-crisp. If they remain in the hot skillet or wok, they will continue to cook, even if the heat has been turned off.

Steaming

Steaming is a quick, healthful way to cook most vegetables. Cleanup is easy and minimal energy is expended. To steam vegetables, pour water in the bottom of a saucepan to a depth of about one inch. Place a collapsible stainless steel basket or fitted steamer insert in the saucepan, and add the vegetables to it. Bring the water to a boil, cover the pan tightly with a lid, and reduce the heat to medium. Steam the vegetables for the amount of time specified, or until they are cooked to your liking. *Begin timing the cooking when steam forms.*

Several vegetables may be steamed easily at the same time. This not only makes the task of steaming simpler, it also aids in cleanup. Start with the longest-cooking vegetables (such as potatoes, winter squash, or carrots). Then, part-way through the cooking time, place the vegetables with shorter cooking times (such as spinach, mushrooms, or scallions) on top of the not-quite-tender, longer-cooking ones. Steam the vegetables just until everything is tender-crisp. Remove the steamer basket from the saucepan as soon as the vegetables are tender. If the vegetables remain in the saucepan they will continue to cook, even if the heat has been turned off and the lid has been removed, since the hot water will continue to produce steam.

Steamed vegetables taste best when they are served immediately. If you are unable to serve them at once, you can refresh them with cold water to stop the cooking process. To do this, place the steamer basket directly under the tap, and run cold water over the vegetables. The steamer basket will allow the water to flow through and drain off.

Grilling or Broiling

Cooking with direct dry heat, which includes grilling and broiling, is an exquisite treatment for many vegetables. When thinly cut vegetables are cooked in this fashion, their outer surface is quickly seared while the interior becomes silky and tender.

Times are not listed for grilling or broiling vegetables as the interval required to reach tenderness varies greatly depending on the moisture content of the vegetables and how they are prepared. Vegetables broil fastest when they are sliced very thinly. This also helps to ensure that the outside of the vegetable will not be charred while the inside remains undercooked. Test with a fork to check for doneness; then do a taste test to be sure.

Because this method of cooking exposes the vegetables to high heat for a very brief time (otherwise they would burn), moderately firm and juicy vegetables (for example, mushrooms, onion wedges, summer squash, thin asparagus, halved bell peppers, very thinly sliced eggplant, whole cherry tomatoes, snow peas, etc.) that tend to cook quickly will generally have the best results. For denser, longer cooking vegetables (such as potatoes, string beans, carrots, thick asparagus, cauliflower, or broccoli), first blanch them or steam them until they are almost tender-crisp, and use grilling or broiling as a finishing method.

To broil or grill vegetables, coat them lightly with oil. This can be done by misting the exposed surfaces of the vegetables with a thin layer of nonstick cooking spray or brushing them lightly with oil. The oil helps to transfer heat and flavor and seal in the juices of the vegetables. However, for totally fat-free cooking it is not necessary to use any oil at all.

Another option is to baste the vegetables with a seasoned marinade before and/or during cooking. For the deepest flavor, marinate raw or blanched vegetables three to eight hours prior to grilling or broiling them. The tofu and tempeh marinade recipes on page 154 are also excellent marinating and basting sauces for grilled or broiled vegetables.

Before heating the grill or oven, mist the cold grill or broiler pan with a little nonstick cooking spray to keep the vegetables from sticking to it. Arrange the vegetables in a single layer directly on the grill or, for broiling, on a pan which should then be placed just a few inches from the heat source. When the side of the vegetables that is exposed to the heat is lightly browned and blistered, turn the vegetables over to finish cooking them. Watch closely so they

do not burn. Direct dry heat can rapidly scorch foods! Remove the vegetables from the grill or pan as soon as they are tender to your liking. Season them with salt, pepper, and fresh herbs *after* cooking so the seasonings do not burn.

Slow-Roasting

Contrary to stir-frying, grilling, or broiling, which are designed to keep vegetables crisp through brief cooking, slow-roasting brings out the more mellow, rich flavors of nature's bounty. This process incorporates searing the vegetables and slow-roasting them using high heat to caramelize their natural sugars. This way a multitude of magnificent, complex flavors are developed.

Unlike stir-frying, cooking with direct dry heat, or steaming, larger, dense vegetables respond best to slow-roasting. Very moist vegetables, such as tomatoes, tend to weep their juices and steam instead of caramelizing. Let the density, moisture, and natural sugar content of the vegetables be your guide. The only rule of thumb for slow-roasting is to avoid smaller, overly juicy vegetables.

Slow-roasting can be accomplished with just a small amount of olive oil or canola oil to help transfer the heat and flavor, or for totally fat-free roasting, a little water or vegetable broth can be used to help start the cooking process until the vegetables release their own juices for steaming.

Slow-roasting really brings out the natural sugars and mature flavor of root vegetables, whether they are cooked in or out of their jackets. Try white potatoes, sweet potatoes, carrots, parsnips, beets, onions, shallots, turnips, or rutabagas, or a mix of several of these.

Vegetables that are less dense, such as summer squash and eggplant, will lose quite a bit of moisture during roasting and will be significantly reduced after cooking. Leave their thin outer skins intact to contain the flavors. Peppers will also lose much of their juice during roasting and will shrivel because of their hollow centers. Fennel and peeled winter squash are delicious roasted. Other vegetables such as broccoli, cauliflower, and Brussels sprouts, which have a low sugar content, will have limited caramelization and will need a little extra water or vegetable broth to help get the roasting process going.

Here are general directions for slow-roasting vegetables:

1. Peel the vegetables, if appropriate, and cut them into small, equal-size pieces. Toss them with a little olive oil or canola oil, salt and pepper, spices, and/or fresh herbs.

2. Transfer the vegetables to a deep, 4-quart or 6-quart casserole dish with a lid. Add a little water or vegetable broth to get the cooking started. Cover the casserole dish tightly with the lid, and place it in a preheated 400°F oven on the lowest rack. The use of a lid controls browning and shelters the vegetables from the direct heat, allowing gentle cooking to take place.

3. Roast the vegetables for about 20 to 30 minutes.

4. Stir the vegetables, and return them to the oven to finish cooking and browning for about 20 to 60 minutes longer, depending on their size and density. Remove the lid for most or all of the second half of the cooking. This will raise the direct heat and start the browning and caramelization process which creates a rich, sweet flavor.

For specific examples of how to slow-roast vegetables, see the recipes for Slow-Roasted Broccoli Hoagies, p. 98, and Harvest Bake, p. 120.

COOKING VEGETABLES
Quantities For Two

The following section lists approximate quantities for two servings of vegetables. Increase the amount called for if the vegetables are going to be the center of your meal or if you are trying to appease particularly ravenous appetites.

Artichokes - two 10-ounce artichokes

Asparagus - 1/2 pound (approximately 1 cup of pieces)

Beans: Green, purple, and yellow wax - 1/2 pound (approximately 1 1/3 cups of pieces)

Beets - 1/2 pound (approximately 1 1/3 cups cubed)

Broccoli - 1/2 pound (approximately 2 cups florets)

Brussels sprouts - 1/2 pound (approximately 2 cups)

Cabbage - 1/4 of a 1 pound head (approximately 2 cups sliced)

Carrots - 1/2 pound (about 1 1/2 cups sliced)

Cauliflower - 1/2 of a 1 1/2 pound head (about 1 1/2 cups florets)

Celery - 2 stalks (1 1/4 cups sliced)

Corn - 2 cups of kernels

Corn on the Cob - 2 ears

Eggplant - 1 small Western or 1 large Asian (about 1/2 pound; approximately 2 1/2 cups of cubes)

Fennel - 1 large head (about 1 1/2 cups chopped)

Greens: Beet, Collard, Kale, Mustard, Turnip - 1/4 pound (about 4 cups of leaves torn)

Jicama - 8 ounces (about 1 cup of cubes)

Kohlrabi - 1/2 pound (about 1 1/2 cups julienne strips)

Leeks - 3/4 pound (about 1 1/2 cups sliced)

Mushrooms: White Button or Criminis - 1/2 pound (about 2 cups sliced)

Okra - 1/4 pound

Onions - 1 medium

Parsnips - 3/4 pound (2 cups sliced)

Pea Pods (Snow Peas) - 1/4 pound (about 1 cup)

Peppers, Bell: Green, Red, Yellow or Orange - 1 large (about 1 1/4 cups rings or strips or squares)

Rutabagas - 1/2 pound (about 1 1/2 cups cubed)

Spinach - 1/2 pound (about 5 to 6 cups torn)

Squash: Acorn, Delicata, Golden Nugget - 1 pound

Squash: Banana, Buttercup, Butternut, Hubbard, Turban - 1 pound (or a 1-pound piece)

Squash: Pattypan, Sunburst, Yellow and Zucchini - 1/2 pound (about 2 cups sliced)

Squash: Spaghetti - one 2-pound squash

Swiss Chard - 1/2 pound (about 6 cups torn)

Turnips - 1/2 pound (about 1 1/4 cups cubed)

Vegetable Medley Suppers

Some of my most memorable meals have consisted of a simple assortment of raw, baked, broiled, sautéed, steamed, or grilled vegetables attractively arranged on a plate accompanied with a scoop of cooked grain, or a potato, or thick slices of fresh whole grain bread, and perhaps a colorful mound of cooked beans. Nothing could be easier or more beautiful.

The only secret to a successful Vegetable Medley Supper is to use the freshest organically grown vegetables and incorporate a kaleidoscope of colors. (A plateful of all green or all white vegetables can be terribly boring.) Also, try varying the shapes and sizes for visual excitement and appeal.

For seasoning, garnish the vegetables with fresh herbs, a light sprinkle of seeds or nuts, a pinch of salt, or a splash of lemon juice or soy sauce. However, you'll most likely find that freshly picked, seasonal vegetables require little assistance to bring out their peak flavor.

As a general guideline, select three to five vegetables. More than this can become cumbersome to prepare and overwhelming to eat, and fewer than three is usually not sufficient to be enticing or satisfying. Let your appetite be your guide as to how much to prepare. To get you started, here are a few medley possibilities:

1. Baked acorn squash
Steamed kale
Corn on the cob
Fresh tomatoes garnished with fresh
   basil leaves
Whole grain rolls

2. Steamed green beans sprinkled with sesame
   seeds
Thinly sliced eggplant slices and red
   bell pepper strips, brushed with olive
   oil or canola oil and grilled or broiled
Rice garnished with lemon zest and
   fresh parsley

3. Baked potato with Tofu Sour Cream, p. 73,
   and snipped chives or scallions,
   or Ranch-Style Spread & Dip, p. 109
Steamed swiss chard garnished with
   fresh lemon slices and fresh enoki
   mushrooms
Diagonally sliced carrots, steamed

4. Baked spaghetti squash topped with toasted
   sunflower seeds, chopped fresh tomatoes, and torn fresh basil leaves, minced
   parsley, or chopped cilantro
Steamed asparagus spears or broccoli trees
   with fresh lemon juice
Whole grain bread

5. Sliced turnips and rutabaga brushed
   lightly with olive oil and baked
Steamed mustard greens
Canned red kidney beans, rinsed,
   drained, warmed through, and seasoned with a tiny bit of olive oil, salt or
   soy sauce, and ground black pepper
Yankee Corn Muffins, p. 39

6. Steamed or baked carrots and parsnips
Sautéed collard greens with garlic, black-
   eyed peas, and fresh lemon juice
Cornmeal Biscuits, p. 43, with applesauce or
   apple butter

7. Sautéed portobello mushrooms
Fresh or broiled thick tomato slices
Steamed spinach garnished with
sesame seeds
Wild rice

8. Steamed broccoli trees lightly sprinkled with
chopped, toasted walnuts
Grilled or broiled onion slices
Steamed or broiled yellow summer squash
Red skinned potatoes steamed in their jackets, drizzled with a tiny bit of olive oil
and garnished with fresh rosemary

9. Steamed Brussels sprouts sprinkled with
lemon pepper
Apple slices sautéed in a tiny bit of canola
oil with a pinch of cinnamon
Julienned carrots, lightly steamed
Cooked bulgur (medium ground) with
raisins

10. Baked butternut squash filled with steamed
green peas and pearl onions
Steamed cauliflower florets sprinkled with
vegetable-seasoned salt
Whole grain herb bread

11. Baked yams, split and topped with apple
sauce and cinnamon
Sliced cooked beets
Salad of fresh spinach and mushrooms,
drizzled with lemon juice and a tiny bit
of olive oil, or a fat-free dressing

12. Quinoa tossed with grilled or sauteed
onions, red bell peppers, zucchini, shi-
itake mushrooms, and toasted walnut
pieces
Salad of romaine lettuce and grated carrot
tossed with fresh lime juice and a tiny bit
of olive oil

A Note From Michael:

Bundled or packaged produce tends to come in portions that are just a bit too much for us to use at one sitting. Therefore, we tend to accumulate small amounts of vegetables throughout the week because there's never enough left over for another complete meal or recipe. My solution is to make a "Steamed Vegetable Medley," and almost any vegetable can be included.

First, I heat up the water in my steaming pot and place the longest cooking vegetable in the steamer basket. After a few minutes, I add the next longest cooking vegetable and continue in this fashion until everything is tender at the same time. If we have a few water chestnuts sitting in the fridge or some nuts or herbs, I just throw them on top near the end of the cooking time.

If the vegetables are starting to get a little overdone, I place the steamer basket under the faucet and run cold water over the vegetables. This instantly stops the cooking process and prevents the vegetables from becoming mushy.

Stir-Fries Tonight!

It's very easy to create exciting stir-fries and, if you like, they can be unique every time you make them. Stir-fries are also a great way to use up small amounts of odds and ends hiding in your refrigerator.

The following is a general outline of some ingredients you could select and their approximate quantities for a two-person stir-fry extravaganza. Serve the finished stir-fries over your favorite cooked grain, polenta, or pasta.

1 to 2 teaspoons canola oil (this is one of the best oils for stir-frying since it has a high flash point)

VEGETABLES:
Use a total of 3 to 4 cups of vegetables, incorporating 3 to 6 different kinds (such as asparagus, bell pepper, bok choy, broccoli, cabbage, carrots, cauliflower, celery, collard greens, corn, peeled fennel, green beans, jicama, kale, mushrooms, onions, frozen peas, scallions, shallots, snow peas, spinach, summer squash, swiss chard, water chestnuts, zucchini)

SEASONINGS OF YOUR CHOICE (optional - select one or more):
1 to 3 Tablespoons fresh herbs, or 1/2 to 1 teaspoon dried herbs (individual herbs or a blend)
1 to 2 cloves garlic, minced or pressed
1/2 to 1 teaspoon fresh gingerroot, minced
1/2 teaspoon curry powder, or to taste
1/2 teaspoon chili powder, or to taste
a splash of soy sauce
a few drops of toasted sesame oil

OPTIONAL INGREDIENTS (select one):
1 cup cooked beans, drained
1/4 pound tofu, diced (may be browned separately before adding, if desired)
1/4 pound tempeh, cubed (may be browned separately before adding, if desired)
1/2 to 1 cup seitan, sliced into strips or chunks
3 to 4 Tablespoons raisins

NUTS OR SEEDS (optional):
1 to 3 Tablespoons sunflower seeds, pumpkin seeds, whole blanched almonds, or chopped nuts (toasted or raw)

1. Slice the vegetables into bite-size pieces so they will all cook evenly and quickly.

2. Place the the oil in a large skillet, wok, or 4 1/2-quart Dutch oven, and heat it over medium-high. When the oil is hot, add the vegetables and stir-fry them for several minutes, or until they are tender-crisp.

3. When the vegetables are tender, remove them from the skillet at once, and spoon them over cooked grain, pasta, or polenta.

Yield: 2 main dish servings

The Cook's Secrets:
Quick-cooking vegetables such as spinach, chard, mushrooms, or bean sprouts should be added last, when the other vegetables are just a few minutes shy of being done. Fresh herbs are best when added near the end.

For a moister stir-fry, or to keep the vegetables from sticking to the pan without adding more oil, add a tablespoon or two of water, wine, lemon juice, or vegetable broth during cooking.

Autumn Boiled Dinner with Warm Dijon Dressing

This peasant-style dish incorporates an assortment of fall and winter vegetables and is topped with a delicate mustard sauce. Its elegance is its simplicity. With a minimum of added seasonings, the individual flavors of the vegetables truly shine.

HAVE READY:
1 recipe Creamy Dijon Dressing, p. 72

2 medium carrots, pared and cut into chunks
2 medium parsnips, pared and cut into chunks
1 large onion, cut into wedges
1 small rutabaga, peeled and cut into chunks
1/2 of a very small cabbage, cored and cut into wedges
1 large yam, peeled and cut into chunks
2 bay leaves

1 1/2 cups water

salt and ground black pepper, to taste

1. Place the vegetables and the bay leaves in a 4 1/2-quart saucepan or Dutch oven. Peel and slice the yam last so it will not discolor.

2. Pour the water over the vegetables, and bring it to a boil. Reduce the heat to medium, cover the saucepan with a lid, and simmer the vegetables for 25 to 30 minutes, or until they are all equally tender, stirring occasionally. Remove the saucepan from the heat, and discard the bay leaves.

3. Using a slotted spoon, place the vegetables into wide, shallow soup bowls or onto dinner plates.

4. Drizzle the Creamy Dijon Dressing over the vegetables. Then lightly sprinkle them with a little salt and pepper. Serve warm.

Yield: 2 main dish servings

Per serving: Calories: 341, Protein: 5 gm., Fat: 3 gm., Carbohydrate: 73 gm.

The Cook's Secrets:
Be sure to save the liquid from this recipe. It makes fantastic soup broth, a lovely base for gravy, or a great liquid for cooking grains.

A Note From Anne & Matt:
Be seasonal—vary your menu with organic produce that is available locally.

Harvest Bake

Roasting brings out the deep, rich flavors of winter vegetables. This dish makes a generous and delectable cold weather meal and requires no other accompaniments. It takes a long while to bake, but once it's in the oven, you can put your feet up and relax.

2 Tablespoons water

1 medium carrot, pared, cut in half lengthwise, then cut into bite-size chunks
1 medium parsnip, pared, cut in half lengthwise, then cut into bite-size chunks
1 medium yam, peeled and cut into bite-size chunks (see The Cook's Secrets at right)
1 large onion, cut into wedges
1 small turnip, peeled and cut into bite-size chunks
1 very small rutabaga, or 1/2 of a medium rutabaga, peeled and cut into bite-size chunks
6 to 8 cloves garlic, sliced or very coarsely chopped

2 to 3 teaspoons olive oil

salt and ground black pepper, to taste

1/3 cup fresh parsley, chopped

1. Move one of the oven racks to the lowest level. Preheat the oven to 400°F.

2. Place the water in the bottom of a deep 4-quart or 6-quart casserole dish. Then place the vegetables in the casserole dish. Drizzle the oil over the top of the vegetables. Cover the casserole dish with a lid, and roast the vegetables in the oven on the lowest rack for 30 minutes.

3. Remove the casserole dish from the oven. Stir the vegetables, replace the cover, and return the casserole dish to the oven for 30 minutes.

4. Remove the casserole dish from the oven, and stir the vegetables again. Remove the lid, and finish roasting the vegetables uncovered for 20 to 30 minutes longer, or until everything is tender.

5. Remove the casserole dish from the oven. Season the vegetables with salt and pepper, to taste. Stir in the parsley or sprinkle it over the top of each serving as a garnish. Serve hot.

Yield: 2 main dish servings

Per serving: Calories: 243, Protein: 3 gm., Fat: 6 gm., Carbohydrate: 44 gm.

The Cook's Secrets:
To prevent the yam from discoloring after it has been peeled and chunked, place the pieces in a bowl of water to which a little lemon juice has been added. When the remaining vegetables are ready, place the yam chunks in a colander and rinse off the lemon water thoroughly before proceeding with the recipe.

"Fried" Tomatoes

Fried tomatoes were one of my childhood favorites. I fondly remember dredging the firm, thick slices in flour, and frying them in a deep pool of butter. Now that we are all wiser, I've created a simple "no-fry" version incorporating more wholesome ingredients. Nevertheless, this recipe is just as tasty as the old rendition, and it is much less messy to prepare and clean up.

CORNMEAL BREADING:
1/2 cup dry whole wheat bread crumbs (see The Cook's Secrets, below right)
1/2 cup yellow cornmeal
1/4 cup nutritional yeast flakes
1/2 teaspoon paprika
heaping 1/4 teaspoon salt
1/8 teaspoon ground black pepper
1/8 teaspoon cayenne pepper

1/2 cup whole wheat pastry flour

1 cup water, as needed

2 large, firm, ripe tomatoes

1. Preheat the oven to 375°F. Mist a baking sheet with nonstick cooking spray, and set it aside.

2. To make the cornmeal breading, place the bread crumbs, cornmeal, nutritional yeast flakes, paprika, salt, black pepper, and cayenne pepper in a shallow mixing bowl, and mix them together well.

3. In two separate shallow mixing bowls, place the flour and the water.

4. Slice the tomatoes horizontally into 1/2-inch-thick rounds.

5. Bread each tomato slice one at a time. To do this, first dredge the slice in the flour, coating it well all over. Then dunk the slice in the water, submerging it completely. Remove the slice from the water, and immediately dredge it in the breading meal, coating it well all over.

6. Place each tomato slice on the prepared baking sheet as soon as you finish breading it. When all the slices have been breaded, mist the tops lightly with nonstick cooking spray.

7. Bake the tomato slices for 30 minutes, turning them once after 15 minutes. Serve while hot.

Yield: 2 to 3 side dish servings

Per serving: Calories: 327, Protein: 14 gm., Fat: 1 gm., Carbohydrate: 63 gm.

The Cook's Secrets
To make dry bread crumbs, toast 1 or 2 slices of whole grain bread. Cool the toasted bread and tear it or dice it into small pieces. Whirl the pieces in a food processor fitted with a metal blade until they are finely crumbed, or rub them on the side of a grater. Measure out the amount you need, and store any leftover crumbs in an airtight container. Alternately, purchase packaged whole wheat bread crumbs. They are available in natural food stores and many supermarkets.

"Fried" tomatoes will become soggy if they are allowed to cool on the baking sheet. They will be at their crunchy best if they are eaten while they are still hot. If it is necessary to let them cool, transfer them to a cooling rack immediately after baking, and eat them as soon as possible.

Stuffed Vegetable Rolls

This is a variation of stuffed cabbage rolls using vibrant kale or collard greens in place of the cabbage leaves. Kale and collard greens are exceptionally nutritious. Nevertheless, because many people aren't familiar with them, they often get overlooked. This simple recipe is a delicious way to incorporate these magnificent greens into your repertoire. Serve them with Favorite Mashed Potatoes, p. 141, or Instant Mashed Potatoes, p. 142.

6 very large, beautiful kale leaves or collard green
   leaves

1/2 cup water or vegetable broth
1/2 cup zucchini, diced
1/2 cup red bell pepper, chopped
1/3 cup bulgur (medium ground)
2 Tablespoons raisins
1/2 teaspoon dried basil leaves, crushed
1/4 teaspoon dried marjoram leaves, crushed
1/4 teaspoon garlic granules
slightly heaping 1/4 teaspoon salt
1/8 teaspoon ground black pepper

1/4 cup walnuts, coarsely chopped
1 teaspoon fresh lemon juice

1 8-ounce can tomato sauce (1 cup)
several drops Tabasco sauce, or to taste
   (optional)

1. Carefully remove the stems from the kale or collard greens. Carefully place the whole leaves in a steamer basket or steamer insert in a large saucepan filled with an inch of water. Bring the water to a boil. Cover the saucepan with a lid, and reduce the heat to medium. Steam the leaves until they are wilted and very tender, about 12 to 18 minutes. Remove the steamer from the saucepan, and allow the leaves to cool until they can be handled.

2. Meanwhile, place the water, zucchini, red bell pepper, bulgur, raisins, herbs, garlic, salt, and black pepper in a 2-quart saucepan. Bring the mixture to a boil. Reduce the heat to medium. Cover the saucepan with a lid, and simmer the mixture for 8 minutes. Remove the saucepan from the heat, and let the mixture rest covered for 5 minutes.

3. Preheat the oven to 400°F.

4. Stir the walnuts and lemon juice into the cooked bulgur mixture.

5. Lay the cooked kale or collard green leaves on a flat surface. Place about 1/3 cup of the bulgur mixture on each leaf in a strip near the stem end. Fold in the two lengthwise sides. Then, starting at the unfolded edge of the stem end, carefully roll up each leaf to enclose the filling, forming a neat packet. (Save any extra filling to serve on the side.)

6. Stir the Tabasco sauce into the tomato sauce. Then spoon 1/3 cup of the tomato sauce into a 10-inch glass pie plate or a shallow 2-quart baking dish.

7. Place the vegetable rolls, seam side down, in a single layer in the tomato sauce. Spoon the remaining sauce over the rolls.

8. Place a lid on the casserole dish, or cover it with foil. Bake the vegetable rolls for 20 minutes. Serve hot.

Yield: 6 vegetable rolls (2 to 3 main dish servings)

Per roll: Calories: 105, Protein: 3 gm., Fat: 3 gm., Carbohydrate: 15 gm.

A Note From Glenn:
Generally, it's useful to work towards discovering a few good, quick, fail-proof recipes. Often, I'm not in the mood to experiment. Speaking of experiments, I used to approach a kitchen like a chemistry lab. Rest assured, cooking errors and deviations from recipes will not take out half of your kitchen. In time, I discovered how to add different ingredients and "season to taste" rather than always following a recipe precisely.

Red Cabbage & Apples

A popular palate pleaser, this sweet-sour recipe always conjures up fond memories.

2 cups red cabbage, shredded or very thinly sliced
1 small, tart, red apple, peeled and diced
1/4 cup onion, chopped
2 Tablespoons apple juice concentrate
1 Tablespoon water
1/2 teaspoon whole caraway seeds, or 1/4 to 1/2 teaspoon ground caraway seeds

1 Tablespoon red wine vinegar

1. Place the cabbage, apple, onion, juice concentrate, water, and caraway seeds in a 2-quart saucepan, and toss them together well.

2. Bring the cabbage mixture to a boil. Reduce the heat to medium-low, and cover the saucepan with a lid. Simmer the cabbage until it is tender, about 8 to 12 minutes.

3. Stir in the red wine vinegar, and toss the mixture to coat the cabbage thoroughly. Serve hot or warm, using a slotted spoon.

Yield: 2 side dish servings

Per serving: Calories: 97, Protein: 1 gm., Fat: 0 gm., Carbohydrate: 22 gm.

Grandmother's Peppers & Tomato

Laraine Flemming contributed this recipe, and she fondly remembers her Grandmother Mazzoli preparing it. Laraine says her family has traditionally served peppers this way for generations. The soy sauce, however, was her own special touch. This recipe is so easy and delicious you will certainly want to include it among your own family traditions. It is absolutely wonderful over linguini or other pasta, potatoes, grain, or polenta.

1 large green bell pepper, cut into large chunks
1 large red bell pepper, cut into large chunks
1 small onion, chopped
2 Tablespoons balsamic vinegar
1 Tablespoon soy sauce
2 to 3 teaspoons olive oil
3 to 4 cloves garlic, minced or pressed

1 ripe, medium tomato, chunked

salt and ground black pepper, to taste

1. Move one of the oven racks to the lowest level. Preheat the oven to 400°F.

2. Place the peppers and onion in a deep 4-quart casserole dish.

3. Add the vinegar, soy sauce, olive oil, and garlic. Stir to distribute the ingredients evenly and to thoroughly coat the peppers and onion.

4. Cover the casserole dish with a lid, and roast the mixture on the lowest oven rack for 35 to 40 minutes, stirring once or twice.

5. Remove the casserole dish from the oven, and stir in the tomato chunks. Return the mixture to the oven to roast *uncovered* for 10 minutes longer. Season with salt and pepper, to taste. Serve hot or warm.

Yield: 2 main dish servings when served over pasta (4 to 6 ounces), potatoes, or a grain

Per serving: Calories: 108, Protein: 2 gm., Fat: 6 gm., Carbohydrate: 12 gm.

A Note From Billy:
Being a small business owner and working six days a week, I try to make meal preparation as easy as possible. To save time, I buy soup mixes either from the bulk section of my food co-op or in cup-of-soup packages. For dinner, pasta with a little olive oil, salads, or soups make up my main menus. Sometimes I'll have baked potatoes, stir-fries, or steamed vegetables. I'm not yet very creative with or knowledgeable about cooking, but I'm definitely learning.

Aunt Rose's Marinara Sauce

Dense, rich flavor abounds from the unusual but balanced mix of seasonings in this versatile sauce. It does take a while to simmer, but once it's in the pot you need only stir it occasionally. Marinara sauce is the quintessential topping for pasta, but it is also great to dip bread into or to pour over grains or vegetables. It will keep in the refrigerator for at least a week and will also keep in the freezer for about three months.

2 14.5-ounce cans whole tomatoes, with juice
1 6-ounce can tomato paste
1 large onion, very finely chopped
4 to 6 cloves garlic, minced or pressed
1 Tablespoon olive oil
1 Tablespoon sweetener of your choice
1 Tablespoon dried basil leaves
1 teaspoon salt
1/2 teaspoon dried oregano leaves
1/2 teaspoon dried sage leaves, crumbled
1/2 teaspoon dried rosemary, crushed
1/2 teaspoon dried thyme leaves, crushed
1/8 to 1/4 teaspoon ground fennel seeds, or 2 to
   3 whole fennel seeds
1/4 teaspoon ground black pepper

1/4 cup fresh parsley, minced

1. Place all the ingredients *except the parsley* in a 4 1/2-quart saucepan or Dutch oven. Break the tomatoes apart with the side of a wooden spoon or with your hands. Bring the mixture to a boil. Reduce heat to medium-low, and cover the saucepan with a lid. Simmer the sauce for 45 minutes, stirring occasionally.

2. Remove the lid and simmer the sauce uncovered for 40 to 45 minutes longer, stirring occasionally. Add the parsley during the last 10 minutes of cooking.

3. Use the sauce immediately, or cool it thoroughly and transfer it to a storage container. Store the sauce in the refrigerator. It will develop an even fuller, richer flavor if it is allowed to rest prior to using.

Yield: about 3 cups

Per 1 cup serving: Calories: 181, Protein: 4 gm., Fat: 5 gm., Carbohydrate: 29 gm.

The Cook's Secrets:
If you prefer a smoother marinara, purée all or half of the sauce briefly in a blender or food processor.

The longer the sauce simmers, the thicker and richer it will become.

Pizza Sauce

This sauce is very highly seasoned and concentrated, so a little will go a long way. It is not much work to prepare, however it does take a long while to simmer. Canned or jarred sauces can't hold a candle to the homemade flavor of this sauce, so setting aside the time to make it will prove worthwhile. After all, it's the sauce that really makes the pizza!

1 14.5-ounce can whole tomatoes, with juice
5 Tablespoons tomato paste
3 cloves garlic, minced or pressed
2 teaspoons olive oil
2 teaspoons sweetener of your choice
1/2 teaspoon salt
1/2 teaspoon dried oregano leaves
1/2 teaspoon dried basil leaves

1. Place all the ingredients in a 2-quart saucepan or Dutch oven. Break the tomatoes apart with the side of a wooden spoon or with your hands. Bring the sauce to a boil. Reduce the heat to low, and cook *uncovered* for 45 to 60 minutes, stirring occasionally.

2. Use the sauce immediately, or cool it thoroughly and transfer it to a storage container. Store the sauce in the refrigerator. It will develop an even fuller, richer flavor if it is allowed to rest prior to using.

Yield: about 1 cup

Per 1/4 cup serving: Calories: 68, Protein: 2 gm., Fat: 2 gm., Carbohydrate: 10 gm.

The Cook's Secrets:
Use this sauce for Vegetable Pizza for Two, p. 102, or make quick English Muffin Cheeze Pizzas, p. 103, with it. This sauce is also an excellent spread for bread, imparting a rich burst of flavor.

A Note From Scott:
I don't like to cook large amounts of a particular recipe since I'm usually just cooking for myself. However, it's very useful to cook additional items for use in another recipe if the preparation is the same. For instance, the steamed potatoes used in one day's baked casserole can be doubled for use in another day's potato soup.

This is true of any vegetable—just double the ingredient called for in a particular recipe. Rice and pasta can be spread out as well. Thursday's pasta for minestrone can be doubled so Sunday's pasta with sauce is ready to go. (Just place the pasta in a colander in the sink, and pour boiling water over it to heat it up. The colander allows the water to drain off, and the pasta is hot and ready to use in under a minute.)

Pizza Emergency Sauce

Not as rich and flavorful as long-cooked pizza sauce, but a terrific option when the "pizza emergency" sirens are howling.

6 Tablespoons tomato paste
1/4 cup water
1 to 2 teaspoons olive oil
1 teaspoon sweetener of your choice
1/2 teaspoon garlic granules
1/2 teaspoon onion granules
1/2 teaspoon dried oregano leaves
1/2 teaspoon dried basil leaves
1/4 teaspoon salt, or to taste
1/8 teaspoon ground black pepper

1. Place all the ingredients in a small mixing bowl, and stir until they are well combined.

2. Use the sauce immediately, or transfer it to a storage container. Store the sauce in the refrigerator. It will develop an even fuller, richer flavor if it is allowed to rest prior to using.The sauce will thicken somewhat when refrigerated. Stir it well before using, and thin it with a little water, if desired.

Yield: about 1/2 cup

Per 1/4 cup serving: Calories: 82, Protein: 1 gm., Fat: 4 gm., Carbohydrate: 11 gm.

Tangy Dijon Apricot Sauce

This is an ideal dipping sauce for Crispy Tofu Sticks, p. 158, or Breaded Seitan Nuggets, p. 168. It also readily perks up any grain or vegetable dish and is a delightful sauce for baked or grilled vegetables of any kind. Best of all, it can be made in two minutes flat!

3 Tablespoons fruit-sweetened apricot jam
1 Tablespoon Dijon mustard
1 Tablespoon balsamic vinegar

1. Place all the ingredients in a small mixing bowl, and stir them together until they are thoroughly combined.

2. Serve at once, or, if time permits, let the mixture rest for 10 to 15 minutes before serving to allow the flavors to blend.

Yield: 1/3 cup

Per Tablespoon: Calories: 34, Protein: 0 gm., Fat: 0 gm., Carbohydrate: 8 gm.

A Note From Scott:
Tomato sauce is a cure-all. I like to keep plenty on hand to pour over leftover rice, pasta, vegetables, tofu, or whatever on those nights I don't feel much like cooking.

Quick Brown Gravy

Great on everything from biscuits to mashed potatoes, you're sure to find many uses for this versatile
gravy.

1 Tablespoon cornstarch
1 1/2 Tablespoons soy sauce

2/3 cup water or vegetable broth
1/4 teaspoon garlic granules

1 Tablespoon tahini

1. Place the cornstarch in a 1-quart saucepan,
and stir in the soy sauce to make a smooth, thin
paste.

2. Gradually whisk in the water or vegetable
broth and garlic granules.

3. Place the saucepan over medium-high heat,
and cook the gravy, stirring constantly with a
wire whisk, until it thickens and comes to a
boil.

4. Remove the saucepan from the heat, and
beat the tahini into the gravy using the wire
whisk. Serve the gravy at once, or cover the
saucepan with a lid to keep it warm.

Yield: about 3/4 cup (2 servings)

Per serving: Calories: 70, Protein: 2 gm., Fat: 4 gm.,
Carbohydrate: 6 gm.

Golden Gravy

Nutritional yeast flakes impart a "cheesy" flavor that
is filled with homey warmth. Use this lovely sauce on
vegetables, potatoes, croquettes, grains, or biscuits.

2 Tablespoons nutritional yeast flakes
2 Tablespoons whole wheat pastry flour

3/4 cup water or vegetable broth
1 Tablespoon soy sauce
1 teaspoon olive oil or canola oil

1/8 teaspoon onion granules
pinch of ground black pepper, or to taste

1. Place the nutritional yeast flakes and flour in
a dry 1-quart saucepan, and toast them over
medium heat, stirring constantly, until they are
lightly browned and fragrant.

2. Remove the saucepan from the heat.
Gradually whisk in the water or vegetable
broth, soy sauce, and oil until the gravy is very
smooth. Then whisk in the seasonings.

3. Cook the gravy over medium heat, stirring
almost constantly with the wire whisk, until it is
thickened, smooth, and bubbly. Serve at once.

Yield: about 3/4 cup (2 servings)

Per serving: Calories: 75, Protein: 5 gm., Fat: 2 gm.,
Carbohydrate: 9 gm.

WHOLE GRAINS, POTATOES & PASTA

AN INTRODUCTION TO WHOLE GRAINS

Grains are the edible seeds of members of the grass family. Grains and the products made from them have been food staples in all cultures for thousands of years, and many ancient grains are making a vibrant comeback in vegetarian and gourmet cuisine. All grains are excellent sources of dietary fiber, carbohydrates, protein, and other vital nutrients.

There are three basic parts which make up whole grains: (1) the bran, which is the layer underneath the hull made up primarily of insoluble fiber and small amounts of vitamins, minerals, and protein; (2) the endosperm, the starchy center of the grain containing protein, amino acids, and trace elements of other nutrients; and (3) the germ, the tiny "heart" inside the grain which sprouts and grows to produce new plants. The germ is high in B-complex vitamins, vitamin E, protein, unsaturated fat, minerals, and carbohydrates.

Refined grains have had all or part of the bran and/or the germ removed in processing. What remains is simply the starchy middle. On the other hand, whole grain products are those which contain all three edible parts of the grain and thereby retain the highest amounts of vitamins, nutrients, protein, and fiber. Because the germ is rich in vitamin E, a fat-soluble vitamin which is reactive to light, moisture, and heat, always store whole grains in airtight, bug-proof containers in a cool, dry place. Cracked grain products (such as bulgur or cornmeal) may be stored for brief periods in tightly sealed containers at room temperature, but for longer storage keep them in the refrigerator to prevent rancidity. The best way to keep whole grains fresh is to purchase them in small quantities, store them properly, and use them up regularly.

Depending on the particular grain, a pound can contain anywhere from 2 to 4 1/2 cups worth. Generally speaking, 1/2 to 2/3 cup of raw grain will yield anywhere from 1 to 2 cups of cooked grain, or enough for two main dish servings. For most two-person households, one or two pounds each of four or five different grains should be sufficient for about three to five weeks of meals, depending on your eating patterns.

A Note About Cooking Grains

Always rinse whole grains in water prior to cooking them. The easiest way to do this is to place the grain in a wire mesh strainer and rinse it under running tap water, stirring with your hands or a spoon. Grains should be cooked in a heavy saucepan with a tight fitting lid unless other equipment is specified.

Vegetable broth or plain water may be used as the simmering liquid for grains. Unless otherwise directed, a pinch of salt may be added to the cooking liquid for each 1/2 cup of grain used. Occasionally you may want to change the flavor of the grain itself by adding different seasonings to the raw grain so that the seasoning is absorbed into the kernels while they cook. It is fun to experiment with all the intriguing flavors and textures that various seasonings can add to grains. The following are a few ideas you may find helpful:

Herbs

Fresh or dried herbs and other savory seasonings such as onion, garlic, or a tiny pinch of asafetida* may be added to the washed grain before cooking. About 1 to 2 teaspoons of fresh herbs or 1/4 to 1/2 teaspoon of dried herbs per 1/2 cup of grain will suffice. Some favorite herbs you may want to try are basil, chives, cilantro, marjoram, oregano, parsley, rosemary, sage, savory, tarragon, and thyme. You could also try seasoning the cooking liquid with a little vegetarian bouillon powder, soy sauce, or liquid aminos instead of salt.

Spices

Whole spices added to the rinsed grain before cooking will add variety and flavor to a dish of plain grains. Try a piece of cinnamon stick, whole peppercorns, whole cloves, bay leaves, or star anise. A pinch of turmeric imparts a lovely golden color to rice; saffron bestows a delicate rose shade. Black mustard seeds, crushed green cardamom, and whole cumin seeds add a delightful, exotic Indian flavor to grains and are especially delicious with basmati rice. These spices can be found in Indian grocery stores, gourmet specialty markets, natural food stores, and some supermarkets. (To enhance their flavor, black mustard seeds and cumin seeds can be sautéed briefly in a tiny bit of canola oil before adding them to the rinsed grain.)

Fruit, Nuts & Seeds

Depending on what other foods you are serving with your meal, chopped dried or fresh fruits or a small quantity of chopped nuts or seeds can add interest and flavor to plain grain.

Try adding chopped fresh or dried apple, raisins, snipped dried apricots, toasted or raw sunflower seeds, pecans, black sesame seeds, or pomegranate seeds before or after cooking the grain for a bit of added color and variety.

Vegetables

Some grated carrot, a bit of chopped green pepper, diced celery, or garlic are wonderful additions to longer-cooking grains (such as brown rice or pearl barley) or those prepared with a pressure cooker. For quick-cooking grains, try adding a few frozen peas, some frozen corn, or frozen green beans.

A Note About Pressure Cooking

Pressure cookers can cook whole grains in a flash. They work by locking the steam inside the cooker. This builds up pressure and raises the internal temperature of the cooker from the standard boiling point of 212°F to 250°F. This reduces the cooking time by as much as 50 percent without destroying the grain's nutritional value.

Depending on the size, type, and brand of pressure cooker you have, it can take anywhere from 30 to 60 seconds to bring the pressure up to high. The manufacturer's instruction manual that comes with your pressure cooker will tell you how to recognize when the maximum pressure has been reached. When pressure cooking whole grains, always do so under high pressure (13 to 15 pounds). The guide for pressure cooking whole grains on pages 134-35 is based on cooking under maximum pressure.

Whenever you pressure cook small quantities, you will have the most success if you use a small pressure cooker. A 2 1/2-quart size is highly recommended; however, larger cookers (such as 4-quart or 6-quart sizes) will work adequately.

*A soft resin with a pungent, rich flavor, particularly popular in Indian and Middle Eastern cooking, and often used as a replacement for onions or garlic.

To "quick-release" the pressure in your cooker, follow the instructions in the manual that comes with your equipment, or place the cooker in a sinkful of cold tap water until the pressure has dissipated.

To let the pressure come down naturally, turn off the heat and let the cooker sit until the pressure drops of its own accord. This will generally take anywhere from 3 to 20 minutes. If a recipe's instructions call for letting the pressure drop naturally for 10 minutes, keep the lid in place even if the pressure comes down faster. *Always release any remaining pressure before trying to remove the lid!*

When you remove the lid of your pressure cooker, hold it at an angle facing away from you, even if all the pressure has been released naturally, as there can still be residual steam in the pot.

A Note From Mary:
I'm probably not the best example of a small quantity cook. Having raised a large family, I've become quite used to cooking plentiful amounts. The biggest difference between how I cook now and how I used to cook is that although I still make large quantities of food, I keep leftovers in the refrigerator to use throughout the week. Therefore we have to cook less often. It's also helpful for me to have food prepared and stored in the refrigerator in case company or family stops in unexpectedly.

RICE & GRAINS FOR TWO
Stovetop Cooking Guide
(Amounts of uncooked grain to start with are listed in parentheses.)

Amaranth (1/2 cup)
Heat amaranth and 1 1/4 cups *cold* liquid to a boil. Do not add salt until after the grain is cooked. Reduce heat to low, cover, and simmer 20 to 25 minutes; makes 1 cup.

Barley (pearl—1/2 cup)
Heat 1 2/3 cups liquid to a boil. Stir in the barley and reduce heat to low. Cover and simmer 55 to 60 minutes. Remove from heat and let stand covered 10 minutes; makes 2 cups.

Barley (quick-cooking—1/2 cup)
Heat 1 cup liquid to a boil. Stir in barley and reduce heat to low. Cover and simmer 10 to 12 minutes. Remove from heat and let stand covered 5 minutes; makes 1 1/2 cups.

Buckwheat (kasha—1/2 cup)
If buckwheat is not roasted, you can roast it, if desired, in a dry skillet or saucepan until it is dark brown and fragrant. Add 1 cup liquid and bring to a boil. Reduce heat to low, cover, and simmer 10 to 12 minutes. Remove from heat and let stand covered 5 minutes; makes 1 1/2 cups.

Bulgur (1/2 cup)
Stovetop Method: Heat 1 cup liquid to a boil. Stir in bulgur and reduce heat to low; cover and simmer 20 minutes. Remove from heat and let stand covered 5 minutes; makes 1 1/2 cups.
Soaking Method: Pour boiling liquid over bulgur and soak 30 to 60 minutes. Do not cook. Drain, if necessary, or place bulgur in a wire mesh strainer, and press firmly to express excess liquid; makes 1 1/2 cups.

Couscous (1/2 cup)
Heat 1 cup liquid to a boil. Stir in couscous and reduce heat to low; cover and simmer 1 minute. Remove from heat and let stand covered 5 minutes; makes 1 1/2 cups.

Millet (1/2 cup)
For a richer flavor and fluffier texture, toast millet before simmering it. To toast, heat a heavy skillet over a medium flame. Add the rinsed millet and stir until all of the rinse water has evaporated. Lower the heat slightly and continue to stir until the grains begin to pop, turn a shade darker, and release a roasted aroma similar to popcorn. Add 1 1/4 cups liquid and bring to a boil. Reduce heat to low, cover, and simmer until all the liquid has been absorbed, about 20 to 25 minutes. Remove from heat and let stand covered 5 minutes; makes 1 1/2 cups.

Quinoa (1/2 cup)
Heat 1 cup liquid to a boil. Stir in thoroughly rinsed quinoa and reduce heat to low. Cover and simmer until all the liquid has been absorbed, about 15 minutes. Remove from heat and let stand covered 5 minutes; makes 1 1/2 cups.

Rice, Brown (and brown basmati—1/2 cup)
Heat the liquid to a boil (1 cup plus 2 to 4 tablespoons—short grain brown rice will require the most liquid). Stir in rice and reduce heat to low. Cover and simmer until all the liquid has been absorbed, about 35 to 45 minutes. (Short grain brown rice will require the longer time.) Remove from heat and let stand covered 10 minutes; makes 1 1/2 cups.

Rice, Precooked Brown (quick-cooking—1 cup)
Heat 1 1/4 cups liquid to a boil. Stir in rice, reduce heat to medium, and simmer *uncovered* until all the liquid has been absorbed, about 10 to 14 minutes. Remove from heat and let stand covered 1 to 2 minutes; makes 1 1/2 cups.

Rice, Precooked Brown (instant—1 cup)
Heat 1 cup liquid to a boil. Stir in rice, return to a boil, and reduce heat to low. Cover and simmer until all the liquid has been absorbed, about 5 minutes. Remove from heat, and let stand covered 5 minutes; makes 1 1/4 cups.

Rice, White (basmati or extra long grain—1/2 cup)
Heat 1 cup plus 2 Tablespoons liquid to a boil. Stir in rice and reduce heat to low. Cover and simmer until all the liquid has been absorbed, about 15 to 20 minutes. Remove from heat and let stand covered 5 minutes. Fluff with a fork before serving; makes 1 1/2 cups.

Rice, Wild (1/2 cup)
Heat 1 1/4 cups liquid to a boil. Stir in rice and reduce heat to low. Cover and simmer 50 to 55 minutes, or until most of the rice is "butterflied" (split open). Cover and let stand 10 minutes. If excess liquid remains, drain it off and let the rice steam, covered, for just a few minutes to dry out; makes 1 1/2 cups.

Rice, Arborio (1/2 cup)
Heat 1 cup liquid to a boil. Stir in rice and reduce heat to low. Cover and simmer until all the liquid has been absorbed, about 15 to 20 minutes. Remove from heat and let stand covered 5 minutes. Fluff with a fork before serving; makes 1 1/2 cups.

PASTA
The standard I recommend for determining main dish pasta quantities for two adults is two to four ounces (one-eighth to one-quarter pound) of pasta per person. The following equivalents should help:

1/4 pound (4 ounces)
uncooked spaghetti noodles =
about one 1-inch-thick bundle =
approx. 2 cups cooked

4 ounces uncooked macaroni,
small shells, spirals, or flat noodles =
about 1 1/2 cups dry =
approx. 2 to 3 cups cooked

RICE & GRAINS FOR TWO
Pressure Cooking Guide
(Amounts of uncooked grain to start with are listed in parentheses.)

Amaranth (1/2 cup)
Place amaranth and 1 cup *cold* liquid in pressure cooker. Do not add salt. Lock lid in place and bring to high pressure over high heat. Lower heat just enough to maintain pressure. After reducing heat, cook for 3 minutes. Remove from heat and let pressure come down naturally for 10 minutes; makes 1 cup.

Barley (pearl—1/2 cup)
Place pearl barley and 1 1/2 cups liquid in pressure cooker. Add 1 teaspoon of canola oil to help control foaming. Lock lid in place and bring to high pressure over high heat. Lower heat just enough to maintain pressure. After reducing heat, cook for 18 to 20 minutes. Use "quick release" method or allow pressure to come down naturally; makes 1 3/4 cups.

Buckwheat (kasha—1/2 cup)
If buckwheat is not roasted, you can dry roast it over medium heat in the open pot of the pressure cooker. Stir constantly until kernels are dark brown and fragrant. Add 1 cup liquid all at once, then add 1 teaspoon of canola oil to help control foaming. Lock lid in place and bring to high pressure over high heat. Lower heat just enough to maintain pressure. After reducing heat, cook for 2 minutes. Remove from heat and let pressure come down naturally for 8 minutes; makes 1 1/2 cups.

Bulgur (1/2 cup)
Place bulgur and 1 cup liquid in pressure cooker. Lock lid in place and bring to high pressure over high heat. Lower heat just enough to maintain pressure. After reducing heat, cook for 4 minutes. Remove from heat and let pressure come down naturally for 10 minutes; makes 1 1/4 cups.

Millet (1/2 cup)
If you prefer, millet can be roasted in the open pot of the dry pressure cooker until golden brown and fragrant. Add 1 1/4 cups liquid. Lock lid in place and bring to high pressure over high heat. Lower heat just enough to maintain pressure. After reducing heat, cook for 10 minutes. Remove from heat and let pressure come down naturally for 10 minutes; makes 1 3/4 cups.

Quinoa (1/2 cup)
Place quinoa and 1 cup liquid in pressure cooker. Lock lid in place and bring to high pressure over high heat. Lower heat just enough to maintain pressure. Remove from heat and let pressure come down naturally for 10 minutes; makes 1 2/3 cups.

Rice, Brown (and brown basmati—1/2 cup)
Place rice and 1 1/4 cups liquid in pressure cooker. Lock lid in place and bring to high pressure over high heat. Lower heat just enough to maintain pressure. After reducing heat, cook for 20 minutes. (Short grain brown rice will require an additional 5 minutes of cooking time.) Remove from heat and allow pressure to come down naturally for 20 minutes; makes 1 1/2 cups.

Rice, White (basmati or extra long grain—1/2 cup)
Place rice and 1 cup liquid in pressure cooker. Lock lid in place and bring to high pressure over high heat. Lower heat just enough to maintain pressure. After reducing heat, cook for 2 minutes. Remove from heat and allow pressure to come down naturally for 7 minutes; makes 1 1/2 cups.

Rice, Wild (1/2 cup)
Place rice and 1 1/4 cups liquid in pressure cooker. Lock lid in place and bring to high pressure over high heat. Lower heat just enough to maintain pressure. After reducing heat, cook for 20 to 25 minutes. If most of the rice is not "butterflied" (split open), return it to high pressure for a few minutes or simmer, covered, (but not under pressure), until done. After the cooking time has elapsed, quick-release the pressure or allow the pressure to come down naturally. If excess water remains at the end of the cooking time, drain it off and return the rice to the pot. Let the rice steam, covered (but not under pressure), over low heat, for just a few minutes to dry out; makes 1 1/2 cups.

A Note From Anne & Matt:
The most important advice we could give someone regarding cooking is to plan as completely as possible! Every minute spent planning a menu and a shopping list will be rewarded tenfold. For example, look at your upcoming week, and see when you (or your partner) will be able to cook. Do you have evening meetings or engagements? Do you have a bit more time on certain days? What can be made in larger quantities to be eaten throughout the week? Make a weekly menu according to your schedule, and use this menu to create your grocery list. A thorough grocery list is the biggest time saver of all!

CLEANING & PREPARING POTATOES & SWEET POTATOES

Both potatoes and sweet potatoes should be scrubbed well under running tap water just before cooking, using a stiff vegetable brush. Completely remove any "eyes" and discolored areas. Whenever possible, leave skins on when cooking to lock in the nutrients. Although the skin does contain fiber and iron, it is not necessary to eat the skin since much of the potato's nourishment is just beneath it.

TIP #1: To prevent cut and/or peeled white potatoes from darkening, keep them immersed in cold water until you cook them.

TIP #2: To prevent cut and/or peeled sweet potatoes from discoloring, place them in a bowl of cold water to which a little lemon juice has been added. Just before using, place the sweet potatoes in a colander, and rinse off the lemon water thoroughly.

TIP #3: Keep bite-size steamed potatoes or cooked sweet potato chunks in the refrigerator for handy snacks.

Steamed Potatoes

To steam potatoes or sweet potatoes, place one-inch of water in a 2-quart or 4 1/2-quart saucepan or Dutch oven (depending on the quantity you are preparing). Add the potatoes and bring the water to a boil. Reduce the heat to medium, cover the saucepan with a lid, and cook the potatoes until they are tender. Alternately, place a stainless steel vegetable steamer basket or steamer insert inside the pot so that the potatoes do not sit in the water. Whole potatoes will take about 40 to 45 minutes to cook, depending on their size, and chunked potatoes will take approximately 20 to 25 minutes.

Pressure Cooked Potatoes

You can also steam potatoes in a pressure cooker using the same techniques as steaming. In a pressure cooker, chunks will take about 10 minutes to cook. Small whole potatoes will take about 20 to 25 minutes. Prior to cooking, be sure to prick whole potatoes all over with a fork to prevent them from bursting in the pressure cooker.

TIP: The water left over from steaming potatoes is ideal for bread making. The starchy liquid makes yeast breads soft, moist, and exceptionally light.

Oven Baked Potatoes

To bake potatoes or sweet potatoes, prick them all over with a fork to allow steam to escape during cooking. Place the potatoes directly on the oven rack (sweet potatoes should be placed on a tray because of the syrupy juice that trickles out when they cook). Bake at 375°F for 1 1/2 to 2 hours or 400°F for 1 to 1 1/2 hours, or until a fork slides easily into the center and they feel soft when gently squeezed.

TIP: Always use an oven mitt when handling hot potatoes to keep from getting burned.

Oven "Fried" Potatoes

Yield: 2 side dish servings

Per serving: Calories: 136; Protein: 2 gm., Fat: 2 gm., Carbohydrate: 27 gm.

You may be surprised how easy it is to make healthful "oven-fries." Season them as you like, or serve them with ketchup, the perfect potato condiment.

2 large russet potatoes

1 teaspoon canola oil
1/4 to 1/2 teaspoon paprika
1/4 to 1/2 teaspoon salt, to taste (optional)
ground black pepper, to taste (optional)
garlic granules, to taste (optional)
pinch of turmeric (optional)

The Cook's Secrets:
If you like your fries a little spicier, omit the paprika and instead use 1/2 teaspoon curry powder, garam masala, hot Hungarian paprika, or chili powder.

Leftover cooked potatoes can also be oven "fried." Cut them into chunks and prepare and bake them as directed above. Even though they are already cooked, they will get brown, crusty, and even more tender when prepared in this fashion.

1. Preheat the oven to 400°F.

2. Scrub the potatoes well and remove any eyes and discolored areas. Peel the potatoes, if desired, and cut them into wedges or french fry shapes. Place the pieces in a large mixing bowl.

3. Sprinkle the potatoes with the oil, and toss to coat them evenly.

4. Then sprinkle the seasonings of your choice over the potatoes, and toss them again so all the pieces are evenly coated.

5. Spread the potatoes in a single layer on a large baking sheet. Bake them for 30 to 40 minutes, or until they are golden brown and tender, turning them over once with a metal spatula midway in the cooking cycle.

Twice-Baked Potatoes

Flavor these to suit your personal taste, or make them "restaurant style" with "the works." Children and adults alike enjoy selecting their own special seasonings.

2 large russet potatoes
1/3 cup low-fat, non-dairy milk, more or less as
   needed

OPTIONAL SEASONINGS (select as many as
   you like):
1 small, ripe tomato, seeded and chopped
1 small carrot, pared and shredded
1/3 cup scallions, thinly sliced
1/4 cup red or green bell pepper, minced
1/4 cup leftover cooked vegetables, chopped
1/4 cup black olives, sliced
2 to 4 Tablespoons fresh cilantro leaves,
   chopped
2 to 4 Tablespoons fresh parsley, chopped
2 to 4 Tablespoons other fresh herbs, chopped
2 to 3 Tablespoons nutritional yeast flakes
1 to 2 Tablespoons prepared horseradish (not
   creamed)
1 to 2 Tablespoons onion, minced
1 Tablespoon vegetarian bacon bits
2 to 3 teaspoons poppy seeds, sesame seeds,
   or sunflower seeds
1 to 2 teaspoons olive oil
1 teaspoon anchovy-free Worcestershire sauce
1/2 to 1 teaspoon Dijon mustard
1 to 2 cloves garlic, finely minced or pressed, or
   1/4 to 1/2 teaspoon garlic granules
1/4 teaspoon crushed hot red pepper flakes, or
   to taste
1/2 teaspoon dried herbs, to taste (basil, dill
   weed, oregano, tarragon, thyme, etc.)

1/4 teaspoon salt, or to taste
ground black pepper, to taste
several drops Tabasco sauce, to taste
paprika, as needed (for garnish)

1. Preheat the oven to 400°F.

2. Scrub the potatoes and pat them dry. Prick the potatoes all over with a fork, and place them directly on the center rack in the preheated oven. Bake the potatoes for 1 to 1 1/2 hours, or until they are very tender when gently squeezed (wear an oven mitt!).

3. Remove the potatoes from the oven using an oven mitt. *Do not turn the oven off.* Slice each potato in half lengthwise. Scoop out the pulp of the potato with a spoon, leaving about 1/4-inch of pulp in each shell to help it keep its shape.

4. Place the pulp in a medium mixing bowl. Place the scooped out shells on a dry baking sheet, and set them aside.

5. Using a potato masher, electric hand mixer, or sturdy fork, mash the potatoes until they are smooth.

6. Gradually beat in the milk, using just enough to make the potatoes creamy but not mushy. Then stir in the optional seasonings of your choice, mixing well until they are evenly distributed.

7. Spoon the seasoned potato mixture evenly into the reserved shells. Dust the tops lightly with paprika, if desired.

8. Return the stuffed potatoes to the 400°F oven. Bake them for 20 to 25 minutes, or until they are heated through.

Yield: 2 main dish servings (or 4 side dish servings)

Per serving: Calories: 131; Protein: 2 gm., Fat: 0 gm., Carbohydrate: 30 gm.

The Cook's Secrets:
If you and your dining partner have different seasoning preferences, this recipe is sure to please you both. Simply follow the recipe up to step #6. Beat in the milk, then divide the mixture in half. Keep one half in the original mixing bowl, and transfer the other half to a separate mixing bowl. Season each half as preferred, and proceed with the recipe as directed.

After stuffing them, you can store Twice-Baked Potatoes for several hours in the refrigerator, loosely covered with foil, plastic wrap, or waxed paper. Just add an additional 5 minutes to the final baking time.

Hash Browns

Crisp and tender is the way we like our hash browns. Try them with ketchup or gravy or a little of each.

1 large russet potato, shredded (it is not necessary to peel the potato; just scrub it well)
2 Tablespoons onion, grated or very finely minced
1/4 teaspoon salt
pinch of ground black pepper, or to taste

1. Place all the ingredients in a medium mixing bowl, and toss them together until everything is evenly distributed.

2. Mist a 9-inch or 10-inch skillet with nonstick cooking spray or coat the skillet with a thin layer of canola oil. Place the skillet over medium heat. When the skillet is hot, add the potato mixture, spreading it out into a large, thin patty using a metal spatula or the back of a spoon.

3. Cover the skillet with a lid, and cook the hash browns for 10 to 15 minutes, or until the bottom of the patty is crisp and brown.

4. Using a metal spatula, cut the patty in half, and turn each half over separately. Cook uncovered for 10 minutes longer, or until the bottom of the patty is crisp and brown and the potato is tender.

Yield: 2 side dish servings

Per serving: Calories: 119; Protein: 2 gm., Fat: 0 gm, Carbohydrate: 28 gm.

The Cook's Secrets:
A food processor fitted with a shredding disc will make easy work of preparing the potato. The potato should be cooked immediately; otherwise, it will discolor.

Stuffed Sweet Potatoes

Sweet, creamy and delicious—kids love 'em.

2 large sweet potatoes or yams

1 8-ounce can crushed pineapple, drained
1/4 cup raisins or currants
1 Tablespoon apple juice concentrate
1/4 teaspoon ground cinnamon
1/8 teaspoon ground allspice
1/8 teaspoon ground cloves
salt, to taste

1. Preheat the oven to 400°F.

2. Scrub the potatoes and pat them dry. Prick them all over with a fork, and place them on a dry baking sheet. Bake them for 1 to 1 1/2 hours, or until they are very tender.

3. Remove the sweet potatoes from the oven using an oven mitt. *Do not turn the oven off.* Slice each potato in half lengthwise. Scoop out the pulp with a spoon, leaving about 1/4-inch of potato pulp in each shell to help it keep its shape.

4. Place the pulp in a medium mixing bowl. Return the scooped out shells to the baking sheet, and set them aside.

5. Using a potato masher, electric hand mixer, or sturdy fork, mash the potatoes until they are smooth. Add the remaining ingredients and stir to combine them thoroughly.

6. Spoon the potato mixture into the reserved shells, distributing it among them evenly.

7. Return the stuffed potatoes to the 400°F oven. Bake them for 15 to 20 minutes, or until they are heated through.

Yield: 2 main dish servings (or 4 side dish servings)

Per serving: Calories: 294; Protein: 2 gm., Fat: 0 gm., Carbohydrate: 70 gm.

The Cook's Secrets:
Prior to the second baking, Stuffed Sweet Potatoes may be stored several hours or overnight in the refrigerator, loosely covered with foil, plastic wrap, or waxed paper. Add an additional 5 minutes to the final baking time.
    Reserve the drained pineapple juice—it's delicious to drink.

A Note From Mary:
Ray and I like to make generous quantities whenever we cook, a holdover from raising a large family. We keep the leftovers in the refrigerator and use them in creative ways throughout the week. For instance, if we are making mashed potatoes we'll cook up a huge amount. With the leftovers we might make potato pancakes or patties the following day. Then, the day after that, we might make shepherd's pie. It's fun and challenging to use up leftovers in this way.

Favorite Mashed Potatoes

This basic standard is often overlooked with today's harried schedules—yet homemade mashed potatoes are incredibly quick and simple to make from scratch.

2 1/2 cups potatoes, peeled and cubed (about 1 pound)

1/4 to 1/2 cup low-fat, non-dairy milk, as needed
1 to 2 teaspoons olive oil

1/2 teaspoon garlic granules, or to taste
1/2 teaspoon salt, or to taste
ground black pepper, to taste

1. Place 1 inch of water in a 4 1/2-saucepan or Dutch oven.

2. Add the potatoes and bring the water to a boil. Reduce the heat to medium, cover the saucepan with a lid, and cook the potatoes until they are very tender, about 20 to 25 minutes.

3. Drain the potatoes in a colander, and place them in a large mixing bowl. Alternately, transfer the potatoes from the saucepan to the bowl using a slotted spoon.

4. Add the milk and olive oil to the potatoes. Mash the potatoes using a potato masher, electric hand beater, or sturdy fork until they are smooth. Use only as much milk as necessary to achieve the consistency you desire. The potatoes should be thick and fluffy, not runny.

5. Season the potatoes with the garlic granules and salt and pepper, to taste. Serve hot.

Yield: 2 side dish servings

Per serving: Calories: 240; Protein: 3 gm., Fat: 4 gm., Carbohydrate: 48 gm.

The Cook's Secrets:
If you aren't serving the mashed potatoes immediately, they may be kept hot for about 30 minutes in a double boiler. (A double boiler is an arrangement of two saucepans designed to fit together, one nesting partway inside the other. A single lid fits both saucepans. The lower pot is used to hold simmering water which gently heats the food contained in the upper pot.)

For a more delicate and different taste, try mixing in other cooked, mashed vegetables such as carrots, parsnips, or peeled winter squash which complement the flavor of potatoes nicely. To save washing an additional pot, you can steam these vegetables right along with the potatoes.

Save the potato cooking water to use as vegetable broth. It also is great to use in yeast-risen breads.

Instant Mashed Potatoes

This recipe is for people who don't believe that mashed potatoes really can be made from scratch in under thirty minutes and for those who don't even have thirty minutes to spare. This makes gobs of mashed potatoes—just the way we like 'em.

1 cup water
1 to 2 teaspoons olive oil

1 cup low-fat, non-dairy milk
1 2/3 cups instant potato flakes
1/2 teaspoon salt
1/2 teaspoon garlic granules (optional)
ground black pepper, to taste

1. Place the water and olive oil in a 2-quart saucepan, and bring them to a boil.

2. Turn off the heat and add the milk to the boiling liquid.

3. Using a fork, stir in the potato flakes, and seasonings until the mixture is very smooth and well combined. Serve hot.

Yield: 2 side dish servings

Per serving: Calories: 276; Protein: 5 gm., Fat: 4 gm., Carbohydrate: 50 gm.

The Cook's Secrets:
For a creamier consistency, stir in a tiny bit more milk. For a stiffer consistency, stir in more potato flakes.

If you like, stir fresh snipped chives, whole celery seeds, sautéed garlic, or other favorite seasonings into the hot mashed potatoes.

If you are not serving the potatoes immediately, cover the saucepan with a lid, and serve them within 10 minutes. If you need to keep the potatoes hot longer than that, place them in a double boiler. (See The Cook's Secrets on page 141.)

Old Country Potatoes

This recipe was inspired by one my mother-in-law makes. It's a hearty, peasant-style dish that is exceptionally easy to prepare.

2/3 cup water
2 1/2 cups potatoes, peeled and cubed (about 1 pound)
1 cup onions, coarsely chopped

1 to 2 Tablespoons fresh parsley, chopped
1 to 2 teaspoons olive oil
1/2 teaspoon salt, or to taste
1/4 teaspoon paprika
ground black pepper, to taste

1. Place the water in a 4 1/2-quart saucepan or Dutch oven.

2. Add the potatoes and onions, and bring the water to a boil. Reduce the heat to medium, cover the saucepan with a lid, and cook the potatoes until they are very tender, about 20 to 25 minutes, stirring once or twice.

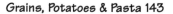

3. Remove the saucepan from the heat. *Do not drain the potatoes.* Add the parsley and olive oil to the pot, and mash the potatoes and onions with the cooking water (right in the pot) using a potato masher or sturdy fork. The potatoes should be slightly chunky and slightly creamy.

4. Season with the salt, paprika, and pepper, to taste. Serve hot.

Yield: 2 side dish servings

Per serving: Calories: 228; Protein: 3 gm., Fat: 2 gm., Carbohydrate: 46 gm.

Aunt Shayna's Potato Cakes

This recipe is from my book *The Uncheese Cookbook*. It's such an easy and delicious dish, and the perfect amount for two, I couldn't resist sharing it with you here.

1 cup low-fat, non-dairy milk

1/2 cup quick-cooking rolled oats (not instant)

1 cup instant potato flakes
2 medium carrots, pared and shredded
1 stalk celery, finely minced
1 small onion, grated
3 Tablespoons nutritional yeast flakes
1/2 teaspoon salt
ground black pepper, to taste

1. Place the milk in a 2-quart saucepan, and bring it to a boil.

2. Remove the saucepan from the heat, and stir in the oats.

3. Cover the saucepan with a lid, and let the mixture stand for 5 minutes.

4. Stir in the remaining ingredients, mixing thoroughly. The mixture will be stiff.

5. Form the mixture into 8 small patties using water-moistened hands. Place the patties on a sheet of waxed paper as they are formed.

6. Mist a 9-inch or 10-inch skillet with nonstick cooking spray, or coat the skillet with a thin layer of canola oil. Heat the skillet over medium-high. When the skillet is hot, add the patties and reduce the heat to medium. Slowly brown the patties on both sides, turning them once with a metal spatula. Depending on the size of your skillet, you will need to cook the patties in several batches. Serve hot or warm.

Yield: 2 main dish servings (4 potato cakes per person)

Per serving: Calories: 327; Protein: 13 gm., Fat: 4 gm., Carbohydrate: 60 gm.

The Cook's Secrets:
To keep the potato cakes warm, place them on a nonstick baking sheet or on a baking sheet that has been misted with nonstick cooking spray. Put the cooked potato cakes in a preheated 300°F oven until all of them have been browned and you are ready to serve them.

Brown Rice Croquettes

These delicious, log-shaped croquettes make a tasty entrée for lunch or dinner or an unusual sandwich filling. Serve them plain or with ketchup or gravy.

1 cup water or vegetable broth
3/4 cup quick-cooking brown rice (not instant)

2 Tablespoons peanut butter or almond butter
   (crunchy or smooth)

2 Tablespoons quick-cooking rolled oats (not
   instant)
1/2 teaspoon dried sage, crumbled
1/2 teaspoon dried marjoram leaves
1/2 teaspoon onion granules
salt and ground black pepper, to taste

1. Preheat the oven to 350°F. Mist a baking sheet with nonstick cooking spray, and set it aside.

2. Place the water or broth in a 1-quart saucepan, and bring it to a boil. Stir in the rice and reduce the heat to medium. Simmer the rice *uncovered* for about 12 to 14 minutes, or until the liquid has been absorbed.

3. Transfer the rice to a small mixing bowl. Stir in the peanut butter or almond butter until it is well incorporated. Then stir in the remaining ingredients in the order given.

4. Form the mixture into 6 finger-length logs using water-moistened hands. Place the logs on the prepared baking sheet as soon as they are formed.

5. Bake the croquettes for 15 to 20 minutes, or until they are hot and the surface is crisp.

Yield: 6 croquettes (2 servings)

Per serving: Calories: 287; Protein: 8 gm., Fat: 9 gm, Carbohydrate: 44 gm.

Pierogies in a Pot

Pierogies are a Polish specialty consisting of half-moon-shaped noodle dumplings stuffed with different minced or mashed mixtures. Some common, traditional fillings include onions, potatoes, cottage cheese, mushrooms, and cabbage. After the pierogies are boiled in water, they are often sautéed in butter and topped with toasted bread crumbs. Karen Bernard concocted this wonderful, healthful recipe to satisfy her craving for pierogies while eliminating the effort and mess that typically goes along with making them.

2 cups green cabbage, shredded or thinly sliced
1 1/2 cups potatoes, peeled and cubed
1 large onion, thinly sliced or chopped

1 1/2 cups rotini (spiral twist pasta), bow tie
   pasta, or wide noodles (egg-free)

salt and ground black pepper, to taste
2 to 3 teaspoons olive oil

1. Place the cabbage, potatoes, and onion in a steamer basket or steamer insert in a large saucepan filled with an inch of water. Bring the water to a boil. Cover the saucepan with a lid, and reduce the heat to medium. Steam the vegetables until the potatoes are very tender, about 40 to 45 minutes.

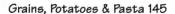

2. Meanwhile, fill a 4 1/2-quart saucepan or Dutch oven halfway with water. Bring the water to a rolling boil. Add the pasta and cook it until it is al dente. Drain the pasta well and return it to the saucepan. Cover the saucepan with a lid to keep the pasta warm, and set it aside.

3. When the vegetables are tender, add them to the pasta in the saucepan. Season the mixture with salt, pepper, and olive oil, to taste. Toss gently and serve.

Yield: 2 main dish servings

Per serving: Calories: 366; Protein: 8 gm., Fat: 6 gm., Carbohydrate: 68 gm.

The Cook's Secrets:
For eye appeal, a small amount of grated carrot, a few pimiento pieces, a pinch of crushed hot red pepper flakes, or a light dusting of paprika may be used as a garnish. Alternately, use spinach rotini or tomato rotini or a colorful combination of both.

Macaroni Skillet Dinner

Both children and adults enjoy this quick pasta dish. Serve it with steamed greens on the side.

1 14.5-ounce can whole tomatoes, with juice
2/3 cup water
1/2 cup onion, chopped

1 cup ziti or penne pasta
4 ounces (1/4 pound) tempeh, grated on the
    coarse side of a grater

3 Tablespoons fresh parsley, minced,
    or 1 Tablespoon dried parsley flakes
1 Tablespoon soy sauce
1 teaspoon dried oregano leaves
1/2 teaspoon dried basil leaves
1/8 teaspoon ground black pepper

salt, to taste

1. Pour the tomatoes and their juice into a 9-inch or 10-inch skillet. Break the tomatoes apart with your hands or the side of a spoon. Add the water and onion, and bring the mixture to a boil.

2. Stir the remaining ingredients *except the salt* into the boiling sauce. Reduce the heat to medium, and cover the skillet with a lid. Simmer the mixture until the pasta is tender, about 15 minutes, stirring occasionally to prevent sticking.

3. Season with salt, to taste. Serve hot.

Yield: 2 main dish servings

Per serving: Calories: 284; Protein: 16 gm., Fat: 5 gm., Carbohydrate: 44 gm.

The Cook's Secrets:
If the pasta is tender but the mixture is too juicy for your liking, simmer it for another minute or two uncovered.

Michael's Hot Pasta Salad

My husband Michael calls this a "desperation dinner." He doesn't really have a recipe for this mixture, but I tried my best to quantify it for you. This dish arose after a particularly grueling workday. I started out making a pasta recipe but was too exhausted to finish it. Michael took over and added his own creative flair. To our amazement it turned out to be great, and it is now one of Michael's "specialties of the house."

1 cup elbow macaroni or other small pasta of
   your choice

2 cups cauliflower or broccoli, cut into bite-size
   florets
1/2 of a red or green bell pepper, chopped
1/2 of a medium onion, coarsely chopped
1/8 teaspoon crushed hot red pepper flakes
1 medium zucchini or yellow squash, sliced in half
   lengthwise and sliced into half moons

approximately 2/3 cup low-fat salad dressing
   (use any of the recipes in this book or your
   favorite low-fat bottled dressing), as needed

salt and ground black pepper, to taste

1. Fill a 4 1/2-quart saucepan or Dutch oven two-thirds full with water. Bring the water to a rolling boil, and cook the macaroni in it until it is al dente. Drain the macaroni well and return it to the saucepan. Cover the saucepan with a lid to keep the pasta warm, and set it aside.

2. Meanwhile, place the cauliflower or broccoli in a steamer basket or steamer insert in a large saucepan filled with an inch of water.

Bring the water to a boil. Cover the saucepan with a lid, and reduce the heat to medium. Steam the cauliflower or broccoli for 5 to 8 minutes, or until the florets are just barely starting to get tender.

3. Layer the bell pepper, onion, and crushed hot red pepper flakes over the broccoli or cauliflower, and steam them for 3 to 4 minutes.

4. Next, layer on the zucchini, and steam all the vegetables for about 5 minutes longer, or until everything is tender to your liking.

5. Stir the steamed vegetables into the reserved pasta in the saucepan (from step #1). Pour in enough dressing to moisten everything sufficiently. Toss well.

6. Season the mixture with salt and pepper, to taste. Toss again gently and serve.

Yield: 2 main dish servings

Per serving: Calories: 183; Protein: 6 gm., Fat: 0 gm., Carbohydrate: 38 gm.

The Cook's Secrets:
For a more substantial meal, cubed tofu, tempeh, seitan, or cooked beans may be placed on the steamer rack along with the vegetables.

   Other vegetables may be substituted for the ones listed here. This recipe is particularly amenable to whatever leftovers or bits and pieces of vegetables you have huddling in your refrigerator. Just put the longest cooking ones in the steamer basket first to let them soften a bit. Then layer on the other vegetables according to their cooking times, putting the shortest cooking vegetables in last.

Peanut Butter Noodles

Yield: 2 main dish servings

Per serving: Calories: 483; Protein: 27 gm., Fat: 16 gm., Carbohydrate: 56 gm.

I devised this dish for my niece Hillary when she was five years old. My sister Peggy said Hillary would never touch tofu, and I wanted to prove her wrong. I told her that these were "Auntie Jo's *famous* peanut butter noodles." (Okay, so I "fibbed a little.") Well—to our surprise she loved them! I omitted the Tabasco sauce for Hillary, but I included it in this version for any adults who prefer a little heat.

1 1/2 cups ziti or penne pasta

4 Tablespoons brown rice vinegar
3 Tablespoons peanut butter (smooth or crunchy)
3 Tablespoons soy sauce
2 Tablespoons tomato paste
few drops Tabasco sauce, to taste (optional)
1/2 pound fat-reduced firm regular tofu, cut into 1/2-inch cubes (press if time permits; see the directions for pressing tofu on p. 155)

1. Fill a 4 1/2-quart saucepan or Dutch oven two-thirds full with water. Bring the water to a rolling boil, and cook the pasta in it until it is al dente. Drain the pasta well and return it to the saucepan. Cover the saucepan with a lid to keep the pasta warm, and set it aside.

2. Place the vinegar, peanut butter, soy sauce, tomato paste, and Tabasco (if using) in a small mixing bowl. Mix well to form a smooth sauce.

3. Stir the sauce into the warm pasta. Then fold in the tofu, taking care not to break apart the cubes. Mix gently but thoroughly. Serve warm or chilled.

A Note From Michael:
Whenever I make pasta with steamed vegetables and the pasta is finished first, I drain the pasta and return it to the pot. Then I add a little non-alcoholic wine to keep the noodles moist. The wine imparts flavor without added fat and keeps the pasta from sticking together when the vegetables are tossed with it.

Baked Macaroni & Vegetable Casseroles

Try this creamy casserole instead of traditional macaroni and cheese. It just might become your preferred new "comfort food."

1 cup elbow macaroni

1 10-ounce package frozen mixed vegetables

3 Tablespoons whole wheat pastry flour
3 Tablespoons nutritional yeast flakes
1/2 teaspoon dried oregano leaves
1/4 teaspoon garlic granules
1/4 teaspoon salt
1/8 teaspoon ground black pepper

1 cup water

4 teaspoons tahini

1 small, ripe tomato, sliced

1. Preheat the oven to 375°F. Coat two 15-ounce or 16-ounce casserole dishes with nonstick cooking spray, and set them aside.

2. Fill a 4 1/2-quart saucepan or Dutch oven halfway full with water. Bring the water to a rolling boil. Add the macaroni and cook it until it is al dente, adding the frozen mixed vegetables during the last 3 to 5 minutes of cooking. Drain the pasta and vegetables well, and return the mixture to the saucepan. Cover the saucepan with a lid to keep the mixture warm, and set it aside.

3. To make a creamy sauce, place the flour, yeast flakes, oregano, garlic granules, salt, and pepper in a 1-quart saucepan, and stir them together until they are well combined. Gradually whisk in the water, stirring briskly until the mixture is smooth.

4. Place the saucepan over medium heat, and cook the sauce, stirring almost constantly with a wire whisk, until it is thickened and bubbly. Remove the saucepan from the heat, and whisk in the tahini.

5. Stir the hot sauce into the drained pasta mixture (from step #2), and toss them together until the pasta and vegetables are evenly coated.

6. Spoon the macaroni and vegetable mixture into the prepared casserole dishes. Bake the casseroles for 10 minutes.

7. Using oven mitts, remove the casseroles from the oven. Top them with the tomato slices, and return the casseroles to the oven. Bake them for 5 minutes longer. Serve hot.

Yield: 2 main dish servings

Per serving: Calories: 368; Protein: 15 gm., Fat: 6 gm., Carbohydrate: 62 gm.

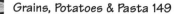

Cabbage & Pasta Bake

One of my husband's favorite recipes, this casserole is hearty, homey, and down-right delicious.

1 cup bow-tie pasta or elbow macaroni

1/2 cup carrots, pared and thinly sliced

3 cups green cabbage, shredded or thinly sliced
2/3 cup water or vegetable broth
3 Tablespoons nutritional yeast flakes (optional)
1 teaspoon whole caraway seeds, or 1/2 teaspoon ground caraway seeds
1/4 teaspoon ground black pepper

1/2 pound fat-reduced, firm regular tofu, rinsed, patted dry, and well mashed
1 Tablespoon prepared yellow mustard

1/3 cup low-fat, non-dairy milk
2 teaspoons cornstarch

2 scallions, sliced

salt, to taste

1. Preheat the oven to 375°F. Coat two 15-ounce or 16-ounce individual casserole dishes with nonstick cooking spray, and set them aside.

2. Fill a 4 1/2-quart saucepan or Dutch oven two-thirds full with water. Bring the water to a rolling boil, and cook the pasta in it until it is al dente. Add the sliced carrots during the last 5 minutes of cooking the pasta. Drain the pasta and carrots well, and set them aside.

3. In the same 4 1/2-quart saucepan or Dutch oven, place the cabbage, water or broth, yeast flakes (if using), caraway seeds, and pepper. Bring the mixture to a boil. Reduce the heat to medium-low, cover the saucepan with a lid, and simmer the mixture for 5 minutes. Then stir in the tofu and mustard.

4. Measure the milk in a small measuring cup, and dissolve the cornstarch in it. Add the milk-cornstarch mixture to the hot cabbage-tofu mixture. Cook over medium-low, stirring constantly, for 2 more minutes.

5. Remove the saucepan from the heat. Stir in the scallions and the reserved pasta and carrots (from step #2). Toss everything together gently but thoroughly. Season with salt, to taste, and toss again.

6. Spoon the mixture equally into the prepared casserole dishes. Bake for 20 minutes, or until the casseroles are heated through and bubbly.

Yield: 2 main dish servings

Per serving: Calories: 324; Protein: 19 gm., Fat: 7 gm., Carbohydrate: 50 gm.

Pasta & Dogs

A childhood favorite revisited, this recipe brings out the kid in us all.

2 cups bow tie pasta or wide noodles (egg-free)

3 low-fat or fat-free vegetarian hot dogs

2 teaspoons canola oil
2/3 cup onions, finely chopped

1/4 cup cold water
1 Tablespoon cornstarch

1/4 cup tomato paste
3/4 cup water
2 teaspoons sweetener of your choice

salt and ground black pepper, to taste

1. Fill a 4 1/2-quart saucepan or Dutch oven two-thirds full with water. Bring the water to a rolling boil, and cook the pasta in it until it is al dente. Drain the pasta well and return it to the saucepan. Cover the saucepan with a lid to keep the pasta warm, and set it aside.

2. Cook the vegetarian hot dogs according to the package directions, and slice them into 1/4-inch rounds. Set them aside.

3. Place the oil in a 1-quart or 2-quart saucepan, and heat it over medium-high. When the oil is hot, add the onions and sauté them until they are very well browned and tender, about 10 to 15 minutes.

4. Meanwhile, measure out the 1/4 cup of cold water in a small measuring cup, and dissolve the cornstarch in it. Set aside.

5. Add the tomato paste, the 3/4 cup water, and sweetener to the browned onions, stirring until they are well combined.

6. Stir the reserved cornstarch mixture (from step #4), then stir it into the onion-tomato sauce (from step #5). Bring the sauce to a boil, stirring constantly. Reduce the heat to medium, and cook, stirring constantly, until the sauce is thickened. Remove the saucepan from the heat, and season the sauce with salt and pepper, to taste.

7. Pour the hot sauce over the reserved pasta in the saucepan (from step #1). Add the reserved hot dog slices (from step #2), and toss everything together until the sauce and hot dog slices are evenly distributed. Serve at once.

Yield: 2 main dish servings

Per serving: Calories: 498; Protein: 22 gm., Fat: 9 gm, Carbohydrate: 80 gm.

Cheezy Macaroni

This stovetop casserole is thick, gooey, and cheesy-tasting, yet it is totally dairy-free and can be ready in a flash.

1 1/3 cups elbow macaroni

1/3 cup nutritional yeast flakes
1/3 cup whole wheat pastry flour

1/2 teaspoon dried oregano leaves
1/2 teaspoon dried basil leaves
1/2 teaspoon garlic granules
1/4 teaspoon paprika
1/8 teaspoon dry mustard

1 cup low-fat, non-dairy milk
1 to 2 teaspoons olive oil

1/2 cup water
2 Tablespoons cornstarch

1 Tablespoon ketchup
1/4 teaspoon salt, or to taste

1. Fill a 4 1/2-quart saucepan or Dutch oven two-thirds full with water. Bring the water to a rolling boil. Add the macaroni and cook it until it is al dente. Drain the macaroni well and return it to the saucepan. Cover the saucepan with a lid to keep the pasta warm, and set it aside.

2. Place the yeast flakes and flour in a 2-quart saucepan, and toast them over medium heat, stirring constantly for several minutes, until they are lightly browned and fragrant. Remove the saucepan from the heat.

3. Stir the herbs, garlic granules, paprika, and dry mustard into the yeast-flour mixture. Then gradually whisk in the milk and olive oil, beating well until the sauce is completely smooth.

4. Measure the water in a glass measuring cup. Add the cornstarch to the water, and stir well until it is completely dissolved. Whisk this mixture into the sauce.

5. Place the saucepan over medium-high heat, and cook the sauce, stirring constantly with a wire whisk, until it is very thick and smooth. Remove the saucepan from the heat.

6. Beat the ketchup and salt into the sauce using the wire whisk. Stir the sauce into the reserved macaroni in the saucepan (from step #1), and serve immediately.

Yield: 2 main dish servings

Per serving: Calories: 446; Protein: 19 gm., Fat: 6 gm., Carbohydrate: 80 gm.

Bean & Bulgur Pilaf

This hearty pilaf makes a satisfying entrée. Just add a side of cooked greens to complete the meal.

1 teaspoon olive oil
1 ripe, medium tomato, peeled, seeded and
    chopped (see The Cook's Secrets at right)

1 small potato, peeled and diced
1 cup canned garbanzo beans, rinsed well and
    drained
1 cup water or vegetable broth

1/2 cup bulgur (medium ground)
1/2 cup green or red bell pepper, chopped

salt and ground black pepper, to taste

1. Place the oil in a 2-quart saucepan, and heat it over medium-high. When the oil is hot, add the tomato. Reduce the heat to medium, and sauté the tomato for 4 to 5 minutes.

2. Then add the potato, garbanzo beans, and the water or vegetable broth. Bring the mixture to a boil. Stir in the bulgur and the bell pepper. Reduce the heat to low, and cover the saucepan with a lid. Simmer the mixture for about 20 minutes, or until the liquid is absorbed and the potato is tender.

3. Season the pilaf with salt and pepper, to taste. Serve at once.

Yield: 2 to 3 main dish servings

Per serving: Calories: 341; Protein: 12 gm., Fat: 3 gm., Carbohydrate: 63 gm.

The Cook's Secrets:

To peel a tomato, first use a sharp knife to cut a small cross in the bottom of the tomato. Turn the tomato over and cut out the core. Immerse the tomato in a pot of boiling water for about 10 to 15 seconds. Remove the tomato from the pot using a slotted spoon, and transfer it to a bowl of cold water. Let it rest for one minute. Remove the tomato from the cold water, and peel off the skin using your fingers—it should peel away easily.

To seed a tomato, cut the tomato in half crosswise and gently squeeze out the seeds.

ENTRÉES

FEATURING TOFU, TEMPEH, SEITAN or BEANS

Tofu, tempeh, seitan, and beans have been grouped together in this section because they are high in protein and easily replace meat in many traditional recipes. For people who are not yet used to a vegetarian diet, these foods can help ease the transition. Additionally, they are delicious in their own right and are extremely adaptable to a wide range of dishes and eating styles.

Tofu, tempeh, and seitan have an uncanny way of absorbing flavors and seasonings. Beans add bite and robustness to meals, and their rainbow of colors can enliven even the most pallid dish. If you are unaccustomed to these amazing foods, I invite you to try the following recipes. At first the ingredients may seem a bit unusual, but the overall concept and outcome should delight you.

A Note From Glenn:
Strive to make cooking an enjoyable and painless endeavor. Avoid attempting lengthy or difficult recipes when you're tired—save them for your day off. A little music in the kitchen can do wonders. It works for surgeons in the operating room (and just try winning a malpractice case!). Occasionally, invite friends over for dinner. Positive feedback is a great motivator. They'll most likely be very impressed with your cooking.

Marinated Tofu, Tempeh & Seitan

Tofu, tempeh, and seitan always relish the chance to bathe in a tasty marinade. Although they may be used immediately after marinating without further ado, marinated tofu, tempeh, and seitan are especially delicious baked, broiled, sautéed, or grilled. Always use firm regular tofu, not silken tofu, for marinating.

The following recipes make sufficient marinade for 1/2 pound of tofu, 1/4 pound of tempeh, or 1 cup of sliced or chunked seitan (two servings).

1. Stir or whisk the marinade ingredients together in a small glass measuring cup.

2. Cut the tofu, tempeh, or seitan into cubes, strips, or slabs, and place the pieces in a wide, shallow, ceramic or glass bowl.

3. Pour the marinade over the tofu, tempeh, or seitan, turning each piece so it is well coated. Cover the bowl with a lid or plastic wrap, and let the pieces soak up the flavors of the marinade for at least 2 hours or longer in the refrigerator. (Overnight is great!) Occasionally, turn the tofu, tempeh, or seitan over gently so all the pieces remain evenly covered with the sauce.

4. Prior to cooking, drain off any excess marinade. Then sauté, bake, broil, or grill the pieces until they are golden brown all over, turning them as necessary. If you like, brush any remaining marinade over the pieces while they cook.

MARINADE #1:

1 Tablespoon fresh lemon juice
1 Tablespoon water
1 Tablespoon soy sauce
1 1/2 teaspoons olive oil
1 1/2 teaspoons fresh gingerroot, grated (opt.)
1 clove garlic, pressed
1/4 teaspoon dry mustard

MARINADE #2:

1 Tablespoon soy sauce
2 teaspoons pure maple syrup
1 teaspoon brown rice vinegar
1 1/2 teaspoons fresh gingerroot, grated (opt.)
1 1/2 teaspoons toasted sesame oil
1 clove garlic, pressed

MARINADE #3:

2 Tablespoons ketchup
1 Tablespoon balsamic vinegar
1 Tablespoon water
1 teaspoon olive oil
1 small clove garlic, pressed

MARINADE #4:

2 Tablespoons red wine vinegar
1 Tablespoon orange juice concentrate
1 Tablespoon soy sauce
1 teaspoon olive oil or toasted sesame oil
several drops Tabasco sauce, to taste

The Cook's Secrets:

If you are exceptionally rushed, you can marinate the tofu, tempeh, or seitan pieces for a minimum of 20 minutes. However, they will not be as well infused with flavor as they would be with the longer marinating time.

A pinch of cayenne pepper or crushed hot red pepper flakes may be added to the marinades if you prefer your food with a little "heat."

If the tempeh's packaging does not state that the tempeh is fully cooked and ready to use, steam the tempeh for 20 minutes prior to marinating it.

Broiling or Grilling Marinated Tofu, Tempeh & Seitan

1. To broil or grill tofu, tempeh, or seitan after marinating, first mist a baking sheet or the cold grill with a little nonstick cooking spray to keep the tofu, tempeh, or seitan pieces from sticking to it. Then heat the broiler or grill.

2. Arrange the pieces in a single layer on the baking sheet, and place them under the broiler or directly on the grill in a single layer, just a few inches from the heat source.

3. When the sides exposed to the heat are lightly browned and blistered, turn the pieces over to finish cooking them. (Watch closely so they do not burn. Direct dry heat can rapidly scorch foods!)

4. Remove the pieces from the broiler or grill as soon as they are browned to your liking. Season them with salt, pepper, and fresh herbs, to taste, *after* cooking so the seasonings do not burn.

Pressed Tofu

Firm regular tofu is at its best when it is pressed. This simple process removes excess moisture, leaving the tofu firmer and with a much denser texture. Pressed tofu is suitable for any of the recipes in this book calling for "regular" (not silken) tofu, and pressing is a particularly choice treatment for tofu that will be marinated. Because the texture of the tofu is significantly improved, I highly recommend setting aside the small amount of time needed to press it.

1. To press tofu, set the solid 1/2 pound block of tofu (the standard portion for 2 servings) between two plates. The best place to do this is in your sink.

2. Place a heavy weight on the top plate. (I like to use a jar of beans, but almost any small, relatively heavy object will do. The idea is to apply firm pressure to the tofu without crushing it.)

3. Let the tofu rest for 15 to 30 minutes. Drain off the liquid and pat the tofu dry with a clean tea towel or paper towels.

4. Cut the tofu into the desired pieces, and proceed with the recipe as directed.

Homemade Seitan

If you do not have access to prepared seitan, or if you simply prefer to fix as many foods as possible from scratch, this is the easiest, tastiest, fastest, and least expensive way I know of to make seitan (cooked wheat gluten) at home. It makes enough seitan for three two-person servings. Seitan keeps well in the refrigerator or freezer, so it is well worth having plenty on hand to use in other recipes in this book. Seitan may also be used as a substitute for chicken and beef in traditional, meat-based recipes.

Use *only* instant gluten flour (not high-gluten wheat flour) in this recipe. Do not substitute any other flour. Instant gluten flour (vital wheat gluten) can be obtained from natural food stores and some bakeries. It can also be ordered directly from The Mail Order Catalog (see page 25).

1 1/2 cups instant gluten flour (vital wheat
  gluten)
3 Tablespoons whole wheat pastry flour (opt.–to
  add fiber back in)
3 Tablespoons nutritional yeast flakes (opt.)
1/4 teaspoon garlic granules
1/4 teaspoon onion granules

1 cup water or vegetable broth, or 1/2 cup water
  + 1/2 cup tomato juice
1/4 cup soy sauce
1 Tablespoon olive oil (optional)

SIMMERING BROTH:
10 to 12 cups cold water
1/2 cup soy sauce
3 to 4 cloves garlic, very coarsely chopped
4 to 6 slices of onion (optional)
2 whole bay leaves (optional)
1 teaspoon whole black peppercorns (optional)

1. Place the gluten flour, pastry flour (if using), nutritional yeast flakes (if using), garlic granules, and onion granules in a medium mixing bowl, and stir them together.

2. Measure the water out exactly, and place it in a small mixing bowl. Add the soy sauce and olive oil (if using) to the water, and pour this liquid into the flour mixture. Mix well. If the mixture still has dry flour around the edges, add a little more water to it (about 1 or 2 tablespoons *only*). You should now have a large, firm, spongy mass in the bowl. This is called *gluten.*

3. Knead the gluten on a flat surface or directly in the mixing bowl for 2 to 5 minutes. Then slice or tear the gluten into 3 equal pieces, and set it aside.

4. Place the ingredients for the Simmering Broth in a 4 1/2-quart saucepan or Dutch oven. Add the gluten pieces to the cold broth, and bring the broth to a boil. Reduce the heat very slightly, and simmer the gluten *uncovered* for 50 to 60 minutes, turning it over occasionally. The water should remain at a fairly brisk simmer during the entire cooking time.

5. Remove the saucepan from the heat, and allow the broth and seitan to cool. (After gluten is cooked it is called *seitan.*)

6. Transfer the seitan to storage containers, and add enough of the broth to the containers to keep the seitan immersed. Cover each container tightly with a lid, and store the seitan in the refrigerator for up to ten days or in the freezer for up to six months. To extend the life of fresh or defrosted seitan indefinitely, boil it in its soy sauce broth for ten minutes two times a week.

Yield: 3 chunks, approximately 2 servings per chunk

Per serving: Calories: 137, Protein: 28 gm., Fat: 1 gm., Carbohydrate: 5 gm.

The Cook's Secrets:

Additional ingredients may be added to the broth for an even richer flavor. Options include sliced ginger-root, celery, carrot, and/or mushrooms.

Additional herbs and spices may be added to the dry ingredients to season the gluten. You can try different combinations depending on your preferences as well as what you will be making with the seitan. Some good choices are ground black pepper, dried basil, chili powder, ground cumin, curry powder, ground fennel, dry mustard, marjoram, oregano, sage, or thyme.

After using the seitan, strain any leftover simmering broth, and use it as a vegetable broth in other recipes. It also makes a great stock for gravy (such as in the recipes on p. 128).

For an extensive look into making and using gluten and seitan, refer to *Cooking with Gluten and Seitan*, by Dorothy Bates and Colby Wingate, available through The Mail Order Catalog (see page 25).

A Note From Glenn:

Although many cookbooks insist that recipes be followed to the letter, I often get excellent results by going my own way. Cooking may be an art, but art takes time. In the struggle between art and hunger, hunger rules!

Crispy Tofu Sticks

These tofu sticks are breaded with a mild, crunchy coating and then baked to a crispy finish. They are delicious plain or served with ketchup, barbecue sauce, or Tangy Dijon Apricot Sauce, p. 127, on the side for dipping (which kids love to do).

1/2 pound fat-reduced, firm regular tofu, rinsed, drained, and patted dry (press if time permits; see the directions for pressing tofu on p. 155)

CORNMEAL BREADING:
1/3 cup dry whole wheat bread crumbs (see The Cook's Secrets below right)
1/4 cup yellow cornmeal
2 Tablespoons nutritional yeast flakes
heaping 1/4 teaspoon salt
1/8 teaspoon cayenne pepper

1/3 cup whole wheat pastry flour, as needed

1 cup water, as needed

1. Preheat the oven to 375°F. Coat a baking sheet with nonstick cooking spray, and set it aside.

2. Cut the block of tofu in half lengthwise. Then slice each half into 3 equal sticks (6 sticks in all). Set aside.

3. To make the Cornmeal Breading, place the bread crumbs, cornmeal, nutritional yeast flakes, salt, and cayenne pepper in a shallow mixing bowl, and stir them together well.

4. Place the flour and water in two separate shallow mixing bowls.

5. Bread the tofu sticks one at a time. To do this, first roll the tofu stick in the flour to coat it well all over. Pat off any excess flour. Immediately dunk the floured stick briefly in the water, submerging it completely. Then, immediately roll the stick in the cornmeal mixture to coat it all over.

6. Place each tofu stick on the prepared baking sheet as soon as you finish breading it.

7. When all the tofu sticks have been breaded, bake them for 25 minutes, turning them over midway in the cooking cycle using a metal spatula. Serve hot.

Yield: 2 main dish servings (3 sticks per serving)

Per serving: Calories: 331, Protein: 22 gm., Fat: 6 gm., Carbohydrate: 46 gm.

The Cook's Secrets:
To make dry bread crumbs, toast 1 or 2 slices of whole grain bread. Cool the toasted bread and tear it or slice it into small pieces. Whirl the pieces in a food processor fitted with a metal blade until they are finely crumbed, or rub them on the side of a box grater. Measure out the amount you need, and store any leftover crumbs in an airtight container. Alternately, purchase packaged whole wheat bread crumbs. They are available in natural food stores and many supermarkets.

Rayaya's Tofu Cutlets

Susan Richter contributed this wonderful recipe in honor of her friend Rayaya, who inspired it. Susan loves the recipe so much that she chose to share it with you here so you too could enjoy its tantalizing flavors. Susan has prepared this recipe for numerous children as well as adults, and everyone adores it! The cutlets make a fantastic sandwich filling as well as a tempting dinner entrée.

1/2 pound fat-reduced, firm regular tofu, rinsed, drained, and patted dry (press if time permits; see the directions for pressing tofu on p. 155)

vegetable seasoned salt (such as Spike or Vegesal), salt-free herbal seasoning, or soy sauce, as needed

1/2 cup nutritional yeast flakes, or as needed

1. Slice the tofu into 1/2-inch slabs, and lay the slabs on a flat surface.

2. Lightly sprinkle the top side of the slabs with the seasoned salt, herbal seasoning, or soy sauce.

3. Place the nutritional yeast on a large plate or in a wide, shallow bowl, forming it into a mound.

4. Place each tofu slab, one at a time, into the mound of nutritional yeast, seasoned side down. Sprinkle the exposed side of the slab lightly with the vegetable seasoned salt, herbal seasoning, or soy sauce. With your fingers, cover the sides and top of the slab with lots of nutritional yeast, gently patting it on in a thick layer. As you finish coating each slab, place it on a sheet of waxed paper. Continue coating each slab of tofu in the same fashion.

5. When all the cutlets have been coated, spread a thin layer of canola oil over the bottom of a 9-inch or 10-inch skillet, and heat it over medium-high. When the oil is hot, place the cutlets in a single layer in the skillet. (You may need to do this in batches depending on the size of your skillet.) Cook each cutlet for about 5 minutes on each side, or until it is crispy and very well browned. Turn the cutlets over once using a metal spatula.

6. Serve the cutlets hot or allow them to cool and store them in a covered container in the refrigerator.

Yield: 2 main dish servings

Per serving: Calories: 214, Protein: 25 gm., Fat: 5 gm., Carbohydrate: 17 gm.

The Cook's Secrets:
The more nutritional yeast you use, the more delicious the crust will be.

The cutlets may be served as an entrée or as a sandwich filling, to which Susan recommends adding lettuce leaves and avocado or tomato slices.

Alternately, the tofu can be sliced into sticks or cubes instead of slabs.

Tofu with Vegetable Spaghetti

This quick, one-dish skillet meal is great for busy evenings. The recipe calls for cooked spaghetti squash, so if you have frozen spaghetti squash on hand, dinner can be on the table in under 30 minutes. Serve it in shallow bowls or on warm plates with crispy bread sticks on the side.

2 cups cooked spaghetti squash (or one 2-lb uncooked squash—see The Cook's Secrets below right and on the next page)

1 1/2 teaspoons olive oil
1 cup onion, chopped
1 small red bell pepper, chopped

1 small zucchini, diced
1 cup mushrooms, sliced
2 cloves garlic, minced or pressed
1/4 teaspoon ground black pepper

1 8-ounce can tomato sauce (1 cup)

1/2 pound fat-reduced, firm regular tofu, rinsed, patted dry and cut into 1/2-inch cubes (press if time permits; see the directions for pressing tofu on p. 155)

salt, to taste
1 to 2 Tablespoons nutritional yeast (optional)

1. Prepare partially-cooked fresh or frozen spaghetti squash according to the package directions or cook fresh spaghetti squash (see The Cook's Secrets at right and on the next page).

2. Pull the strands of the spaghetti squash apart with a fork, and set aside.

3. Place the olive oil in a 9-inch or 10-inch skillet, and heat it over medium-high. When the oil is hot, add the onion and red bell pepper, and sauté them for 5 minutes.

4. Add the zucchini, mushrooms, garlic, and black pepper to the onion-pepper mixture in the skillet. Cook, stirring constantly, for 3 minutes longer.

5. Add the reserved spaghetti squash and the tomato sauce to the other vegetables in the skillet. Cover the skillet with a lid, and simmer the mixture over medium-low for 7 to 10 minutes.

6. Carefully fold in the tofu, taking care not to mash it. Replace the lid on the skillet, and continue to cook the mixture for 5 minutes longer, or until the tofu is heated through.

7. Season the mixture with salt, to taste. Divide the mixture equally between two dinner plates, and serve hot. Sprinkle each serving with some of the nutritional yeast, if desired.

Yield: 2 main dish servings

Per serving: Calories: 284, Protein: 16 gm., Fat: 10 gm., Carbohydrate: 34 gm.

The Cook's Secret:

Use partially-cooked spaghetti squash (available in packages in the produce section of your supermarket) or frozen spaghetti squash if it is available in your area. It can be steamed or boiled in about 6 to 8 minutes.

Alternately, wash, halve lengthwise, and remove seeds from one 2-lb. spaghetti squash. Place the halves cut side down in a baking dish or pan misted with nonstick cooking spray or filled with 1/2 inch of water. Cover and bake in a 350°F oven for 40 minutes, or until fork-tender.

After cooking, use a fork to scrape and pull the flesh away from the thick, tough shell in order to create its characteristic spaghetti-like strands.

Country-Style Scrambled Tofu

After a hard day at work, this "dinner in a skillet" is very soothing. We also like it for breakfast, brunch, or lunch. Serve it with thick slices of whole grain bread and perhaps a glass of sparkling cider for whimsy.

1 medium potato, peeled and cut into 1/2-inch cubes

1 teaspoon olive oil
1/2 cup onion, chopped

1/2 pound fat-reduced, firm regular tofu, rinsed, patted dry and crumbled
1 small zucchini, diced
1 ripe, medium tomato, seeded and chopped (see The Cook's Secrets at right)
1/2 teaspoon garlic granules
1/8 teaspoon turmeric

salt and ground black pepper, to taste

1. Place the potato cubes in a steamer basket or steamer insert in a large saucepan filled with an inch of water. Bring the water to a boil. Cover the saucepan with a lid, and reduce the heat to medium. Steam the potato until it is tender, about 15 to 20 minutes. Set aside.

2. Meanwhile, heat the olive oil in a 9-inch or 10-inch skillet over medium high. When the oil is hot, add the onion and sauté it until it is very tender and browned, about 10 to 15 minutes.

3. Add the reserved cooked potato (from step #1), tofu, zucchini, tomato, garlic granules, and turmeric to the cooked onion. Cook, stirring almost constantly, until the zucchini is just barely tender, about 8 minutes.

4. Season the mixture with salt and pepper, to taste. Serve hot.

Yield: 2 main dish servings

Per serving: Calories: 226, Protein: 15 gm., Fat: 7 gm., Carbohydrate: 26 gm.

The Cook's Secrets:
To seed a tomato, cut the tomato in half crosswise and gently squeeze out the seeds.

Tofu Cacciatore

A terrific remake of an Italian classic. Serve it over pasta or rice.

1 teaspoon olive oil
1/2 cup onion, chopped
2 cloves garlic, minced or pressed

1/2 cup green bell pepper, chopped

1 cup mushrooms, sliced
2 Tablespoons red wine vinegar

2 ripe, medium tomatoes, peeled, seeded, and
   chopped (see The Cook's Secrets at right)
1/2 pound fat-reduced, firm regular tofu, pressed
   and cut into 1/2-inch cubes (see the directions
   for pressing tofu on p. 155)

salt and ground black pepper, to taste

1. Place the oil in a 9-inch or 10-inch skillet, and heat it over medium-high. When the oil is hot, add the onion and garlic, and cook them, stirring often, for 7 to 10 minutes.

2. Add the bell pepper to the onion and garlic, and cook it for 2 minutes.

3. Then add the mushrooms and vinegar, and cook for 1 minute longer.

4. Stir in the tomatoes and the tofu. Reduce the heat to low, cover the skillet with a lid, and simmer the mixture for 5 to 8 minutes.

5. Season the mixture with salt and pepper, to taste. Serve hot.

Yield: 2 main dish servings

Per serving: Calories: 190, Protein: 14 gm., Fat: 7 gm., Carbohydrate: 17 gm.

The Cook's Secrets:
To peel a tomato, first use a sharp knife to cut a small cross in the bottom of the tomato. Turn the tomato over and cut out the core. Immerse the tomato in a pot of boiling water for about 10 to 15 seconds. Remove the tomato from the pot using a slotted spoon, and transfer it to a bowl of cold water. Let it rest for one minute. Remove the tomato from the cold water, and peel off the skin using your fingers–it should peel away easily.

    To seed a tomato, cut the tomato in half crosswise, and gently squeeze out the seeds.

Kraut, Dogs & Dumplings

This casserole is a nod to the pork and sauerkraut meals which many people around the world serve at New Year's Eve celebrations for good luck in the coming year. By making it vegetarian, however, the good luck now can be spread to *all*.

The secret to the success of this dish is baking the sauerkraut for a very long time to make it extremely tender. It hardly requires any attention, though, so even if you prepare this for a special occasion like New Year's Eve, you won't have to work very hard. Serve it with garlic-flavored mashed potatoes for a truly satisfying meal.

KRAUT & DOGS:
2 cups low-sodium sauerkraut, lightly drained
1/2 cup applesauce

3 low-fat or fat-free vegetarian hot dogs

DUMPLING MIX:
1/2 cup whole wheat pastry flour
1 teaspoon non-aluminum baking powder (such as Rumford)
heaping 1/8 teaspoon salt

3 Tablespoons water
2 teaspoons olive oil

1. Preheat the oven to 350°F. Coat two 15-ounce or 16-ounce individual casserole dishes with nonstick cooking spray, and set them aside.

2. Place the sauerkraut and applesauce in a medium mixing bowl, and stir them together until they are evenly combined. Spoon the sauerkraut mixture into the prepared casserole dishes. Cover the casserole dishes tightly with a lid or silver foil, and bake them for 1 hour.

3. Cook the hot dogs according to the package directions, and slice them into 1/4-inch rounds. Stir half of the rounds into each casserole, tucking them under the sauerkraut as best as possible.

4. To prepare the dumplings, place the flour, baking powder, and salt in a small mixing bowl, and stir them together. Pour the water and oil into the flour mixture, and stir until the dry ingredients are evenly moistened. The dough will be stiff. Drop the dough by spoonfuls on top of the casseroles to create 4 dumpling mounds (2 per casserole).

5. Bake the dumpling-topped casseroles *uncovered* until the dumplings are golden brown, about 14 to 18 minutes. Serve hot.

Yield: 2 main dish servings

Per serving: Calories: 315, Protein: 17 gm., Fat: 8 gm., Carbohydrate: 41 gm.

The Cook's Secrets:
Although these may be eaten directly from the casserole dishes, I like to spoon the contents onto dinner plates, keeping the dumplings intact and on top of the sauerkraut and hot dogs.

Shepherd's Pie

These power packed casseroles rely on convenience foods to recreate a vegetarian version of an old favorite. Mixed vegetables are combined with an herb-seasoned sauce, then topped with a mashed potato crust, and baked to a delectable golden brown.

CASEROLE FILLING:
1 16-ounce package frozen mixed vegetables (any kind; your choice)

1 teaspoon canola oil
1 medium onion, finely chopped
2 cloves garlic, minced or pressed

1/4 cup whole wheat pastry flour
1 teaspoon dried thyme leaves, crushed
1/2 teaspoon dried basil leaves

3/4 cup low-fat, non-dairy milk

1/2 pound fat-reduced, firm regular tofu, rinsed, patted dry, and cut into bite-size cubes

1/2 teaspoon salt, or to taste
ground black pepper, to taste

POTATO TOPPING:
2/3 cup water
1 teaspoon olive oil or canola oil (optional)
2/3 cup low-fat, non-dairy milk
1 1/2 cups instant potato flakes
1/4 teaspoon garlic granules
1/4 teaspoon salt
ground black pepper, to taste

paprika, for garnish

1. Preheat the oven to 400°F. Mist two 15-ounce or 16-ounce individual casserole dishes with nonstick cooking spray, and set them aside.

2. Cook the vegetables according to the package instructions. Drain them well in a colander. Place them in a large mixing bowl, and set aside.

3. Place the oil in a 2-quart saucepan, and heat it over medium-high. When the oil is hot, add the onion and garlic. Reduce the heat to medium, and sauté the onion and garlic for about 10 minutes, or until the onion is tender.

4. Stir the flour and herbs into the cooked onion, and continue to cook for 1 minute longer.

5. Then, gradually pour in the milk, about 1/4 cup at a time, stirring constantly until the sauce is smooth. Cook, stirring constantly over medium heat, until the sauce has thickened.

6. Stir the sauce into the reserved vegetables in the mixing bowl (from step #2). Fold in the cubed tofu, and season the mixture with salt and pepper, to taste.

7. Spoon the mixture equally into the prepared casserole dishes, and set aside.

8. To prepare the mashed potato topping, place the water and oil (if using) in a 1-quart or 2-quart saucepan, and bring to a boil. Remove the saucepan from the heat, and stir in the milk. Using a fork, stir in the potato flakes, garlic granules, salt, and pepper, to taste. Mix well until the potatoes are smooth.

9. Spoon the potatoes equally over the filling in the casserole dishes, spreading the mixture out to the edges using a fork. If desired, create an attractive design on the top of the potatoes using the tines of the fork. Dust the potatoes lightly with paprika.

10. Bake the casseroles *uncovered* for 20 to 25 minutes, or until they are hot and bubbly and the tops are golden brown.

11. Remove the casseroles from the oven (using oven mitts or pot holders). Let the casseroles rest for 5 minutes before serving.

Yield: 2 main dish servings

Per serving: Calories: 510, Protein: 23 gm., Fat: 9 gm., Carbohydrate: 81 gm.

A Note From Glenn:
My shopping trips always begin by browsing through cookbooks and planning what I'm going to make. This way I'm less likely to buy food I don't need. (That bargain-priced case of perishable food will cease to be a bargain when the leftovers mutate into a virtual petri dish!) I always keep plenty of aseptically packaged soy milk and silken tofu, nutritional yeast and canned goods on hand because they have a long shelf life.

Tofu & Vegetable Ragoût with Cornmeal Dumplings

An easy but full-flavored dish that needs only a crisp green salad to accompany it.

RAGOÛT:
1 cup water or vegetable broth
2 Tablespoons Dijon mustard
1 1/2 teaspoons dried dill weed
2 to 4 cloves garlic, minced or pressed

1/2 pound fat-reduced, firm regular tofu, rinsed, patted dry, and cut into 1/2-inch cubes (press if time permits; see the directions for pressing tofu on p. 155)
1 1/2 cups mushrooms, sliced
1/2 cup carrots, pared and thinly sliced on the diagonal
1/2 cup leeks, sliced (use only the white bulb and tender green parts; see The Cook's Secrets on next page)

1/4 to 1/2 teaspoon salt, to taste
ground black pepper, to taste

CORNMEAL DUMPLING MIX:
1/4 cup yellow cornmeal
1/4 cup whole wheat pastry flour
1 teaspoon non-aluminum baking powder (such as Rumford)
1/8 teaspoon salt

1/4 cup water
2 teaspoons olive oil

THICKENER:
1 Tablespoon cold water
1 teaspoon cornstarch

1. Place the water or vegetable broth, mustard, dill weed, and garlic in a 4 1/2-quart saucepan or Dutch oven. Stir to combine them well. Then stir in the tofu, mushrooms, carrots, and leeks. Bring the mixture to a boil. Reduce the heat to medium, and cover the saucepan with a lid. Simmer the ragoût for 10 minutes, stirring once or twice. Season the ragoût with salt and pepper, to taste.

2. While the ragoût is simmering, prepare the dumpling mix. To do so, place the dry ingredients in a small mixing bowl, and stir them together. Pour the water and olive oil into the cornmeal-flour mixture at the same time. Mix until all of the dry ingredients are evenly moistened. The dough will be stiff.

3. After the stew has simmered for 10 minutes, drop the dough by spoonfuls on top of the simmering ragoût to form 4 dumpling mounds. Cover the saucepan with a lid, and simmer the dumpling-topped ragoût for 10 minutes longer.

4. With a large spoon, transfer the dumplings to two warm soup bowls or dinner plates.

5. Place the water and cornstarch in a small mixing bowl or measuring cup, and stir them together until smooth. Stir this thickener into the hot ragoût. Cook over medium, stirring constantly, until the ragoût's sauce is slightly thickened and bubbly, about 30 seconds. Spoon the hot ragoût over the dumplings, and serve immediately.

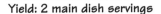

Yield: 2 main dish servings

Per serving: Calories: 346, Protein: 17 gm., Fat: 12 gm., Carbohydrate: 40 gm.

The Cook's Secrets:

To clean a leek, rinse it thoroughly to remove sandy grit and dirt. The easiest way to do this is to slice halfway through the bulb lengthwise and separate the leaves gently so the inner sections of the leek are exposed and can be readily cleaned.

A Note From Glenn:

Many cookbooks assume more knowledge about cooking than many of us have. Don't hesitate to ask a good cook for pointers!

Breaded Seitan Nuggets

These tasty little chunks of seitan are a popular entrée or snack food. Serve them with your favorite dipping sauce such as ketchup, cocktail sauce, barbecue sauce, or Tangy Dijon Apricot Sauce, p. 127.

BREADING MEAL:
1 cup whole grain cracker crumbs or dry whole
   wheat bread crumbs (see The Cook's Secrets
   below right)
2 Tablespoons nutritional yeast flakes
heaping 1/4 teaspoon salt
1/4 teaspoon paprika
1/8 teaspoon poultry seasoning
1/8 teaspoon ground black pepper

1/2 cup whole wheat pastry flour

1 cup water, as needed

1 cup seitan, pressed firmly between the palms
   of your hands to remove excess moisture and
   cut into 1 1/2-inch chunks

1. Preheat the oven to 350°F. Mist a baking sheet with nonstick cooking spray, and set it aside.

2. To make the breading meal, place the cracker crumbs or bread crumbs, nutritional yeast flakes, salt, paprika, poultry seasoning, and pepper in a shallow mixing bowl, and mix them together well.

3. Place the flour and water in two separate, shallow mixing bowls.

4. Bread each seitan chunk one at a time. To do this, first dredge the chunk in the flour, coating it well all over. Then immerse the chunk in the water, submerging it completely. Remove the chunk from the water, and immediately dredge it in the breading meal, coating it well all over.

5. Place each nugget on the prepared baking sheet as soon as you finish breading it. When all the nuggets have been breaded, mist the tops lightly with nonstick cooking spray.

6. Bake the nuggets for 20 to 25 minutes, turning them once after 10 minutes. Serve while hot.

Yield: 2 main dish servings (approximately 5 to 6 nuggets per person)

Per serving: Calories: 428, Protein: 36 gm., Fat: 3 gm., Carbohydrate: 63 gm.

The Cook's Secrets:
To make whole grain cracker crumbs, break whole grain crackers into small pieces, and whirl them in a food processor fitted with a metal blade until they are finely crumbed. Alternately, place the crackers between two sheets of waxed paper, and roll over them firmly with a rolling pin until they are finely crushed.

To make dry bread crumbs, toast 2 to 4 slices of whole grain bread. Cool the toasted bread and tear it or slice it into small pieces. Whirl the pieces in a food processor fitted with a metal blade until they are finely crumbed, or rub them on the side of a box grater. Measure out the amount you need, and store any leftover crumbs in an airtight container. Alternately, purchase packaged whole wheat bread crumbs. They are available in natural food stores and many supermarkets.

Store any leftover breading meal in an airtight container at room temperature. Use it to bread more seitan at a later time or to bread sliced zucchini, summer squash, peeled eggplant, tomatoes, or tofu according to the method described above. The breading meal will keep for about a month.

Seitan Swiss Steak

Swiss steak has never been this tender or this easy! Just like Mom used to make only better because it's faster, more healthful, and meat-free. I like to serve it with Favorite Mashed Potatoes, p. 141, or Old Country Potatoes, p. 142. To round out the meal, add a side dish of steamed, fresh green beans and a few slices of whole grain bread—essential for sopping up any stray gravy.

1/2 cup water
1/2 of a medium onion, or 1 small onion, thinly
   sliced
2 stalks celery, sliced
1 medium carrot, pared and thinly sliced
1 to 2 Tablespoons soy sauce, to taste
2 cloves garlic, minced or pressed
1/2 teaspoon dried oregano leaves
1/4 teaspoon dried marjoram leaves
1/8 teaspoon ground black pepper

2 Tablespoons tomato paste

1 large, ripe tomato, chopped
1 cup seitan, thinly sliced

1. Place the water, onion, celery, carrot, soy sauce, garlic, and seasonings in a 9-inch or 10-inch skillet. Bring the mixture to a boil. Reduce the heat to medium, and cover the skillet with a lid. Simmer the mixture for 15 minutes, stirring once or twice.

2. After 15 minutes, add the tomato paste to the skillet, mixing well until it is thoroughly incorporated. Then add the chopped fresh tomato and seitan slices. Stir to mix well.

3. Cover the skillet with a lid, and simmer the mixture for 2 to 5 minutes longer, or just until the seitan is heated through. Serve hot.

Yield: 2 main dish servings

Per serving: Calories: 181, Protein: 25 gm., Fat: 1 gm., Carbohydrate: 18 gm.

Saucy Beans & Franks

Children love this dish because it's fun to eat and tastes terrific. Adults love it because it's a quick, nutritious last-minute entrée. Serve it with whole grain rolls or biscuits and coleslaw.

1 16-ounce can beans (pinto, white beans, or any other bean you prefer), rinsed and drained
1/3 cup ketchup
2 low-fat vegetarian frankfurters (hot dogs), cooked according to package directions and sliced into 1/4-inch rounds
1 Tablespoon soy sauce
1 Tablespoon light molasses, sorghum syrup, pure maple syrup, or other liquid sweetener of your choice
1 teaspoon brown rice vinegar or balsamic vinegar
1/2 teaspoon onion granules
1/4 teaspoon dry mustard
few drops liquid smoke (optional)

1. Place all the ingredients in a 2-quart saucepan, and gently stir them together.

2. Place the saucepan over medium heat, and simmer the mixture, stirring occasionally, until it is hot and bubbly. Serve at once.

Yield: 2 main dish servings

Per serving: Calories: 463, Protein: 25 gm., Fat: 3 gm., Carbohydrate: 83 gm.

Chili Bean Topping for Grains or Pasta

Chili seasonings and red beans join together to make a lively topping for rice, couscous, bulgur, polenta, or your favorite pasta—and it cooks up in under 15-minutes!

1 14.5-ounce can whole tomatoes, with juice
1 cup canned kidney or pinto beans, rinsed well and drained
1 small green bell pepper, sliced into 1/4-inch by 2-inch strips
2 Tablespoons tomato paste
1 Tablespoon chili powder
1 teaspoon olive oil (optional)
1/4 teaspoon salt, or to taste
1/4 teaspoon garlic granules
1/4 teaspoon ground cumin

2 Tablespoons water
1 Tablespoon cornstarch

1. Place the tomatoes and their juice in a 2-quart saucepan. Break the tomatoes apart with your hands or the side of a wooden spoon. Stir in the remaining ingredients *except the water and cornstarch,* and mix well.

2. Bring the mixture to a boil. Reduce the heat to medium, cover the saucepan with a lid, and simmer the mixture for 10 minutes, stirring occasionally.

3. Meanwhile, place the water in a small measuring cup. Add the cornstarch and stir until it is well dissolved.

4. Stir the cornstarch mixture again. Then stir it into the tomato-bean mixture in the saucepan. Continue to cook over medium, stirring constantly, until the sauce is thickened and bubbly. (This will take just a few minutes.) Cook for 1 minute longer, then serve at once.

Yield: 2 main dish servings (if served over 6 ounces of pasta, polenta, or a grain)

Per serving: Calories: 184, Protein: 9 gm., Fat: 0 gm., Carbohydrate: 35 gm.

Easy Baked Beans

A time-honored classic made so much easier by the use of canned beans.

2 teaspoons canola oil
1 large onion, finely chopped
3 cloves garlic, minced or pressed

1/4 cup tomato paste
2 Tablespoons soy sauce
1 Tablespoon light molasses, pure maple syrup, sorghum, or other liquid sweetener of your choice
1 teaspoon Dijon mustard

1 15-ounce can kidney beans, pinto beans, or navy pea beans, rinsed well and drained

1. Preheat the oven to 350°F. Mist two 15-ounce or 16-ounce individual casserole dishes with nonstick cooking spray, and set them aside.

2. Place the oil in a 9-inch or 10-inch skillet, and heat it over medium-high. When the oil is hot, add the onion and garlic, and sauté them until the onion is well browned and very tender, about 10 to 15 minutes.

3. Meanwhile, place the tomato paste, soy sauce, sweetener, and mustard in a large mix ng bowl, and stir them together to form a smooth, thick sauce. Add the beans and mix well.

4. When the onion is finished cooking, stir it into the mixing bowl with the beans and sauce. Mix gently but thoroughly.

5. Divide the mixture evenly between the two prepared casserole dishes. Cover the casserole dishes with a lid or foil, and bake them for 30 minutes. Serve hot.

Yield: 2 main dish servings

Per serving: Calories: 444, Protein: 18 gm., Fat: 6 gm., Carbohydrate: 78 gm.

Red Flannel Hash

For busy people, this homey "comfort food" is a delight. Its uncomplicated taste and straightforward appearance are reminiscent of traditional diner fare. This hash makes a soothing entrée when accompanied by steamed mixed vegetables (perhaps broccoli and squash) and a bowl of applesauce. Serve it with Golden Gravy, p. 128, or Quick Brown Gravy, p. 128, and/or ketchup.

2 medium potatoes, peeled and cut into 1/2-inch cubes

2 teaspoons canola oil or olive oil
1 very large onion, chopped

1 16-ounce can dark red kidney beans, rinsed well, drained and mashed (see The Cook's Secrets at right)

1/4 teaspoon garlic granules
salt and ground black pepper, to taste

1. Place the potato cubes in a steamer basket or steamer insert in a large saucepan filled with an inch of water. Bring the water to a boil. Cover the saucepan with a lid, and reduce the heat to medium. Steam the potatoes until they are fork-tender, about 12 to 18 minutes. Set aside.

2. Meanwhile, place the oil in a 9-inch or 10-inch skillet, and heat it over medium-high. When the oil is hot, add the onion and sauté it, stirring frequently, until it is tender and browned, about 10 to 15 minutes.

3. Add the reserved cooked potatoes (from step #1), mashed kidney beans, and seasonings to the browned onion in the skillet. Continue to cook over medium-high heat, stirring or tossing the mixture constantly, until everything is heated through, about 5 minutes.

4. Serve at once, or cover the skillet with a lid, and keep the hash warm over very low heat until serving time.

Yield: 2 main dish servings

Per serving: Calories: 472, Protein: 19 gm., Fat: 5 gm., Carbohydrate: 86 gm.

The Cook's Secrets:
To mash the kidney beans, use a potato masher, a fork, or your hands.

New Orleans Peasant-Style Red Beans

Soupy, spicy red beans are a Southern specialty. Serve them in a bowl over hot rice, or with Yankee Corn Muffins, p. 39, or whole grain bread to dip into the delicious broth. A plate of steamed fresh greens is the ideal complement.

2 teaspoons olive oil
1 cup onion, chopped
1/2 cup celery, finely chopped

1 small red or green bell pepper (or half of each), chopped
2 cloves garlic, minced or pressed

1 cup water or vegetable broth
1 15-ounce can kidney beans, rinsed well and drained
3 Tablespoons vegetarian Worcestershire sauce
1/4 to 1/2 teaspoon Tabasco sauce, to taste
1/4 teaspoon ground black pepper
1 whole bay leaf

2 Tablespoons fresh parsley, chopped (for garnish; optional)

1. Place the oil in a 2-quart saucepan, and heat it over medium-high. When the oil is hot, add the onion and celery. Reduce the heat to medium, and sauté the onion and celery for 10 minutes.

2. Add the bell pepper and garlic to the onion and celery in the saucepan, and continue to sauté them for 5 minutes longer.

3. Stir in the remaining ingredients *except the parsley*, and bring the mixture to a boil. Reduce the heat to medium-low, cover the saucepan with a lid, and simmer the mixture for 20 minutes, stirring occasionally.

4. Discard the bay leaf. Ladle the beans and broth into two large soup bowls, distributing them equally. Garnish each serving with fresh parsley, if desired. Serve hot.

Yield: 2 main dish servings

Per serving: Calories: 354, Protein: 17 gm., Fat: 5 gm., Carbohydrate: 59 gm.

A Note From Anne & Matt:
Rice and beans are staples for us—we have them at least twice a week. Due to our "revolving door" schedules, canned beans are extremely handy. Rinse them very well before using, though, since this can remove up to half of the sodium.

Italian Beans & Bows

Garbanzo beans in a rich tomato sauce are mated with bow tie pasta. It's a knockout with both children and adults. A dark green leafy salad or any green leafy vegetable will make an attractive and healthful accompaniment.

2 cups bow tie pasta

1 15-ounce can garbanzo beans, rinsed well and
   drained
1 cup water
1/2 cup tomato paste
1 Tablespoon sweetener of your choice
1 teaspoon olive oil
1/4 teaspoon garlic granules
1/4 teaspoon onion granules
1/4 teaspoon dried oregano leaves
1/4 teaspoon dried basil leaves
1/4 teaspoon salt, or to taste
1/8 teaspoon ground black pepper

6 to 8 small black olives, sliced (optional)

1. Fill a 4 1/2-quart saucepan or Dutch oven two-thirds full with water. Bring the water to a rolling boil, and cook the pasta in it until it is al dente. Drain the pasta well and return it to the saucepan. Cover the saucepan with a lid to keep the pasta warm, and set it aside.

2. Meanwhile, place the remaining ingredients *except the olives* in a 2-quart saucepan. Stir them together until they are well combined, then bring the mixture to a boil. Reduce the heat to low, cover the saucepan with a lid, and simmer the mixture for 15 minutes, stirring occasionally.

3. Stir the olives, if using, into the beans and sauce.

4. Pour the hot beans and sauce over the reserved pasta (from step #1), and toss them together well. Divide the mixture equally between two serving plates, and serve at once.

Yield: 2 main dish servings

Per serving: Calories: 610, Protein: 23 gm., Fat: 7 gm., Carbohydrate: 110 gm.

A Note From Karen:
Canned beans are a real lifesaver when my daughter is hungry but I'm too pooped to cook. We like to mix kidney or pinto beans with whole grain elbow macaroni or with rice, frozen corn, and green bell pepper. My daughter loves the taste, and I have a quick, nutritious meal on the table in no time.

Spicy Soy Crumble & Kraut

This dish wins accolades for its hearty, homey taste. We like it served with mashed or baked potatoes and fresh, steamed green beans.

4 ounces (1/4 pound) tempeh, grated on the coarse side of a grater (see The Cook's Secrets at right)

1/4 teaspoon dried oregano leaves
1/4 teaspoon ground fennel seeds or ground caraway seeds, or 1/2 teaspoon whole caraway seeds
1/4 teaspoon garlic granules
1/4 teaspoon salt
1/8 teaspoon ground black pepper
pinch of cayenne pepper, to taste

2 teaspoons canola oil
1 cup onion, sliced

1 cup low-sodium sauerkraut, very lightly drained
1 small apple, peeled, cored, and sliced into 8 to 10 wedges

1. Place the tempeh in a medium mixing bowl, and stir in the oregano, fennel or caraway, garlic granules, salt, pepper, and cayenne, to taste. Mix well and set aside.

2. Place the oil in a 9-inch or 10-inch skillet, and heat it over medium-high. When the oil is hot, add the onion. Reduce the heat to medium, and sauté the onion until it is golden and tender, about 10 to 15 minutes.

3. Stir the reserved tempeh mixture (from step #1) into the onion in the skillet, and brown it for about 5 minutes, stirring constantly.

4. Add the sauerkraut and apple slices to the tempeh-onion mixture in the skillet. Cover the skillet with a lid, and cook the mixture until the sauerkraut is heated through and the apple is tender-crisp, about 6 to 8 minutes. Serve at once.

Yield: 2 main dish servings

Per serving: Calories: 242, Protein: 11 gm., Fat: 9 gm., Carbohydrate: 30 gm.

The Cook's Secrets:
Unless the tempeh package directions state that the tempeh is fully cooked, it should be steamed for 15 to 20 minutes and cooled until easily handled.

To prevent the apple from discoloring, peel, core and slice it just before using.

Tempeh & Eggplant Pot Pies

Chunky, individual vegetable pies topped with a biscuit-style crust—honest food at its robust best.

FILLING:
2 cups eggplant, diced (about 1 very small Western eggplant or 1 to 2 Asian eggplants)
1 8-ounce can tomato sauce (1 cup)
1/2 cup onion, chopped
1/2 cup celery, chopped
4 ounces (1/4 pound) tempeh, cut into 1/2-inch cubes
1 teaspoon olive oil (optional)

salt and ground black pepper, to taste

BISCUIT CRUST:
1/2 cup whole wheat pastry flour
1 teaspoon non-aluminum baking powder (such as Rumford)
pinch of salt

1/4 cup water
2 teaspoons olive oil

1. Preheat the oven to 350°F. Coat two 15-ounce or 16-ounce individual casserole dishes with nonstick cooking spray, and set them aside.

2. To make the filling, place all the filling ingredients *except the salt and pepper* in a 4 1/2-quart saucepan or Dutch oven. Place the saucepan over high heat, and bring the mixture to a boil. Reduce the heat to medium, cover the saucepan with a lid, and simmer the mixture, stirring once or twice, for 15 minutes.

3. Remove the saucepan from the heat, and season the filling with salt and pepper, to taste.

4. Divide the filling evenly between the prepared casserole dishes, and set aside.

5. To prepare the biscuit crust, place the flour, baking powder, and salt in a small mixing bowl, and stir them together. Pour the water and oil into the flour mixture at the same time, and mix just until the dry ingredients are evenly moistened. The dough will be stiff.

6. Drop the dough by 4 small spoonfuls on top of each casserole (2 per casserole). Then carefully spread the dough out with the back of the spoon so it evenly covers the top of the filling.

7. Bake the pot pies until the crust is golden, about 20 to 25 minutes. Serve hot.

Yield: 2 main dish servings

Per serving: Calories: 332, Protein: 15 gm., Fat: 8 gm., Carbohydrate: 47 gm.

Tempeh & Vegetable Skillet Delight

Yield: 2 main dish servings

Per serving: Calories: 242, Protein: 13 gm., Fat: 7 gm., Carbohydrate: 30 gm.

Serve this spicy-sweet vegetable dish over hot brown rice.

1/2 cup carrots, pared and sliced diagonally

1 to 2 teaspoons olive oil
2 cloves garlic, minced or pressed

10 asparagus spears, sliced diagonally into 1-inch pieces
4 ounces (1/4 pound) tempeh, cut into 1/2-inch cubes (see p. 18)

1/2 cup water chestnuts, drained and sliced
1/4 cup water
1 Tablespoon orange juice concentrate
1 Tablespoon apple juice concentrate
1 Tablespoon soy sauce
1/4 teaspoon crushed hot red pepper flakes

1. Fill a 1-quart saucepan halfway with water, and bring the water to a boil. Add the carrots and blanch them for 2 minutes. Drain the carrots well in a colander, and set them aside.

2. Place the olive oil in a 9-inch or 10-inch skillet, and heat it over medium. When the oil is hot, add the garlic and sauté it for 1 minute. Then add the asparagus and tempeh, and cook them, tossing often, for 2 minutes longer.

3. Add the reserved carrots (from step #1) and the remaining ingredients to the skillet. Mix well. Cover the skillet with a lid, and simmer the mixture until the asparagus pieces are tender, about 5 minutes longer. Serve hot.

DESSERTS:

THE FINISHING TOUCH

In our household, dessert is served only on special occasions, most often when we have company. At those times, a full-size dessert recipe is generally what's called for. More typically, however, if we want something sweet, and it's just the two of us, we'll grab a piece of ripe fruit or a few organic grapes to quash our craving. A fruit dessert is simple, easy, nutritious, and essentially fat-free.

Sometimes, however, a plain fruit dessert just doesn't satisfy, particularly when a meal has been on the lighter side, such as with a soup or salad entrée. Many of the sweeter recipes in the "Breakfast Fare & Breads" section are quite suitable for dessert.

Keep a carton or two of low-fat, non-dairy "ice cream" or sherbet in your freezer. It's a delicious treat when you're in the mood for something sweet. For a special but easy dessert, spoon a little softened vanilla or raspberry frozen dessert on a small plate and top it with sliced kiwi fruit, sliced strawberries, and fresh whole blueberries.

Other handy, packaged dessert items are low-fat, dairy- and egg-free cookies and brownies, fruit leathers, non-dairy "ice cream" sandwiches, and dairy-free puddings and pudding mixes. If you stock up on a few healthful, low-fat desserts, you can avoid the temptation to indulge in something less than nutritious.

Almond Fudge Cookies

Festive and rich, these cookies are delicious when served with a glass of ice-cold, non-dairy almond milk.

12 whole almonds, blanched

1/2 cup whole wheat pastry flour
1/4 cup oat flour (for information on oat flour see p. 10)
3 Tablespoons unsweetened roasted carob powder, sifted (see The Cook's Secrets below right)
1/4 teaspoon non-aluminum baking powder (such as Rumford)
1/8 teaspoon salt

1/4 cup pure maple syrup
2 Tablespoons canola oil
1/2 teaspoon vanilla extract

1. Preheat the oven to 350°F. Coat a baking sheet with nonstick cooking spray, and set it aside.

2. To blanch the almonds, place them in a 1-quart saucepan, and cover them with water. Bring the water to a boil, and boil the almonds for 2 minutes. Drain the almonds in a colander or wire mesh strainer, and rinse them under cold tap water. To remove the skins, pinch the base of the almonds between your thumb and forefinger. The skins should slip off easily. Pat the almonds dry and set them aside.

3. Place the flours, sifted carob powder, baking powder, and salt in a small mixing bowl, and stir them together.

4. Measure the maple syrup in a small measuring cup. Then stir in the canola oil and vanilla extract. Pour this mixture into the dry ingredients (from step #3), and mix thoroughly. The dough will be stiff.

5. Form the dough into 12 walnut-size balls using water-moistened hands, and place them on the prepared baking sheet.

6. Press one whole blanched almond in the center of each ball, pressing it down lightly.

7. Bake the cookies for 12 minutes. Transfer them to a cooling rack using a metal spatula. Cool the cookies completely before storing them.

Yield: 1 dozen

Per cookie: Calories: 76, Protein: 1 gm., Fat: 3 gm., Carbohydrate: 11 gm.

The Cook's Secrets:

If you prefer, whole walnuts or pecans may be substituted for the almonds.

Carob powder should be sifted because it tends to lump, and once it is mixed with a liquid the lumps are almost impossible to smooth out. Sifting will eliminate any lumps from the start. If you do not own a sifter, simply measure out the quantity of carob powder you need, place it in a wire mesh strainer, and stir it through the strainer directly into your mixing bowl.

Schoolyard Oatmeal Cookies

The best darn cookies this side of the playground!

1/2 cup whole wheat pastry flour
1/2 cup quick-cooking rolled oats (not instant)
1/4 teaspoon non-aluminum baking powder (such as Rumford)
1/4 teaspoon ground cinnamon
1/8 teaspoon salt

1/4 cup light molasses or sorghum syrup
2 Tablespoons canola oil
1 Tablespoon water
3/4 teaspoon vanilla extract

1/4 cup walnuts, coarsely chopped
1/4 cup raisins

1. Preheat the oven to 350°F. Coat a baking sheet with nonstick cooking spray, and set it aside.

2. Place the flour, rolled oats, baking powder, cinnamon, and salt in a small mixing bowl. Stir them together and set aside.

3. Measure out the molasses or sorghum syrup in a small measuring cup. Then stir in the canola oil, water, and vanilla extract. Mix well. Pour this mixture into the dry ingredients (from step #2) along with the walnuts and raisins. Mix thoroughly.

4. Drop the dough by 12 rounded spoonfuls onto the prepared baking sheet. Flatten each cookie lightly with the back of a spoon.

5. Bake the cookies for 12 to 14 minutes, or until they are lightly browned.

6. Transfer the cookies to a cooling rack using a metal spatula. Cool the cookies completely before storing them.

Yield: 1 dozen

Per cookie: Calories: 99, Protein: 2 gm., Fat: 4 gm., Carbohydrate: 14 gm.

Peanut Butter Cookies

Only four ingredients? These unbelievably simple cookies will both surprise and please you with their effortless directions and straightforward flavor.

1/4 cup pure maple syrup
1/4 cup peanut butter (smooth or crunchy)
1/2 teaspoon vanilla extract

1/2 cup whole wheat pastry flour

1. Preheat the oven to 350°F. Coat a baking sheet with nonstick cooking spray, and set it aside.

2. Place the maple syrup, peanut butter, and vanilla extract in a small mixing bowl, and cream them together. Stir in the flour to form a stiff dough. Mix thoroughly.

3. Form the dough into 12 walnut-size balls, and place them on the prepared baking sheet.

4. Flatten the cookies with the tines of a fork, first in one direction and then in the opposite direction to create a cross-hatch design.

5. Bake the cookies for 12 minutes, or until the bottoms are lightly browned.

6. Let the cookies rest on the baking sheet for 1 full minute. Then carefully loosen them, and transfer them to a cooling rack using a metal spatula. Cool the cookies completely before storing them.

Yield: 1 dozen

Per cookie: Calories: 65, Protein: 2 gm., Fat: 2 gm., Carbohydrate: 8 gm.

Sunflower Cookies

A very rich, chewy dessert that is simply out of this world and so very easy to make. My personal favorite.

1/4 cup pure maple syrup
1/4 cup tahini
3/4 cup quick-cooking rolled oats (not instant)
1/4 cup raw (not roasted) sunflower seeds

1. Preheat the oven to 350°F. Coat a baking sheet with nonstick cooking spray, and set it aside.

2. Place the maple syrup and tahini in a small mixing bowl, and cream them together. Then stir in the oats and sunflower seeds, and mix well.

3. Drop the dough by 12 rounded spoonfuls onto the prepared baking sheet. Flatten each cookie slightly with the back of a spoon.

4. Bake for 15 to 18 minutes, or until the cookies are lightly browned.

5. Let the cookies rest on the baking sheet for 5 full minutes. Then carefully loosen them and transfer them to a cooling rack using a metal spatula. Cool the cookies completely before storing them.

Yield: 1 dozen

Per cookie: Calories: 87, Protein: 2 gm., Fat: 5 gm., Carbohydrate: 10 gm.

Carob Fudge Sauce

Finding a delectable chocolate substitute has truly been a challenge, but this fantastically rich and gooey fudge sauce at long last fits the bill. Use it as a topping for vanilla or raspberry non-dairy frozen dessert or as a luscious dip for fresh strawberries and bananas—let your imagination run wild!

1/2 cup low-fat, non-dairy milk
1 1/2 Tablespoons cornstarch

1/2 cup granulated sweetener (such as Sucanat or turbinado sugar)
3 Tablespoons unsweetened roasted carob pow-
   der, sifted (see The Cook's Secrets at right)
1/2 teaspoon non-caffeinated coffee substitute
   crystals (i.e. Pero, Postum, Kaffree Roma, etc.)
pinch of cinnamon

2 to 3 teaspoons tahini
1/2 teaspoon vanilla extract

1. Place the milk in a 1-quart saucepan. Add the cornstarch and mix with a wire whisk until it is well dissolved.

2. Stir the sweetener, carob powder, coffee sub-stitute, and cinnamon into the cornstarch mix-ture, and mix thoroughly.

3. Place the saucepan over medium-high heat, and bring the mixture to a boil, stirring con-stantly with a wooden spoon. Reduce the heat to low, stirring constantly and vigorously until the mixture is thick, about 3 minutes.

4. Remove the saucepan from the heat. Still using the wooden spoon, stir in the tahini and

vanilla extract, beating well until the sauce is completely smooth and glossy.

5. Serve warm or chilled. Store leftovers in the refrigerator (see The Cook's Secrets below).

Yield: about 1 1/4 cup

Per 1/4 cup serving: Calories: 122, Protein: 1 gm., Fat: 1 gm., Carbohydrate: 26 gm.

The Cook's Secrets:
Carob powder should be sifted because it tends to lump, and once it is mixed with a liquid the lumps are almost impossible to smooth out. Sifting will elimi-nate any lumps from the start. If you do not own a sifter, simply measure out the quantity of carob pow-der you need, place it in a wire mesh strainer, and stir it through the strainer directly into your mixing bowl.

   If the sauce has been refrigerated, bring it to room temperature before using it. Then beat it again with a fork or a wooden spoon until it is very smooth.

Peanut Butter Fudge Sauce: Omit the tahini and beat in 2 to 3 teaspoons smooth peanut butter.

Carob Fudge Frosting: Follow the directions for Carob Fudge Sauce, but increase the cornstarch to 2 tablespoons. Use this low-fat frosting for your favorite sweet muffins to instantly transform them into cupcakes!

Baked Apple Slices

The aroma of these spiced apples is as magnificent as their taste. Serve them plain or over a scoop of non-dairy vanilla "ice cream."

2 Tablespoons pure maple syrup
1/4 teaspoon ground cinnamon

3 to 4 Tablespoons walnuts, chopped
2 Tablespoons dried currants or raisins

2 baking apples (Granny Smith, Jonathan, Rome Beauty, Cortland, Northern Spy, York Imperial, etc.), peeled and sliced into 16 pieces (8 slices per apple)

1. Preheat the oven to 400°F. Mist a medium-size casserole dish or glass pie plate with non-stick cooking spray, and set it aside.

2. Place the maple syrup and cinnamon in a small mixing bowl, and stir them together until they are well combined. Then stir in the walnuts and currants or raisins.

3. Place the apple slices in a medium mixing bowl. Add the walnut-currant mixture, and toss until everything is evenly distributed.

4. Place the apple slices in the prepared casserole dish or pie plate, arranging them in a single layer. Cover the dish with a lid or foil, and bake the apple slices for 20 to 25 minutes, or until they are fork-tender. Serve warm.

Yield: 2 servings

Per serving: Calories: 242, Protein: 2 gm., Fat: 8 gm., Carbohydrate: 40 gm.

Flying Saucer Candy Bars

Satisfy your craving for a sweet and crunchy dessert with this kid-pleasing favorite.

2 plain rice cakes
2 to 3 Tablespoons peanut butter (smooth or crunchy)
2 Tablespoons Carob Fudge Sauce, p. 182, or Carob Fudge Frosting, p. 182
2 teaspoons shredded coconut
2 Tablespoons raisins

1. Spread the peanut butter evenly over the rice cakes.

2. Spread the Carob Fudge Sauce or Frosting equally over the peanut butter.

3. Sprinkle the coconut evenly over the Carob Fudge Sauce or Frosting.

4. Scatter the raisins over the top of each "candy bar," pressing them in lightly. Serve.

Yield: 2 servings

Per serving: Calories: 227, Protein: 6 gm., Fat: 11 gm., Carbohydrate: 25 gm.

Maple Banana Custard

Whenever you're in the mood for something soothing and rich-tasting, this simple custard is sure to make you smile.

1 10.5-ounce package fat-reduced, firm silken tofu
1 large ripe banana, mashed
1/4 cup pure maple syrup
1 Tablespoon fresh lemon juice
1 teaspoon vanilla extract

1. Place the tofu, banana, maple syrup, lemon juice, and vanilla extract in a blender or a food processor fitted with a metal blade.

2. Process the mixture for several minutes, until it is very smooth and creamy.

3. Serve the custard at once, or transfer it to a covered container, and chill it in the refrigerator. The flavor will improve greatly when the custard has a chance to chill, and the flavors have an opportunity to mingle.

Yield: 3 to 4 servings

Per serving: Calories: 123, Protein: 6 gm., Fat: 1 gm., Carbohydrate: 22 gm.

The Cook's Secrets:
If the packaged tofu is chilled prior to preparing the recipe, the custard will be cold and ready to be served immediately after preparation.

Banana Popsicles

Karen Bernard relies on these simple but nutritious treats to satisfy her young daughter's sweet tooth. Frozen bananas are nature's ice cream. What a terrific snack idea!

1 large, ripe banana
2 popsicle sticks

1. Cut the banana in half horizontally. Do not peel it, as the peel helps to keep the banana from splitting apart.

2. Carefully insert one popsicle stick into the center of the cut side of each half, about an inch or so deep.

3. Peel the banana halves and wrap them tightly in plastic wrap. Place them in the freezer for several hours, or until they are frozen. (They will keep in the freezer for several days.) Eat them like a popsicle.

Yield: 2 servings

Per serving: Calories: 53, Protein: 1 gm., Fat: 0 gm., Carbohydrate: 12 gm.

INGREDIENT INDEX

The following index will provide you with a convenient way to plan your menus around what you have on hand. The ingredients listed are either the main ingredient in the recipe, a principal ingredient, or a food that gives the recipe its distinctive flavor.

General Index